Calling All Cars

Calling All Cars

*Radio Dragnets and the
Technology of Policing*

KATHLEEN BATTLES

UNIVERSITY OF MINNESOTA PRESS

MINNEAPOLIS • LONDON

The University of Minnesota Press gratefully acknowledges financial assistance provided by Oakland University for the publication of this book.

Published by the University of Minnesota Press
111 Third Avenue South, Suite 290
Minneapolis, MN 55401-2520
http://www.upress.umn.edu

Library of Congress Cataloging-in-Publication Data
Battles, Kathleen.
Calling all cars : radio dragnets and the technology of policing /
Kathleen Battles.
p. cm.
Includes bibliographical references and index.
ISBN 978-0-8166-4913-6 (hc : alk. paper) —
ISBN 978-0-8166-4914-3 (pb : alk. paper)
1. Police communication systems. 2. Law enforcement—Technological innovations. 3. Criminal investigation—Technological innovations.
4. Police—Equipment and supplies. I. Title.
HV7936.C8B38 2010
363.2´32—dc22
2009012461

17 16 15 14 13 12 11 10   10 9 8 7 6 5 4 3 2 1

CONTENTS

Heeding the Call

Its effect is electrifying as it falls on the ears of the men pledged to combat crime. It hurls an army of public protectors into battle formation. As in the days of '49, it is a cry that heralds a battle of hardship and a fight to the death. What is this verbal symbol of modern adventure?

"Calling all cars!"

—Michigan State Police radio broadcast

Calling the police! Calling the g-men! Calling all Americans to war on the underworld!

—*Gang Busters* radio program opening

As historians of policing generally agree, radio in combination with the automobile represented a significant shift in police practices during the years of the Depression. Radio became a technological solution to a number of problems facing police, many of which were tied to the increasing use of the automobile. The automobile enabled increasingly fast mobility for criminals, taxing the fragmented arrangement of law enforcement in the United States. Radio and automobiles formed a powerful rejoinder to criminal mobility. For example, Kelling and Moore (1996) argue, "The patrol car became the symbol of policing during the 1930s and 1940s; when equipped with radio, it was at the limits of technology. It represented mobility, power, conspicuous presence, control of officers, and professional distance from citizens" (83). Yet even a cursory look through a variety of sources of the 1930s, including specialized literature aimed at police professionals and city managers and popular literature aimed at the general public, indicates that radio represented more: police radio symbolized excitement, speed, efficiency, centralized command of geographic space, the promise of inevitable apprehension, two-way communication, masculine prowess, and modernity itself. So exciting was police radio that the Michigan State

Police (1936), among the earliest to develop radio for policing, celebrated their ability to conquer space and time by invoking that symbol of modern adventure, "Calling All Cars." Comparing the excitement generated by police radio to the thrill of the gold rush, and celebrating its ability to liven up the most intimate domestic settings, the Michigan State Police glorified their new technologies as a way to herald their own success as a modern agency of crime fighting.

The most memorable versions of this call, however, emanated not from the police radio stations but from the growing number of commercial radio entertainment programs that told stories of crime-fighting efforts by either police or vigilante heroes. The most vivid and widely circulated call was featured on the nationally broadcast docudrama *Gang Busters,* which purported to give its audience the real facts about police activities. Each week, the program's opening featured a potent sonic cocktail of machine-gun fire, marching feet, and wailing sirens that served as backdrop to the emphatic hail of the announcer, who, speaking through a filter device meant to signify the radio itself, called on the audience to join this crusade against crime. In the American Southwest, listeners could hear the weekly call on the appropriately titled regional docudrama *Calling All Cars.* In keeping with the air of authenticity the show worked to convey, each episode began with a simulated police radio call issued by actual Los Angeles Police Department dispatcher Sergeant Rosenquist, who commanded squad cars to keep a lookout for the suspect whose capture was the subject of the week. Even fictional programs featured their own forms of the call. The most memorable was issued by *The Shadow,* the alter ego of man-about-town Lamont Cranston, who used his "power to cloud men's minds" to render himself invisible in order to fight crime. Using radios and extrasensory perception, Cranston/Shadow frequently hailed his faithful assistant Margot Lane to assist him in his crime-fighting efforts.

That radio programs would draw on the power of police radio as a central part of their program offerings was not a foregone conclusion during the Great Depression. A new group of reformers, including members of various civic institutions, concerned citizens, and those from within the ranks of police forces, found police facing, in the new term of the era, a "public opinion" problem. In addition to a whole host of social changes, police were dealing with an array of representations that were only rarely flattering. The most popular among them were the fictional images of the inept police of Hollywood gangster lore and the stereotypical Irish flatfoot of film and fiction. The clamoring press of the period offered little rectification as it reported on the disastrous legacy of Prohibition and widely publicized the scathing findings of a federally financed crime commission. At the same time, citizens exhibited little faith in the police. Middle-class citizens expressed their fear of social turmoil in the wake of the Lindbergh baby kidnapping and concerns over property crime. Members of the working class and different ethnic groups voiced their opposition to their frequent victimization by the police who were issued the responsibility of breaking strikes and enforcing vice laws. The images and discourses produced by the press, popular culture, and citizens themselves swirled together, forming a vitriolic popular image of police corruption and ineptitude. Battling the perception that police were incompetent, ineffectual, and violent grew as a dominant element of what historians recognize as the second-wave police reform movement. Police would attend not merely to the social problem of crime but also to the cultural problem of image management. In this light, the excitement of the radio call became especially significant.

The thrill of radio was central both to the reorganization of policing and to attempts to improve the dismal public image of the police. The phrase "calling all cars" is situated at the nexus of cultural changes in the United States involving multiple shifts related to technology, authority, power, and identity during the key years of the Great Depression. These changes were central to developments in both policing and commercial radio broadcasting. The practices and discourses of both were linked through the radio in a mutually constitutive relationship. Key to this relationship was the ability of radio to effectively blur traditionally discrete cultural and social categories, including the public and private, the mobile and fixed, the real and representational, and the police and commercial entertainment interests. For police forces, the phrase symbolized the attempt to construct a technologically enhanced, organized, hierarchal, modern, and efficient agency. Radio became a key instrument in the efforts of police reformers to professionalize policing and remove debates about the meaning and focus of policing from the public sphere. For those in the radio industry, "calling all cars" symbolized the excitement and adventure necessary to attract and retain audiences on behalf of corporate sponsors while at the same time allowing them to claim that they were operating on behalf of the public rather than merely for profit. Together they created a narrative form that blended dramatic and documentary elements in order to celebrate the achievements of modern police forces. In doing so, these stories created a cultural space that did not simply celebrate but became a key site of struggle over the meaning of policing and the control of discourses of policing, citizenship, and criminality. The results of this interconnection continue to echo today.

Drawing on archival materials related to the history of commercial radio and policing, as well as on recordings, the popular press, and literature of the period, this project argues that radio—as a technology, an institution, and a site for circulating discourses—played a key role in the construction and naturalization of an emerging form of policing aimed at the control of forms of social and physical mobility during the turbulent years of the Depression. Radio was a significant site for overhauling the dismal public image of policing, turning them into cultural heroes. Yet it was not simply the elevation of the public image of police that was at stake. Policing itself was undergoing a profound transformation involving the control of physical and social mobility. This transformation required the redefinition of a number of the relationships central to policing, including those between citizens and police, between police officers and police authority, and between policing and politics. The definition of the police function shifted from one centered on the performance of tasks related to social maintenance to one focused on the delivery of criminal apprehension as a professional service performed on behalf of the public. Radio proved a new space through which to struggle over of the meaning of these changes. Using radio, reformers sought to control the symbolic terrain through which citizens made sense of, developed expectations of, and interacted with the police. During a time of tremendous social strife, when ideas about the state, class, gender, ethnicity, and national identity were all in flux, they worked to elevate the public perception of the police as part of their broader efforts to turn policing into a modern profession. This discourse of social control found its roots in the changing Progressive ideas about the relationship between expert authority and a mass public as articulated in the second wave of the Progressive police reform movement and representations of the police on commercial broadcast radio.

The thrill of police radio cannot be underestimated. Cover of *Radio News* 11, no. 5 (November 1929).

The radio became not simply a space for circulating discourses about police professionalizing but also a technology through which to imagine the meaning of policing and the stories produced about them. First, radio's technical ability to cross the threshold between public and private allowed police to speak directly to citizens in their homes. The particular demands of addressing dispersed audiences in their domestic spaces often necessitated more intimate forms of address. Radio helped forge an intimate authority between police and citizens at the same moment that the automobile threatened to increase the gap between them. Second, the phrase "calling all cars" gained its affective power through its articulation in both popular and professional spheres of discourse, which were linked through the metaphor of the "net." The net metaphor was central to the description of commercial radio as a network, describing multiple functions: radio's creation of space for circulating discourses, its ability to convene simultaneous national audiences, its functioning as a social institution that contributed to American ideas of imagined community, and its status as medium considered so powerful the government demanded that it be used in the public interest. In professional police discourse, the metaphor of the net was deployed to describe the dragnet. The term once referred to the routine rounding up of suspects in lower-class neighborhoods. During the 1930s, the dragnet came to refer to the police use of radio in creating an "invisible web" over large geographic areas to ensnare mobile criminals. When it came to representing this power, radio dramas were able to simulate the very experience of radio through dramatizations that emphasized radio's ability to collapse space and time. This led to the creation of the "dragnet effect," the imagination of a constantly available police force. In both the popular discourses of commercial broadcasting and the professional discourses of policing, radio served as the key technology through which to alleviate or arrest the social disjuncture caused by mobility.

This project links several often disparate histories, including radio history, urban history, police history, the history of technology, and histories about mass culture and the Depression, to contribute to our understanding of radio and culture during the Depression. This book makes three key contributions toward that goal. First, at its core, it addresses a gap in the growing literature on the cultural history of radio. Despite an explosion of significant scholarship, radio crime dramas remain little discussed. Second, the project makes an important theoretical and methodological contribution to radio scholarship and scholarship on policing and popular culture. It explores the relationship between radio programming and a very specific historically situated set of discourses and material practices, linking radio to the micropolitics of policing. Rather than focusing on a wide swath of programming, the book analyzes a narrow set of programs, concentrating on four docudramas—*Police Headquarters, Calling All Cars, G-Men,* and *Gang Busters*—and two vigilante programs—*The Shadow* and *The Green Hornet.* This focus allows for an intensive analysis of the programs that more clearly delineates the links between these shows and the struggle over the meaning of policing. This book is marked further by a sustained engagement with the discourses of policing as a tangible site through which to understand more fully the cultural meaning of radio. The focus on the discourses of police reform is important for considering the ways that radio crime dramas differed significantly from other forms of Depression-era mass culture. Finally, this book offers a theoretical and methodological contribution to our understanding of radio as a medium. This project is grounded on a close analysis of radio programming with attention to multiple material artifacts, including recordings, scripts, correspondence, and other matter related to the production of radio crime dramas. In addition, this project seeks to understand radio as a unique communicative space in order to understand how the conventions of the radio crime dramas were shaped by the technological and industrial organization of radio as this form intersected with specific elements of the police reform discourse.

RETHINKING THE RADIO CRIME DRAMA

Despite being among the most memorable programs of the radio's golden age, crime dramas have received scant attention from radio scholars. It is perhaps the constant exhortation that "crime never pays" that makes it difficult for scholars to take radio crime dramas seriously. After all, their themes are so frequently "corny" and their stories so straightforwardly didactic that it is tempting to dismiss them as simpleminded entertainment, or at least as an entertainment the meaning of which is so obvious that it does not beg for further analysis. Certainly, radio crime dramas lack the darkness and grit of the their pulp-fiction cousin, the hard-boiled detective story. They further lack the narrative sophistication achieved by nineteenth-century classic detective fiction and early Depression-era gangster films. Each of these forms has received an increasing amount of scholarly attention.[1] Radio crime dramas, on the other hand, have been largely ignored by scholars of radio's cultural history and of the cultural history of the Depression era more generally. This is not to say these programs do not continue to resonate with old-time radio fans and collectors. They have been given nostalgic consideration.[2]

At the same time, other forms of radio programming generally offer greater narrative sophistication, entertainment value that is more comprehensible and enjoyable to modern ears, and more obvious connections to the current cultural studies' interest in categories of race, class, gender, and even sexuality. Comedy, prestige dramas, religious broadcasters, even the lowly soap opera and bizarre border blasters, have been explored for the ways that they mediated changing ideas of social identity at a time of social change.[3] Other scholars have recently turned to understanding radio audiences, the relationship between radio and an emerging consumer culture, and the relationship between radio and nationalism.[4] As a unique cultural space that consistently threatened to upset cultural boundaries regarding public and private space, gender norms, ethnic and racial identities, local and national identities, and class norms, radio has been the subject of interest of an increasing number of scholars who have helped us develop a sophisticated understanding of both a medium and cultural time that many in media studies dismiss as simply the prelude to the more "significant" cultural force, television.

One of the most enduring critical examinations of the radio crime drama remains J. Fred MacDonald's chapter "Detective Programming and the Search for Law and Order" in his classic work *Don't Touch That Dial! Radio Programming in American Life, 1920–1960* (1979). MacDonald offers a key early insight into the Depression-era crime dramas, which he labels "realistic," arguing that their documentary style and emphasis on realism made them an ideal space for celebrating advances in law enforcement. This observation is part of his larger examination of detective shows as social and cultural symbols that functioned to reaffirm a democratic vision of social order. He argues that in a world where religion held less sway, and where a sense of right and wrong was required, detective stories functioned as something like secular passion plays, with detectives themselves acting as secular saviors. More particularly, he makes the connection between radio crime dramas and "the middle class, property owning society which spawned them," arguing that "their heroes were agents of bourgeois America, there to tell criminals and citizens that crime did not pay, and that good was always victorious" (193). Despite these important observations, he generally views the programs as "secular allegories" consisting of "the simple pattern of Good over Evil, Truth over Lie, and Civilization over Anarchy" (193). While making many important observations, MacDonald's work is focused on understanding radio programming more generally and does not draw on any specific connections between radio crime dramas and the politics of police reform.

More recent studies examine the radio crime dramas with a fuller sense of the historical context of the Depression years but do not fully deal with the politics of policing. Russo (2002) draws a connection between the political situation of the Great Depression and World War II and the content of this vigilante crime drama in his exploration of the relationship between *The Green Hornet* and the New Deal. He argues that the program offered a specific counter discourse to the New Deal's faith in the ability of the state to manage the country through its continued focus on civic corruption. Loviglio (1999) argues that *The Shadow* served as a "means for dramatizing and resolving the interrelated crises of public space, mass culture, and national/racial outsiders" (314). One of the most significant aspects of the program is that the main character functioned as what Lippmann (1922) termed an intelligence worker, a figure who used his expert knowledge to deal with an increasingly complex and incomprehensible world. Loviglio draws a clear connection between the broader concerns about radio itself and national anxieties of invasion, demonstrating that the program was not simply escapism and that its content should not be dismissed as merely didactic. Razlogova (2006) examines the ways that *Gang Busters* served as a site for radio professionals and radio audiences to negotiate the meaning of commercial broadcasting during the Depression and into World War II. She examines correspondence from listeners who dispute the ways they were represented in the program. She concludes that while the creators of the program tried early on to accommodate correspondents, as commercial radio became more powerful, their voices mattered less.

These recent studies more fully situate the radio crime drama within the social context of the Depression and within dominant political and cultural trends of the era. However, given the overlap between police discourses and radio discourses about police, they still do not explore the connection between the two. Radio crime dramas like *Gang Busters* and *Calling All Cars* dramatized solved police cases often in cooperation with various law enforcement agencies. In doing so, they encountered the discourse of the second-wave police reform movement initiated during the Depression. While the programs spoke to broader cultural anxieties about publicity and privacy, ethnicity, race, class, gender, and the meaning of broadcasting, they also spoke in very specific ways to developments in policing that continue to shape both police and broadcast practices to this day. Understanding this relationship necessitates moving beyond more general discursive shifts of the Depression era to more fully examine the development of policing during the era and hence an engagement with literatures concerning theoretical approaches to representations of policing, police history, and the dominant images of policing during the Depression era.

POLICE STORIES/POLICE HISTORY

This project is driven by two important, interconnected methodological moves. The first involves the level of analysis of programming, and the second involves the connection between programming and a specific set of historical discourses and practices. In terms of programming, this project focuses on a narrow set of programs belonging to a single genre and covers only material produced during the Depression years. Rarely do radio scholars give focused attention to such a select group of programs. One of the key advantages of this approach to analysis is the ability to connect radio programming to the historically specific practices of policing. It also allows for a complex understanding of the development of this programming form and simultaneously promotes a better understanding of the important role of radio programming in the cultural landscape of the Depression more generally and of its role in articulating a concrete set of practices and discourses more particularly.

The specific and concrete set of historical conditions explored in this project is the struggle over the meaning of policing during the years of the

Depression. This effort draws on the work of scholars in a number of fields who have explored the relationship between policing practices and representations of policing. There is a strong tendency when exploring the relationship between broadcasting and policing to think of policing and culture as existing in two separate spheres, independent of each other. A common result of this view is to examine representations of policing through the lens of accuracy in order to determine if a representation is, first, correct, and second, "positive" or "negative." The result is to treat all representations of policing as if they were merely instrumental, and thus the job of the critic is simply to gauge to what extent cultural texts accurately display what the police do. This is problematic on several counts. First, it gives the police the power to determine the nature of the representation. That is, the approach, even if critical of police practices, upholds police agencies as the central source for meanings about policing and crime. Second, accuracy arguments assume some basic agreement on what police actually do or some agreement on the meaning of policing.

More recently, a number of scholars have persuasively argued that the representations of policing, produced across a range of sources, and the practices of policing are better understood as interconnected rather than discrete. Additionally, scholars have insisted on understanding the meaning of policing as historically variable and contested. Police scholars, citizens, and even the police themselves do not always agree on any precise definition of policing. These scholars insist on historically situating our understanding of policing. This book therefore engages with particular discourse of the second wave of the police reform movement and its relationship to the shifts in Progressive ideas about democracy during the 1920s and 1930s that were based on a profound lack of faith in citizens to reasonably rule themselves in a mass society. As the police reform movement adopted the mantle of professionalization, its self-image clashed with what many see as the populist leanings of Depression-era mass culture.

Policing and Representation

While radio scholars have not fully engaged with the representations of authority in crime dramas, scholars in a number of fields, including English, film studies, media studies, and sociology, have. Scholars working in the cultural studies tradition have begun to explore the theoretical relationship between policing and popular cultural representations, arguing that the symbolic production of images of the police (both by the police and by the culture more generally) and the material practices of the police are continuous rather than discrete processes. Drawing from a range of theoretical perspectives, these scholars consider the ways that the mass media, including the press and popular culture, have intervened in, shaped, and negotiated the meanings of policing in democratic societies. For these authors, mass culture products do not instrumentally reflect what police "actually" do but form part of the cultural terrain over which societies make sense of authority. From the creation of crime waves to the ways that fiction shapes the imaginative horizon of police work, these theoretical, historical, critical, and literary studies point to the constitutive nature of representations, understanding them not through the concept of distortion and accuracy but as contributing to, shaping, negotiating, and imagining cultural ideas about criminality, citizenship, authority, and the state. Drawing from a range of theoretical perspectives, these scholars provide a rich foundation for thinking more seriously about radio crime dramas and the ways they articulated historically specific definitions of policing.

The key work in the exploration of the connection between symbolic production and material practice in negotiating the meaning of policing is Stuart Hall and colleagues' *Policing the Crisis: Mugging, the State, and Law and Order* (1978). The authors examine the "crisis" surrounding an ostensible rash of muggings in early 1970s Britain and the invocation of the notion that a "crime wave" was sweeping urban areas. Arguing that the response to these muggings was out of proportion with the "reality" of the situation, they contend that "mugging" is better understood as a moral crisis. Without denying that there are real criminals and real victims, Hall and colleagues seek a "shift of attention from the deviant act (i.e., 'mugging'), treated in isolation, to the relation between the deviant act and the reaction of the public and the control agencies to the act" (16). The authors more fully draw a connection between social discourses and practices of the police, press, and courts. They include an insightful examination of the role of the press in not simply reporting the "reality" of crime but, through routine practices, developing "spirals" of "mutual reinforcements and reciprocities" between the law and its representation, effectively helping to create the "panics" they purport to merely observe. The authors argue that

Once this point has been grasped, it is difficult to continue to consider the agencies of public signification and control, like the police, the courts and the media, as if they were passive reactors to immediate, simple and clear-cut crime situations. These agencies must be understood as actively and continuously part of the whole process to which, also, they are "reacting." They are active in defining situations, in selecting targets, in initiating "campaigns," in structuring these campaigns, in selectively signifying their actions to the public at large, in legitimating their actions through the accounts of situations which they produce. They do not simply respond to "moral panics." They form part of the circle out of which "moral panics" develop. It is part of the paradox that they also, advertently and inadvertently, amplify the deviancy they seem so absolutely committed to controlling. (52)

For Hall and his coauthors, the definition and assessment of a crime "wave" is not created by the actions of criminals alone but by all of the routine actions of differently situated actors across the fields of law and the mass media. The definition of crime is thus a complex social process rooted in questions of cultural authority to speak about any matter rather than a strictly legal process.

Scholars from diverse fields have examined the symbolic aspects of policing and cultural representations of policing. Some argue that the production of the symbolic meaning is actually a key component of police work. Criminologist Lovell (2003) takes on the specific relationship between police reform and the mass media, arguing that innovations in mass media create cultural lags between public and police use of new communications technologies that open up spaces where citizens are able to examine and critique police practices, thus creating the impetus for police reform. Drawing on media scholarship and the study of social interactionism, Lovell considers the "more subtle ways that media influence policing patterns through the reinforcement of policing definitions and roles, including the construction of the police as crime fighters, the 'good cop' fictional persona, and the very real 'bad cop' of police work" (15). For Lovell, the mass media are the source of legitimacy for the police. He argues that the police themselves use appearances "to dramatize their effectiveness as the keepers of social control" as "they struggle to create a sense of law and order within the body politic" (15).

Ian Loader (1997) is a key scholar examining the cultural dimensions of policing. Even though policing is "a bureaucratic, professionalized and goal-directed set of practices," as he argues, "this does not mean that it is not also shaped and legitimated by various structures of social belief and affect" (7). Loader asserts that as scholars, it is not enough to examine the history of police agencies as autonomous social agencies who produce meaning internally. Instead, the meanings and practices of policing must also be understand as produced through an engagement with broader cultural structures of meaning. Yet Loader does not stop there; he further insists that "policing too communicates meaning and plays its part in the creation of culture" (7). The meanings produced by police are important because "the way we police, represent policing to ourselves, and position it within an overall sense of order, makes a difference to both the construction of individual subjectivities, and the quality and character of social relations" (7). For Loader, it is important to recognize cultural influence on policing and the influence of policing on the cultural landscape because both are key sources of police legitimization and power. While many criminologists and sociologists think of policing in terms of bureaucratic power, patterns of organization, and interaction with criminals, Loader argues that the cultural work produced by the police and culture in general is an equally important site for understanding police power. Policing is always embedded in a broader set of cultural meanings that shape and are shaped by debates over authority.

Christopher Wilson (2000), in his study of the cultural authority of policing, draws on Loader to examine relationships between symbolic production and material practices of policing. He writes:

> Yet my interest, by contrast, falls on what Loader has recently denominated the police's symbolic authority: that is, the neglected parts of police power that involve story-making, the mobilization and differentiation of audiences, the engagement with media, the engineering of consent. By this I certainly mean those elements of police work we customarily deem public or (in softer forms) community relations. But like Loader, I also mean to question the notion that there is a "hard and fast distinction" between supposed real police labor (e.g., solving crime) and these symbolic or meaning-making functions; indeed, I think the functionality of police symbols (like the badge, or the

billy club, or the black-and-white cruiser) points to the opposite conclusion. Thus I intend to suggest how the storytelling capacities I describe above, which play off of and feed back from media formation, become not separate from everyday routines of police work, but actually encoded in them. (12)

Thus, for Wilson, symbolic representations of policing do not say something about the "reality" of policing and are not merely derivative representations that reflect or distort policing practices. By doubling back into police practices, such representations serve as a site of negotiation over the meaning of policing. Arguing that representations of policing produced from a variety of sources are "products of a complex negotiation within what some critics these days often call a given 'field' of social struggle and cultural representation," he asserts the importance of examining the links between "the material conditions of story-making, the affective and imaginative feel to police power that writers clue us in to, and the institutional forms of media that provide the tactical positions and the vehicles for cultural representation of police power" (13).

Additionally, Wilson points to a growing problem in the way ideas about policing increasingly are used in cultural studies discourses: the tendency to think of policing through a Foucauldian lens and thus as a more generalized set of practices associated with the social nexus of "discipline and punish" (Foucault 1979) rather than as a historically variable set of shifting material practices. Wilson insists that in order to understand police power, scholars must engage more thoroughly with the historically shifting discourses and practices of policing, as articulated across a range of sources and institutions. In *Cop Knowledge*, he focuses primarily on journalistic and ethnographic accounts of policing through the twentieth century and does reference popular culture texts, but those produced for film and television rather than radio. Significantly, he argues against accounts of crime and detective fiction that fail to take into account changing historical conditions, reducing changes in crime fiction simply to generic mutations or to an overly broad sense of historical changes. To that end, two works deal with the relationship between the FBI and mass culture during the Depression. Powers (1983) examines the ways that J. Edgar Hoover used the popular culture trope of the action hero to turn FBI agents into cultural icons, thus building public faith in a federal police force. Potter (1998) examines the ways that mass culture served as a central site of struggle over the meaning of federal authority during the Depression era.

While some scholars focus on the production of symbolic meanings of policing produced by the police, largely in the press or in documentary-style narratives, other scholars have examined more closely the relationship between forms of detective fiction and developments in policing and the relationship between fictional imagination and advancements in police methods. For example, in *Detective Fiction and the Rise of Forensic Science* (1999), Ronald Thomas explores the intertwined development of detective fiction and forensic science from the mid-nineteenth century until the early part of the twentieth century, exploring "the production and dissemination of narratives that established the authority of a class of experts that could read someone's body like a text with the precision of a machine" (5) in both popular and professional discourses. For Thomas, detective fiction does not merely "reflect" changes taking place in the nineteenth century but participates in the construction of an imaginative horizon involving the possibility of identification in an increasingly mobile society.

This work leads to some key conclusions about policing and culture. First, the symbolic construction of meanings about policing is not separate from the material practices of policing and should not be reduced to an instrumental relationship based on a reflection thesis. Symbolic representations of policing are not well understood through the lens of accuracy or distortion, which suggest that mediated representations exist independent of material practices. Instead, the symbolic meanings produced about policing, both by the police and throughout the broader cultural field, play a constitutive role in material practices. The creation of symbolic meanings, such as media representations, is a contested process and often involves the efforts of police to gain the authority to shape public understanding about the meanings of policing, criminality, and citizenship. Second, therefore, in understanding the production of symbolic meaning as constitutive, it is key to understand that policing is not static or clearly defined. Understanding the creation of these meanings involves an exploration of the concrete historical development of policing. Theorizing the relationship between the symbolic and material is not enough; unpacking the relationship between them requires an exploration of the specifics of the historic moments in question. In the case of the Great Depression, police forces found themselves facing a number of problems involving the urbanization, mobility, labor, ethnicity, race, and class. In the process of dealing with these changes, the very definition of policing in the United States began to change.

Understanding Police Reform

In putting radio crime dramas in conversation with the history of policing, it is important to set out the key contours of the reform movement, the relationship between the reform movement and social changes of the first part of the twentieth century, and the important shifts made in the definition of policing. This is not to set this as the "truthful" backdrop but as part of the symbolic terrain over which the crime dramas traversed. In particular, it is important to lay out the relationship between policing and significant shifts in Progressivism and to clearly define the meaning of police professionalization and the adoption of criminal apprehension as the dominant goal of policing. These changes created a model of policing that stressed the professional authority of the police to speak as experts on matters involving crime and policing and attempted to minimize citizen involvement in and criticism of police operations. They further shaped the ways that the technologies of the automobile and radio would be adapted for use by police forces.

The Progressive Diagnosis

The "problems" that police reformers found themselves facing by the onset of the Depression cut across the swath of a larger set of transformations in U.S. society and culture: increasing urbanization and mobility; the shift to a consumer-based, pleasure-seeking ethos; changes wrought by developments in communication and transportation technologies; the emergence of professions and the professionalization of an increasing number of social functions, such as education, social work, and health; attempts to control the activities of immigrants and various ethnic groups; a waning faith in the ability for democracy to survive in an era of mass culture; and the growth of the federal state that required a renegotiation of the relationship between the local and the national. As a whole host of demographic, infrastructural, technological, and industrial changes began to reshape national life at many levels, issues surrounding how to maintain the integrity of the social order came to the fore. As reformers at many different levels worked to deal with these changes, the nature of policing went through significant changes. The Progressive police reformers of the late nineteenth and early twentieth centuries had come from the professional classes, such as law, and operated as private citizens working to enhance a public function. By the late 1920s, a small but significant number of reformers came from within the very ranks of police departments. Although crime commissions continued to be manned by civilians, reform discourse was increasingly generated from within rather than outside police forces. Embracing the mantra of professionalization, they came to understand policing as a specialized field of expertise with its own claim to knowledge.[5]

Citizens and police forces agreed that if the social order was to be effectively stabilized, some kind of change was necessary. This was exactly the conclusion reached by numerous crime commissions set up during the 1920s. However, when the National Commission on Law Observance and Enforcement, more commonly called the Wickersham Commission (in deference to its head, former U.S. Attorney General George Wickersham), published its findings in January 1931, few in the police reform movement were surprised by its conclusions.[6] However, widespread publicity about the report, its status as a national rather than municipal or state study, and concerns about the social dislocation caused by the Depression, including what many must have seen as an increasing rift between police and citizens, gave the report a great deal of merit. Reflecting the strong influence of the first wave of the Progressive police reform movement, its writers diagnosed a series of problems remarkably consistent with those of previous crime commissions. However, as the general thrust of the Progressive movement itself began to shift, and as reformers faced a new host of problems caused by the use of transportation and communication technologies, the second wave of the police reformers began to articulate a new model of policing centered on the control of social and physical mobility in the name of a narrowed concern with crime control as the number-one priority of policing. By advocating policing as a profession, reformers set out to redefine the relationship between police forces and local politicians, between police leadership and street officers, and between police and citizens.

As had the generation of reformers before them, members of the Wickersham Commission concluded that the key hindrance to good police work was the strong tie between urban ward politicians and policing, which resulted in rampant corruption, inconsistent enforcement of the laws, and a lack of standards in the hiring, training, and promotion of police officers. If this critique echoed those of the past, changes in the ways criminals operated and technological innovations in transportation and communication both exacerbated existing problems and created new ones. Prohibition had inadvertently led to the creation of the modern crime syndicate, while the Depression led to a sharp spike in rural banditry. In addition, police reformers saw themselves facing, in the new term of the era, a "public relations" problem as negative images of the police circulated through the press and popular culture.

Public faith in the police was particularly low in the wake of the notorious failure of federal and local officials to enforce Prohibition. Failure alone would be one thing, but the Wickersham Commission concluded that the Bureau of Prohibition was utterly unsuccessful at enforcing antiliquor laws and that the tendency toward violence and conflict exhibited by those entrusted to enforce the legislation had alienated them from the public they were supposed to serve (Cohen 1990; Potter 1998). Reformers were well aware that vice laws placed them in an antagonistic relationship with the public. Christopher Wilson (2000) notes that "the inner lesson reformers had learned, particularly from Prohibition, was not that criminality was beyond containing, but that the public had not really wanted it to be" (67). In fact, Progressive reformers had long seen an important link between vice laws and public perception of police work. Central reform figure August Vollmer (1932) argued that "legislative bodies have heaped upon the police innumerable regulatory and inhibitory measures. Many of these are ill advised and absolutely unenforceable. Quite aside from their unenforceability is the hostile attitude of the public, not only toward these regulations but also toward the police (716). The unfortunate result was that citizens lost faith in the police, the police were unable to do their jobs, and reformers, in an effort to control the problem, simply created more vice laws. Therefore, vice laws not only had limited effect on the very behaviors they were meant to curtail but also directly caused a host of additional problems that police were forced to confront. This situation was exacerbated in U.S. cities as large immigrant communities understood that the enforcement of vice laws was largely directed against them.

The Wickersham Commission expanded on its critique of the failure of law enforcement to enforce Prohibition laws to assert that the use of violence was in fact a routine part of police work. A key section of the report, "Lawlessness in Law Enforcement" (1931), detailed a pattern of police brutality and incivility by police forces across the nation. Among the abuses recorded were the routine use of beatings with fists or other objects, such as rubber hoses, and overly long interrogations, threats, and illegal detention (Hopkins 1931; Walker 1977). Walker notes, for example, that "suspects were suspended by their ankles out of upper story windows until they confessed" and that "in Cleveland one suspect was stripped, made to lie naked on the floor, and repeatedly lifted up by his genitals. Detroit police occasionally took suspects 'around the loop,' transporting them from police station to police station to keep them isolated from friends, family, or legal counsel" (133). The report itself might have proved short-lived fodder for public discussion in the press had Ernest Jerome Hopkins not seized upon its findings and sensationalized them in the popular book *Our Lawless Police: A Study of the Unlawful Enforcement of the Law* (1931), heightening public distrust of and hostility toward the police. Noting that there were three kinds of lawlessness, that of the "average man," the "criminal," and the "law enforcing authorities" (3), he devoted his book to outlining and explicating the Wickersham committee report on the lawlessness of police officers.

Reformers noted that working-class, ethnic immigrant, and African American citizens were most often confronted with the daily reality of police brutality. As the findings of the Wickersham Commission pointed out, the police relationship with the ethnic working classes was especially troubled. By and large, the most likely victims of the "third degree," or excessive interrogation techniques, were those lowest in the social hierarchy. So common was the practice that the authors of the report rejected police defense of their practices as an effective tool against lawlessness, arguing that the third degree actually encouraged the immigrant poor to lose respect for the law and that, by encouraging public distrust of policing, threatened the viability of the justice system itself (Johnson 2003, 141). If the urban ethnic and working classes sought relief from police pressure, the middle classes clamored for more effective protection against a perception of a growing crime wave (Potter 1998).

Between the voices of the Wickersham Commission and various publics, reformers began to argue that public discourse was devoid of any reasoned assessment of the work they performed and the improvements they sought to institute. One of the most famous police experts of the era, Bruce Smith (1929b), was especially critical of news press, arguing that even the "most enlightened editorial policies, through which might be secured able discussion of police problems, have often been offset by a news policy designed to appeal to the unschooled and the ignorant." For Smith, the one place where the public might expect clear information about policing was utterly failing, "condemning the police when they were right, and praising them when they were wrong" (1). In fact, he argued, there were "few influences at work of the instruction of the public in the realities and the objective standards of police duty" (1–2). For reformers, this public opinion problem was central to reforming police practices.

The Post-Progressive, Professional Cure: Narrowing the Police Function

Growing out of the Progressive movement and a century-long attempt to define the meaning of policing in a swiftly modernizing nation, a key motive of many reform efforts centered on ways to manage access to and define the proper avenues for social mobility. As Fogelson (1977) effectively argued, from its very beginnings in the late nineteenth century, police reform, under the influence of the Progressive movement, was tightly linked to the desire of middle-class reformers to control the social mobility of newly arriving immigrant groups. The main tenets of Progressive reform took direct aim at this goal and were based on three assumptions that would last well into the later part of the twentieth century:

> In the first place, public service was not a means of social mobility. The big-city police were supposed to provide the best possible service at the lowest possible cost and not to supply jobs for first- and second-generation newcomers whose sole qualification was party loyalty. In the second place, local control was not a source of political legitimacy. No matter how commanding their majorities at the polls, the ward leaders had no right to interfere in departmental affairs, which were the exclusive province of the chiefs, mayors, and other city-wide officials. In the third place, immigrant life-styles were not an expression of American culture. The police forces were supposed to apply the criminal sanction not only to prevent crime but also to impose the

conventional morality on the newcomers and their families. This consensus, which was the great legacy of the first generation of reformers, shaped the nationwide debate over the policies and practices of the big-city police down through the second third of the twentieth century. (262)

This concern with controlling social mobility played a key role in police reform throughout the twentieth century. For example, Laythe (2002) examines turn-of-the-century police history in Eugene, Oregon, and argues that the city's self-identification as morally superior "required a consistency in its vision against 'dangerous outsiders'" (98). While Laythe insists on the historical specificity and distinctiveness of local police histories, he nonetheless points to the broader relationship between policing and the control of social mobility.

In the 1930s, as police reformers began what many police scholars agree is the beginning of the second wave of the reform movement, their attitudes toward the public shifted. It was no longer enough to use reform to manage access to social mobility. Police would now also actively seek to manage public opinion by finding ways to control perception. The police reform movement was part of the general adoption of Progressive and post-Progressive state-building policies during the period that witnessed the end of classic liberalism and the emergence of the new culture of professional expertise or liberal realism. It was during the years of the New Deal, Wilson (2000) argues, that "in historian Dorothy Ross's terms, a certain branch of liberal thought emphasize[d] 'the removal of issues from the political arena of conflict over values and ends to a technical arena in which issues are reduced to an adjustment of means'" (15). While the removal of policing from highly localized concerns in an attempt to prevent policing from being a source of social mobility had been a concern of the Progressive police reform movement since the turn of the century, by the 1930s, "some of the characteristic features of this liberal realist tradition surface in policing: administrative approaches to the consent of the governed, doubts about the rationality of that selfsame democratic public, pragmatic reshapings of community power and hierarchy that begin to place order as a prerequisite of democracy rather than effect" (15).

In his work on the relationship between hard-boiled fiction and the New Deal, Sean McCann (2000) describes this important political development:

By the New Deal era, that paradoxical assumption had come to seem, as Stevens implied—and as artists and intellectuals throughout the culture recognized—a comforting but increasingly untenable myth. The professionalization of legal and literary practice that had proceeded rapidly over the first third of the century made the public and democratic features of both seem less plausible. Law and literature belonged increasingly to specialists and functionaries. And while that development raised the possibility that each might be modernized and made more innovative, or efficient, or progressive, it also came to exemplify the basic problem of the liberal democracy shaped by industrial capitalism: that it was far from democratic, yet nevertheless lacked the political structures necessary to govern a complex society. American intellectuals in the decades leading up to mid-century faced a nation that was harshly divided between rich and poor, the powerful and the weak, and that at the same time did not appear to have the leadership or the state capacity to render its capitalist economy more secure, let alone more just. (306)

The 1930s was a period when more authority was invested in expert knowledge, and such expert knowledge was increasingly centralized and organized by the federal government and other local governmental agencies. A key component of this progressive ideology, as discussed by Loviglio (1999), McCann (2000), Slotkin (1992), and Wilson (2000), was a distrust of the public. Decision making was best left to this class of experts rather than to a public easily manipulated, deluded by outmoded ways of thinking, and incapable of grasping the complexities of modern life. Citizenship was to be marked by deference to such authority rather than a more democratic involvement in decision making about important social issues of the day.

At the federal level, the growth of the federal police powers was likewise tied to the desire to maintain U.S. cultural hierarchies. Potter (1998) argues that "during Roosevelt's first term, the confrontations between the G-men and the bandit, the Bureau of Investigation and the gang, became arenas for articulating nationalist narratives about the benefits of an interventionist state" (4). Thus,

the war on crime became a tangible, nationalist rallying point for a new interventionist state and a vernacular arena for envisioning a national public committed to the New Deal across party lines. This argument becomes even

stronger when we note that the crime of lynching, which represented a
deep and racialized split in both parties, was never written into the crime
bill, nor did Roosevelt ever endorse such legislation. Rather, during the war
on crime, Hoover and Cummings successfully capitalized on preexisting
anticrime sentiment among middle-class white voters by projecting a vision
of a moral and efficient state that transcended political and cultural differences to unite law-abiding citizens against common dangers. . . . A campaign
against bandit crime was thus a crucial political and cultural moment, under-
lining a New Deal commitment to enlarging federal intervention without
fundamentally disturbing the race and class hierarchies that middle-class,
white voters imagined when they spoke the word "community." (110)

While policing had been heavily politicized in the United States, during
the New Deal the concept of professional, depoliticized policing played an
important role in the political expansion of the role of the federal government into increasing areas of public and private life.[7] In addition, depoliticization through the trope of professional expertise and centralization at
the federal, state, and local levels was tightly linked with attempts to maintain U.S. cultural hierarchies.

Dealing with these changes meant that the very nature of policing under-
went profound changes. Because Progressive reform involved the creation
and professionalization of a number of urban social services, second-wave
reformers were in a stronger position to more aggressively pursue the narrowing of the police function. Increasingly, effectiveness in police work was
measured by the success in identifying and capturing criminals (Kelling
and Moore 1996; Walker 1998; Wilson 2000). Up to the mid-1920s, urban
police had operated as general functionaries, performing an array of services
for city residents. In line with the general tenets of the Progressive movement, with its faith in science and emphasis on professionalization rather
than politics, reformers worked to turn policing into a modern profession.
Rather than using a military analogy as a guide for police reform, reformers
like August Vollmer adopted a professional model. Police would work like
other modern, professional organizations, such as doctors or lawyers. They
would produce their own specialized knowledge; organize themselves as a
hierarchy like other modern organizations; and provide professional, scientific training for officers.

The most significant development in Depression-era policing, therefore, was the move to create a procedural apparatus based on the idea that if standardized police procedures and technologies were used, combined with communication and cooperation among various police forces, all criminals eventually would be apprehended. Wilson (2000) argues that between the 1920s and the early 1950s, policing "became a matter of professional crime-busting techniques and proper procedures, a bureaucratic code word for anticipating future criminal actions by following an actuarial logic, based on past cases" (63). Adapting communications and transportation technologies to police work, reformers developed the call-and-response model of policing (Kelling and Moore 1996). Citizens were encouraged to think of policing as a public service focused on crime control. Should they be involved in or witness a crime, they were to call their police station. Police reformers used these technologies to guarantee a speedy response. In this way, citizens were positioned by reformers as outsiders to the processes of police decision making. Citizen interaction would be controlled by the police. Convincing the public to accept police claims to professionalization, the narrowing function of policing, and their contained relationship with the police emerged as a key concern of the era.

Post-Progressive Reform versus Populist Popular Culture

This specific focus on the micropolitics of policing in the United States also sheds light on the complicated nature of radio programming and popular culture in the 1930s. The developments in policing are somewhat at odds with what many see as the populist, leftist orientation of Depression-era mass culture. Cohen (1990), Denning (1996), Douglas (1999), May (2000), McCann (2000), McFadden (2003), Razlogova (2006), and Russo (2002) examine the ways that popular culture, as expressed in film, broadcasting, pulp fiction, theater, documentary, and magazines, often articulated working-class sentiments and specifically critiqued the U.S. cultural hierarchies as produced by the institutions of capitalism and the state. At the same time, scholars such as Hilmes (1997), Lacey (2002), Loviglio (2005), and Susman (1984) argue that commercial cultural institutions, particularly broadcasting, reinforced certain aspects of American race and gender relations and the centrality of capitalism, often through nostalgia. Despite these arguments about the potentially conservative nature of broadcasting, there are many ways that during the social crisis of the Depression, popular culture expressed populist leanings to both the left and the right. This populist tendency is best evidenced in the public fascination with Prohibition era gangsters and Depression-era bandits. In fact, the infamous gangster films were among the most popular movies of the early years of the Depression. Their popularity with working-class audiences, creation of what Denning (1996) called "the first 'ethnic' hero in American popular culture" (254), and seeming celebration of criminality made the films a lightning rod for middle-class reform interests. As several scholars have argued, the gangster emerged as terrain on which the concerns of ethnic and working classes were negotiated and struggled over. David Ruth (1996) argues that the gangster figure was a cultural invention who helped deal with changes brought by urbanization and corporatization of America. The gangster epitomized style, glamour, and individual success in a culture that increasingly demanded conformity to corporate institutions. As America entered an era when identity was increasingly defined by consumption rather than personal character, the culture of personality replaced the culture of character (Susman 1984). The gangster represented cultural anxieties involved in this new culture of superficiality (Munby 1999; Ruth 1996). Carlos Clarens (1980) argues that the dynamic activity of on-screen gangsters, as portrayed by actors such as Edward G. Robinson and James Cagney, made them extremely attractive to movie audiences of the era.

The glamorization of the gangster at the expense of the official forces of law and order was met with disapproval by moral and police reformers and from "a wide range of public opinion and editorial commentary" (Doherty 1999, 156). While some silent films during the 1910s and 1920s dealt with urban underworld crime, they did so with a Progressive bent, presenting the underclass in order to teach moral lessons (Clarens 1980; Munby 1999). The cycle of morally ambiguous, pre–Hays code gangster movies of the early 1930s broke with that tradition, portraying cocky, confident urban gangsters without conveying a clear moral message.[8] These films represented a kind of social critique. Their gangster heroes achieved a Horatio Alger level of success, but a success that Munby (1999) points out was more subversive of the dominant cultural order than supportive of it. He writes, "If anything, the gangster's corrupt capitalist practices reveal the exclusionary features of the Alger myth of success. As most gangster films demonstrate, they are less about reinforcing ideals of capitalist success than about the rules and prejudices that bar specific social groups from access to power" (73). The movie gangsters' urban style, kinetic energy, and appeal to urban, ethnic, working-class populism made them tremendously popular with movie audiences. The gangster film's reversal of normative capitalist relations and celebration of the class mobility of its Irish and Italian main characters was no doubt as much a cause of concern to police and moral reformers as was the film's violent content. More than simply a source of personal gain or survival, these films clearly represented crime as, if not legitimate, then at least an acceptable way to raise their class status in a nation where their ethnic identities severely limited their economic opportunities.

To make matters worse, the official forces of law and order were unable to offer any reasonable threat to the gangster. One of the most famous movie gangsters, *Public Enemy*'s Tommy Powers, dies at the hands of rival gangsters, not at the hands of the police. Richard Slotkin (1992) writes that "in the world of *Public Enemy* the party of order and progress is marginal: the real battle is between a 'good' gang that lives by the code of masculine loyalty and brotherhood, and a 'bad' gang that 'schemes' its way to power and tortures the helpless instead of going at it with straightforward violence" (164). In the end, Tommy's corpse is delivered to the front door of his mother's house by rival gangsters. Even when the police intervene in the gangster's career, they are not the cause of his downfall. For example, Rico Bandello, known as *Little Caesar,* meets his end in a cascade of bullets fired by the police, but the circumstances that lead to his end are less a result of police effort than of his uncontrolled ambition.

Added to this was the increasing public fascination with rural bandits like John Dillinger, who wantonly flaunted their ability to easily escape the police in the process of committing daring bank robberies and kidnappings, using automobiles to quickly escape apprehension. In targeting precisely those institutions that many citizens blamed for the Depression, they achieved a degree of notoriety equaled only by Prohibition-era gangsters. Public fascination with desperado figures like Bonnie and Clyde was a pervasive part of the popular culture landscape (Powers 1983; Potter 1998). Popular culture representations of gangsters, bandits, and even detectives were part of what many scholars see as the populist meaning of Depression-era mass culture.

In specifically dealing with solved police case files, often provided by police agencies, radio crime dramas would have to negotiate this terrain. Given populist support for criminals, representing the police as heroes would require a great deal of cultural work. On the one hand, as the second-wave police reform movement became increasingly informed by the post-Progressive loss of faith in the public, dramas about policing frequently stressed the authority of state to arrest forms of social and physical mobility that threatened to too radically transform the U.S. political and economic structures. At the same time, these dramas were never fully consistent, and as much as they stressed the authority of the police, they also reveled in the exploits of those figures who so strongly symbolized the failings of capitalism, urban gang members and rural bandits. Moreover, vigilante dramas, though relegated to the realm of juvenile programming, continued to offer significant resistance to the claims of police reformers.

Programs such as *True Detective Mysteries, Police Headquarters, Calling All Cars, G-Men, Gang Busters, The Shadow,* and *The Green Hornet* struggled over the shifting definitions of policing. While police reformers might have wanted a strongly post-Progressive definition of policing to emerge from these dramas, radio producers and commercial sponsors understood that gaining audiences required some nod to populist sentiments. These nods, however, were clearly situated within Depression-era understandings of criminality. The post-Progressive construction of policing in these dramas represents their most enduring contribution to the relationship between broadcasting and policing and demonstrates that many of the conservative trends in broadcasting, such as the construction of a normative white, middle-class identity, had their roots in the years of the Depression.

RADIO'S POWER: THE INTIMACY OF AUTHORITY AND THE CONQUERING OF SPACE AND TIME

Radio was not simply another space for the circulation popular culture constructions of policing and criminality. As a new medium with its own institutional and technological logics, radio would not simply "tell" stories. Instead, this book argues that radio crime dramas played off of the unique features of radio in ways that highlighted some key parts of the reform movement, often to foster listener faith in the technological prowess of modernizing police force but sometimes to suggest unease. This understanding of radio is influenced by Williams's (1974) understanding of radio as both technology and cultural form, Lastra's (2000) articulation of film as an assemblage, and by an engagement with the literature of those trying to make sense of how to communicate through this powerful new medium (Arnheim 1936; Barnouw 1939; Cantril and Allport 1935; Wylie 1939). Williams and Lastra examine the uniqueness of separate media forms but avoid ontological reductionism and determinism. For example, Williams argued that the development of technologies such as the television or radio were not abstract processes separate from culture but rather were the result of purposeful decisions of historical actors embroiled in specific historical processes. This more complex way of thinking allows for an understanding of radio as part of the sociohistorical process rather than as something transhistorical. One of the primary historical processes that led to the development of radio as a form of centralized transmission and privatized reception in the United States is what Williams termed "mobile privatization." Broadcasting developed at a time when there were contradictory social changes involving both increased mobility through modern transportation and increased privatization of the home, which was shrinking into a nuclear family unit. Broadcasting mediated this contradiction by allowing for communication between distances and allowing a connection between the privatized home and the larger world. In this discussion, while radio creates a unique communicative space, it is not the technology but the actions of historical actors who develop and use the technology in particular ways that determine its form and content.

While Williams offers a rich way for thinking about radio, his work ignores the more subtle complexities of technological and textual development. Lastra's (2000) argument to think of film as an assemblage furthers these understandings. In his attempt to avoid the determinism that characterizes apparatus theory, he suggests thinking of film as an assemblage of what he terms devices, discourses, practices, and institutions, which "encompass material objects, their public reception and definition, the system of practices in which they are embedded, and the social and economic structures defining their use" (13). While Lastra's model is geared toward film, it offers a rich way to think of radio itself as an assemblage of devices such as microphones, receiving sets, wires, and transmitters; as discourses, such as those surrounding the tension between radio's commercial and public service functions or theories about radio audiences and their relationship to programming; as practices, such as the routines of radio professionals and the behaviors of audiences; and as institutions, such as commercial broadcast networks, advertising agencies, and corporate sponsors. This model is significant for thinking about the complicated ways that radio produced meanings about policing. While drawing on existing discourses of policing and criminality, their articulation through the radio medium would contribute to their development in unique ways. This project considers the ways that radio's textuality was strongly structured by its technical and institutional possibilities. It examines the ways that meanings about policing were connected with certain experiences of radio, such as its organization into regional and national networks; its ability to simultaneously communicate over vast geographic spaces; its ability to cross the division between the public and the private; and its unique qualities of intimacy, dailiness, and liveness.

These were precisely the qualities that those working in the radio industry grappled with as they worked to communicate with their dispersed, privatized audiences. The decisions they made intersected with the many parts of the radio assemblage to highlight specific aspects of the police reform movement. First, the programs worked within the confines of an aural medium to use both the style and content of speech to clearly differentiate police from criminals and, more significantly, to distinguish the police in the radio crime drama from their less flattering popular culture cousins in film and pulp fiction. Second, writers of the crime dramas played on radio's domestic reception in the development of intimate modes of address meant to enter but never disturb the sanctity of the private space of the home. In dramatizing the activities of police, the crime dramas developed a form of intimate authority by bringing the police into the private space of the home and allowing them to directly address home listeners. Police might have been tough on crime, but intimate authority suggested that they did so on behalf of their radio listeners, who could rest snug in their homes, assured that their communities were now safe from mayhem.

Finally, radio crime docudramas articulated the commercial notion of the network with the police use of radio and played with radio's ability to collapse time and space to create the dragnet effect, the cultural construction of police forces as an always-available presence that could conquer the problem of criminal mobility. It is in the dragnet effect that radio content and form merged, producing a powerful double effect. What better medium to convey the radio's sense of invisible omnipresence than one that could communicate by sound alone into the private space of the home, creating a sense of enveloping presence. The interconnection and interdependence of radio's form and content rendered it a unique space for constructing an apprehension-based model of policing. The dragnet effect rested on the idea of guaranteed police response central to the emerging model of call-and-response policing. The same qualities of the medium were also used to create a more uneasy series of effects in vigilante dramas that challenged the emerging model of policing.

In these ways, radio programming became a unique site for negotiating the changing meaning of policing in an increasingly complex society. It was about police involvement in crime control rather than other social services. It was about the state of policing in urban areas, growing in both geographical area and population. And it was about connecting people as previously geographically isolated areas were linked through improvements in transportation and communication. For some writing about the history of policing, the radio and the automobile are mere short discussions of technological innovation in policing, but in the crime drama and in police discourse, they are central to imagining of policing, as they are indeed central to the broader history of the nation. If intimate authority shaped understandings of policing, criminality, and citizenship, the dragnet effect shifted ideas about criminal behavior from the thrill of speed on the open road to one of desperation under the unbearable burden of inevitable apprehension. This was all achieved through radio.

chapter 1

Policing Perception

Public Image Management and the Creation of the Radio Crime Docudrama

> Good evening friends. Tonight is the 100th broadcast of *Calling All Cars*. It was with a certain amount of misgiving that I appeared on that first broadcast a hundred weeks ago tonight. But my desire to bring the policeman's side of the story to the public outweighed the fear of possible criticism. The public spirit and civic-mindedness of the Rio Grande Oil Company in maintaining these broadcasts and the unflagging zeal of William S. Robson, their author and producer, in dramatically presenting them, have justified my decision.
>
> —"Lt. Crowley Murder," episode of *Calling All Cars,* 1934

Like the soap opera and variety program, among others, the radio crime docudrama drew on existing cultural forms but was nonetheless unique to radio. While vigilante-styled dramas had clear precedents in pulp fiction, the origin of those programs that claimed to present true stories of policing is less obvious and ultimately more complicated. Created in cooperation with police forces intent on improving their public image, by advertising agencies devoted to furthering the commercial interests of their commercial clients, for broadcast on commercial radio networks concerned with government interference in their efforts, the programs grew out of the contradictory attempts to please a range of interests. This confluence of interests is evident in Los Angeles Police Department Captain James E. Davis's address to radio listeners at the beginning of the regionally broadcast radio crime docudrama *Calling All Cars.*

Given the negative images of policing circulating through the cultural landscape, listeners of the time would not be surprised to learn that Davis had originally approached the project with "a certain amount of misgiving."

Yet as image management came to increasingly occupy the attention of reformers, what better way to feature "the policeman's side of the story" than to cooperate with radio professionals? For corporate sponsor Rio Grande Oil Company, it appeared entirely fitting to parlay its contract as the exclusive supplier of gas to the Los Angeles Police Department's growing fleet of motor cars into the sponsorship of a radio program through which it could receive weekly praise not only for the quality of its product but for its "public spirit and civic-mindedness." Program creator William Robson could proffer his "unflagging zeal" as proof of his commitment to the program's public service goals. And for the sponsor and network, what better way to ensure consistent audience attention than the creation of what Davis asserted was a "splendid," "interesting," and "thrilling" program? Is it any wonder that radio crime dramas became a staple of broadcast schedules during the golden age of radio (Fink 1981, 189; MacDonald 1979, 155)?

The radio crime docudrama was a unique program form that drew from a range of generic influences. MacDonald suggests that the first reality-based drama was *True Detective Mysteries,* which debuted on radio in 1929. Adapted from the Bernarr Macfadden publication, the show achieved moderate success. No doubt there were other attempts at reality-styled police programs, but it was not until the 1930s that the more successful ventures began. Syndicated program *Police Headquarters* was produced in 1932. Recorded on electrical transcription disks, the program was sold to various NBC West Coast radio stations, which were then free to fill the lengthy music segments of the recording with local advertising. While not directly based on solved police cases, it attempted to tell authentic police stories (Sies 2000, 632). *Calling All Cars* debuted in 1933 on the regional Don Lee Network.[1] Nineteen thirty-five marked the debut of the FBI-endorsed and controlled *G-Men,* produced by radio showman extraordinaire Phillips H. Lord, sponsored by Chevrolet, and airing on NBC. After airing a mere thirteen episodes in early 1936, Lord retooled the formula and premiered *Gang Busters* on CBS for sponsor Colgate-Palmolive. This program would stay on the air, making several shifts of network and sponsorship, through 1957.[2]

The radio crime docudrama grew out of the historical confluence of the not-always-reconcilable needs of a group of historical actors, including police forces, radio professionals, corporate sponsors, advertising agencies, and the commercial radio networks. Police reformers, actively seeking to improve and control their public image, sought ways to educate the public about the developing professionalism of police forces. Those involved in the radio industry, however, sought to attract audiences to their radio sets as a venue for the messages of corporate sponsors. Sponsors, in the anti-business climate of the Depression, sought to improve their own public image while simultaneously selling their products. For those in the radio industry, programs had to be entertaining. As these groups clashed over the purpose of the programs, their concerns intersected with existing generic precedents. In the process, the programs made significant breaks with both classic and hard-boiled detective fiction, action hero stories, and confessional magazines. These breaks were key in developing a dramatic form that, if not exactly as reformers might have intended, nonetheless proved significant in forwarding a definition of policing consistent with that imagined by the second wave of reformers.

This chapter details the interactions of these groups and how the interests of police, advertising agencies, sponsors, and networks shaped these uniquely police-centered dramas that, though imperfect, positioned the police as professional authorities. First, the chapter considers the role public image management played in the police reform movement. Second, it examines the ways the programs both drew from and broke from existing generic precedents. The programs made significant breaks from both the classic and hard-boiled detective genres by shifting the narrative action of the programs from detection to apprehension and by placing police in the position of narrative protagonist. This shift was part of the goal of radio professionals to make the programs as entertaining as possible and led to clashes with police over the meaning of the shows. Nowhere was this tension more evident than in the clash between J. Edgar Hoover and Phillips H. Lord over the making of *G-Men*. The programs also broke from another significant generic precedent, the confessional magazine, by replacing a more populist notion of "truth" in storytelling with a more professional notion of "facts," resulting in a valorization of police authority. Finally, the chapter examines the ways that "facts" further served the needs of corporate sponsors and networks, who used the ostensible truth of the programs to claim that they were serving the public interest.

POLICE REFORM AND PUBLIC IMAGE MANAGEMENT

By the late 1920s, reformers began to take on what they increasingly saw as an "image" problem. The publicity of the findings of the Wickersham Commission, the failure of Prohibition, and constant criticism led police forces to feel under attack from a public they were supposed to serve. Popular representations such as the comical Keystone Kops of the 1910s and 1920s and the ineffectual stereotyped police of the popular gangster films did little to suggest that critiques issued from a variety of sources were anything less than valid. In keeping with developing ideas about the public, those in the reform movement believed that such images would prove a key hindrance to the success of reform efforts. One writer commented, "We can sum up the whole matter by saying there are two main reasons why the police experience such difficulty in doing their work: (1) the kind of people they are and (2) the kind of people we are" (Bain 1939, 453–54). While reformers did not deny the many criticisms of the police, they maintained a firm belief that the cultural landscape was so saturated with stereotypes that it was impossible for the public to truly understand and appreciate the police. Bain further noted, for example, that the public walked around with "a caricature of the ordinary policeman on the beat, but it is the 'picture of him in the heads' of many law-abiding citizens. It is one of those stereotyped, categorical myths which abound in our culture. While it may be untrue, it is still a social reality which must be reckoned with so long as numbers of people believe it" (451). Drawing on the language of Walter Lippmann (1922), the most stark of the democratic realists, who argued that the complexity of modern society and nature of modern communications made it increasingly unlikely that participatory democracy would be possible, Bain clearly articulates the police reformers' belief that public attitudes could only be corrected by police control of the information environment.

While reform efforts could improve certain aspects of police performance, many came to realize that these caricatures would prove a real obstacle to redefining policing as a public service focused on criminal apprehension. Given the general level of public mistrust and disregard, finding a cultural space to improve their public image was a key concern. One of the key elements of the professionalization was the development of an expertise in crime fighting that would give police officials the knowledge to define the meaning and nature of police work and criminality. Reformers sought to reconstruct the "pictures in the head" of various classes. Experts were needed to manage the complexity of policing in a modern society and to present the public with the information necessary to understand those efforts. Police work would center on an apprehension model that required citizens to call to report crime but not to engage in questions regarding police policy or behavior. By effectively removing policing from the realm of politics, such a model responded both to middle-class fears of property crime and to ethnic and working-class communities' concern that police were singling them out.

Seeking to improve their public image by countering a range of negative popular characterizations, citizen complaints, and even the poor self-image of rank and file officers, police reformers turned to modern conceptions of image management. This meant that images about the police would have to be initiated and controlled by the police themselves. Emerging as a new cultural space, freed from the interference of the press and filmmakers, municipal and state reformers saw the value of using radio to reach citizens directly. For example, in the fall of 1923, New York City Commissioner of Police Richard Enright (1923) delivered a series of talks about the problems facing police forces. In these talks, Enright attempted to educate the public about the activities of the police and to counter the negative image of the New York City police as politically corrupt. Listeners to KDKA in Pittsburgh, Pennsylvania, had the opportunity to hear William Root (1925) deliver six talks on criminology. On September 15 and September 22, 1932, listeners of station WEAN in Providence, Rhode Island, heard Director of Public Health Lester Round educate his audience on "the issue of scientific crime detection" (Round 1932). He discussed using science to discern a maximum amount of information from the smallest clues with methods such as fingerprinting and the use of instruments such as the microscope, black light, and lie detector test. He ended his first talk offering the Public Health Commission laboratories as a source of aid in police cases. The Michigan State Police used their Flint, Michigan, radio station to broadcast a series of eighteen radio talks outlining their activities for radio listeners. Among the topics deemed important for listeners were the use of science in detective work, the education and training of officers, the radio patrol car, the importance of fingerprinting, and the importance of citizen cooperation with police activities (Michigan State Police 1936).[3]

For local reformers, local radio outlets and their own police radio stations offered a space to gain some control over their community reputation. Nationally, however, the most vocal advocate for shifting the public image of the police was J. Edgar Hoover. While many of his efforts with the FBI drew from and built on existing efforts by municipal and state police reformers, Hoover distinguished himself as a key showman advocating police reform. While seeking to make his image over as America's number-one crime fighter, Hoover was the mastermind behind the Roosevelt administration's much vaunted war on crime. As historians have documented, this war involved sophisticated public relations on the part of Hoover to improve the image of federal crime-fighting efforts in the wake of the disastrous years of Prohibition (Powers 1983; Potter 1998). Hoover was the most aggressive reformer in his attitude toward the public. Adamant about gaining citizen support, he rallied against crooked politicians and lawyers who let criminals free or who held up crime-fighting initiatives and attacked criminologists who argued that criminals deserved leniency and understanding. Average citizens came in for a special drubbing over their refusal to serve on juries or to serve as witnesses against state persecution efforts or, worse yet, for perjuring themselves on the stand out of fear of particular criminals. Hoover found among the public a kind of cowardice and apathy, which needed to be corrected if crime fighting was to be successful. Drawing from the experience of Prohibition, Hoover posited the public as feminine in its sentimentality and weakness. This was a position advocated to Americans in any of a number of ways, and popular books on police work echoed these sentiments, as did Hoover's own frequent public statements.[4]

Already seeing the value of radio as a space from which to directly speak to citizens and to construct their own vision of professional authority, it was perhaps not a stretch to imagine themselves as the heroes of radio dramas. For these reformers, and for a figure like Hoover, radio offered a new cultural space through which they might be able to control their image in order to "educate" the public. If they had hoped for full control, however, they had to contend with new forces: those involved in the creation of the apparatus of radio. Networks, advertisers, and radio professionals each brought their own set of concerns and ideas about the public that were sometimes at odds with those of the police. While police used the radio as a way to gain citizen support for a very particular model of policing, radio professionals, concerned with gaining audience attention, were more flexible in their approaches to representing policing. Dramatizing the successful efforts of the police necessitated an encounter with existing generic models for telling stories about crime, including classic and hard-boiled detective fiction and confessional magazines. While drawing elements of each form, certain aspects were also rejected in order to more fully put the police at the center of the narratives.

THE THRILL OF THE CHASE

For a radio professional like Lord, the most important aspect of a radio program was that it be entertaining and engaging for home listeners. For police reformers, documenting their work in the name of improving their public image necessitated the emphasis on certain features of the reform definition of policing. Because technology and science figured so centrally in reform discourse, it was logical that they were key elements of the programs. It is not surprising, then, that MacDonald (1979) links the docudramas with other early detective programs. He notes that the earliest radio crime dramas focused on the logical process of deductive reasoning in solving crime. A radio adaptation of *Sherlock Holmes* was among the earliest, as was *The Eno Crime Club*. MacDonald argues that these classic detective-based programs were similar in style to the semidocumentary style of series that chronicled the work of the police. He writes, "With its emphasis upon investigation and the inevitability of apprehension, the format of the Realistic Detective series lent itself easily to dramatizations of the activities of police departments. In this way radio, as a medium of entertainment, became a salient disseminator of information regarding the achievements of law enforcement agencies" (165).

While MacDonald includes these programs in the same category as fictional detective programs that likewise focused on logical deduction in solving crimes, there is an important difference. Based on the tradition of classic detection, the "realistic detective" programs featuring fictional, private investigators tended to emphasize detection and identification. The reality-based crime series would alter this formula in a key way. Listeners did not wait for the criminal to be *identified* while matching their own wits against those of the fictional detective; they waited for the criminal to be *apprehended* while marveling at the continued success of the police in fighting crime. This switch developed out of the intersecting interests of police and radio professionals. Police reformers, such as Hoover, offered solved police cases for dramatization because they celebrated success. Dramatizing solved cases meant that the identity of the criminal was known from the outset. What was important was the apprehension rather than identification of the criminal. But this move was equally important to radio professionals, who found that apprehension offered a more thrilling story than detection. Logical deduction might work on the printed page or the movie screen, but producers like Phillips H. Lord were not confident that it would work equally well on radio. Nowhere was the tension between detection and apprehension more contested than in the relationship between Lord and Hoover during the making of *G-Men*.

From Detection to Apprehension

Dramatizing stories of criminal apprehension required a negotiation with the two most strongly delineated genres in crime fiction of the time, classic and hard-boiled detective fictions. A product of the series of concerns key to the social changes of the nineteenth century, classic detective fiction followed set patterns and, according to Cawelti (1976), turned the detection of crime into a game or a puzzle, where an intelligent detective matched wits with intelligent criminals. The emphasis was on the scientific process involved in determining who the criminal was rather than on bringing the criminal to justice. The classic detective functioned as an outsider who came in to deal with the momentary disorder caused by a single crime committed by a single criminal. Most of the crimes took place within the domestic sphere of the middle classes. After the detective solved the crime by identifying the criminal, order was restored, and the world returned to normal. In this way, classic detective fiction stories reaffirmed the normal functioning of the nineteenth-century bourgeois society. Sean McCann (2000) ties the stories even more concretely to the contradictions of classic nineteenth-century liberalism, arguing that they represent "a world in which the freedom of the individual creates an archaic or soulless society" (8). Absent traditional bonds, people pursue their narrow self-interests, leading to a dystopic vision of society. This image is rectified "by banishing a pair of scapegoats (murderer and victim) who embody the worst of those evils" (8).

With their emphasis on domestic action, questions of identity, the uncovering of hidden secrets, and the expertise of the genius detective, the classic detective format spoke to a different set of values and ideas. In the United States, by the early twentieth century, hard-boiled detective fiction emerged as a response to classic detective fiction. The hard-boiled detective novels of writers like Dashiell Hammett broke from the classic detective novel format by shifting "the underlying archetype of the detective story from the pattern of mystery to that of heroic adventure" (Cawelti 1976, 142). The tough-talking, action-oriented, justice-seeking privateeyes of hard-boiled detective fiction offered a masculine alternative to their more effete British classic detective predecessors (Smith 2000). May (2000) argues that by the 1930s, working-class detectives, such as Hammett's Nick Charles, populated the cinema, taking the place of the more mannered, upper-middle-class protagonists of classic detective stories. In fact, hard-boiled detective stories were associated with a leftist populism and tied to social critique (Denning 1996). Whereas the classic detective story focused more on developing the intricate mystery of the crime, the hard-boiled detective drama focused on bringing the criminal to justice, usually through the personal action of the hero.

Cawelti (1976) ties the development of the hard-boiled detective character to the changes wrought by urbanization and capitalism in the early years of the twentieth century and the concomitant destabilization of class status and gender roles. Smith (2000) expands on this analysis by concentrating on the relationship between hard-boiled detective fiction and its working-class readers, arguing that the pulp novels, through their production and consumption practices, became a way for working-class readers to deal with the shift from a production-oriented to a consumption-oriented economy during the 1920s and 1930s. Thus, whereas classic detective fiction was tied to a set of middle-class anxieties, hard-boiled detective fiction was more clearly tied to U.S. working-class culture.

The radio crime docudramas drew from elements of both classic and hard-boiled detective fiction, but one key component of both forms had to be particularly overcome: neither valorized the authority of the state. In the case of classic detective fiction, this was achieved by generally representing police officers as incompetent. In hard-boiled detective fiction, the police were not simply incompetent but corrupt and brutal, frequently sparring with the protagonist. Simply put, neither genre could be reproduced without, if not exactly denigrating state authority, at least reproducing doubt in the power of the state as represented by the police. More problematically, hard-boiled detective fiction spoke to a populist perspective that was precisely what police reformers sought to shift. The kind of professional authority imagined by reformers did not exactly fit within these generic variations.

A clear example of a program that reproduced the classic detective story and its attitude toward state authority was *Eno Crime Clues*.[5] As MacDonald notes of such detective programs, this program invited listeners to participate in solving the crime. It addresses its audience as members of the Eno Crime Club and invites them to join protagonist Spencer Dean, "man hunter," in his search for clues and to figure out the mystery for themselves. Dean is a solid example of the classic detective. In the two-part episode "The .32 Caliber Kiss" (1933), it is through Spencer's individual genius and reasoning powers that he solves a crime of murder that the regular law enforcement officers seem incapable of solving. Throughout the episode, Spencer asks questions that appear incredulous to the sheriff, who several times chastises Spencer for his seeming irrelevance. By the end, however, as the case is carefully reconstructed, it is clear that Spencer had command of the situation from the beginning. As Dove (1982) notes about the portrayal of police in classic detective fiction, it is not exactly that they are bad at their jobs but that they see the situation so narrowly that they are sometimes incapable of solving the crimes they confront. In this case, the sheriff exclaims that he is "plum flabbergasted" by the situation, unable to determine exactly when the murder occurred or who the culprit might be. Adept at gathering clues at the immediate scene, he is incapable of noting the more minute details that Spencer easily notices.

The shift to police-centered programs would mean a shift in narrative action and protagonist. The stories would no longer center exclusively on detection and the uncovering of secrets, nor would they focus on the use of violence alone as a means to secure justice. Action, adventure, and the chase would take center stage in place of detection and identification. Identification mattered less than apprehension. This is evident in one of the earliest programs, *Police Headquarters*. Whether the stories were taken from real police cases or not, the program clearly strives for a kind of realism in its presentation of the work of the police. Straddling a line between the classic detective fiction and hard-boiled detective fiction genres, these fifteen-minute episodes are initiated by a call to police headquarters from a citizen reporting a crime such as murder, kidnapping, or robbery. In a typical episode, the call is forwarded to the proper upper-level officer, who then either attends to the call himself or sends beat cops to investigate. These short episodes work quickly to solve the crime, with half of the thirty-nine episodes operating as classic whodunits and the other half more clearly concerned with the apprehension rather than identification of the criminal.

In those episodes that worked like classic whodunits, police were afforded the position of intelligence usually allotted to the citizen investigator. Logical deduction took center stage, and the audience was given the space to unravel the elements that revealed the identity of the criminal. An example can be found in the "Mrs. North Robbery" (1932) episode. It begins with the typical phone call, this time involving a possible robbery. When the woman calling screams for help and the line goes dead, the operator forwards the details and address to Lieutenant Marshall of the Detective Bureau, who quickly arrives at the scene. As he approaches the door of the woman's apartment, a neighbor from down the hall, Mr. Woods, opens his door to tell the lieutenant he heard a woman screaming. The officers break in the door and find the woman lying on the floor, bound and gagged. As the neighbor goes to get water for the woman, he finds the body of her husband in the bedroom. Noting that the case has all the earmarks of a robbery, Marshall calls for a doctor and for a team from the Identification Bureau to search for fingerprints.

When the doctor arrives, he tells Marshall that the victim suffered two gunshots to the head, which suggests that Mr. North was shot in his sleep. Demonstrating his knowledge of criminal behavior, Marshall tells the doctor that he will have to throw out the robbery theory, as no thief would go out of his way kill someone—that would be too dangerous. Marshall questions Mrs. North about the events of the evening, telling her she needs to pull herself together and stop crying. He asks her where she was when she witnessed the murder. Mrs. North tearfully reports that she heard a window open and then her husband arguing with some men. When she entered the room, one of the men took her and bound her on the sofa while she watched the other struggle with her husband, eventually shooting him. Marshall then leaves the room with the beat cop, and the two discuss their strong belief that Mrs. North is lying to them. Following their suspicions, they go to her neighbor's door, where they knock to ask why he had not heard any gunshots. He claims he had been listening to a radio symphony.

Finally, Marshall brings Mrs. North to the neighbor's apartment and, much to their surprise, tells them they should be acting a lot friendlier toward each other, given that they are "sweethearts." Then, in classic detective fashion, Marshall carefully details for them the mistakes they made that allowed him to conclude they were the murderers. He tells Mrs. North and Mr. Woods that, contrary to Mrs. North's claim, her husband could not have called out to her when the supposed intruder entered, as he was shot when he was asleep; that from the place on the sofa where Mrs. North claims she had been sitting, she could not have seen the bedroom; and that the supposed robber would not have been able to shoot Mr. North in the head from where she claims she saw him. Finally, Marshall tells Mr. Woods that he, too, is a radio fan and knows that the radio symphony Woods claims he was listening to is not scheduled until the following evening.

This episode unfolds like a typical detection story in the classic tradition, including identification of the criminal based on the logical pursuit of evidence, the matching of statements against evidence, and deductive reasoning skills. What is notable is that the police are placed in the privileged position of being able to discern the truth and identify the criminal. While the listener is not invited to participate in solving the mystery in the same way as he or she is by *Eno Crime Clues,* there is nevertheless the opportunity to see how the police work through logical reasoning and keen observation to solve crimes.[6] Other episodes of the short-lived series focus more on the action involved in apprehension than on the process of deduction.

For example, in the "Antonio Moretti" episode, Lieutenant Gray responds to a call from beat officer Mike Ryan concerning a jewelry theft on a downtown street. After questioning the witnesses and collecting fingerprint evidence, Gray and Ryan go back to headquarters and quickly learn that the fingerprints have yielded the identity of the thief. They are looking for an Antonio Moretti, who has already been jailed twice. This all happens fairly quickly, so that even before the halfway point of the fifteen-minute long drama, the audience knows the identity of the criminal. The rest of the episode is spent dramatizing the efforts of Gray and Ryan in apprehending Moretti and his accomplice, Bull Alexander, whom they identify merely on the basis of a description provided by Morretti's landlady. They chase Alexander to a train where they search him for jewels. Finding none, Gray tells Ryan that they will have to go but quickly whispers to Ryan to hide. As they wait, they see a sandwich delivery man enter Alexander's car. When he leaves, they again search Alexander and, lo and behold, find the jewels. It is Gray who understands that the sandwich man was Moretti in disguise. After a chase on the train, they apprehend both men.

In their knowledge of the secret world of criminals, Gray and Ryan take on some characteristics of their generic cousins from classic and hard-boiled detectives. Like a classic detective, they can secure the identification of the criminal through their ability to invade secret, domestic spaces, as indicated by their questioning of Moretti's landlord, and can employ superior investigative abilities, as indicated through their use of fingerprints. Like the hard-boiled detective, they easily traverse the dark corners of urban life, interacting with the criminal world. At the same time, in placing police at the center of the narrative, the program began to challenge some of the assumptions forwarded in both detective fiction and the press. First, despite all the negative publicity suggesting that police were incompetent to deal with a whole range of crimes, in *Police Headquarters,* they always succeed. Second, these officers are dedicated to upholding the law rather than to personal gain that might be had from corrupt practices. Most important, the series began to move away from placing identification as the central narrative problem to be solved and instead focused on apprehension as the source of tension and excitement.

Apprehension in Action: J. Edgar Hoover versus Phillips H. Lord

The reality-based crime series made the most significant break with detection as the source of narrative action. *Calling All Cars, G-Men,* and *Gang Busters* were all based on solved police cases, meaning that the action more fully shifted from detailing and inviting the audience to participate in the process of identification to documenting the process through which police were able to capture criminals. *Calling All Cars* was the earliest series to debut and, as its title suggests, was focused on issues of mobility. Sponsored by Rio Grande Cracked Gasoline, the program was designed to highlight Rio Grande Oil Company's position as the sole provider of gasoline to the Los Angeles Police Department. *G-Men* was the first national program to fully focus on apprehension: it told stories of the FBI's hunt for some of the era's most notorious "public enemies." The Phillips H. Lord–produced program, however, was short lived because Lord and Hoover clashed over control of the content. As an entertainer foremost, Lord sought for the program to be entertaining. As the national symbol of police reform and the most aggressive in reforming the image of federal police efforts, Hoover was adamant in carefully crafting and controlling the image of *G-Men*. After airing thirteen episodes, the program folded, and Lord went on to produce the successful and long-running series, *Gang Busters.*

The clash between Hoover and Lord centered on their different understandings of the purpose of the radio program and their different ideas of how to approach their audiences. If Hoover was a master at berating the public in order to justify the growth of a federal police force, Lord was the consummate showman. Lord began his radio career in 1929 with the creation of *Seth Parker,* a weekly series that took place in the living room of the elderly Seth Parker, played by Lord himself. It combined homey conversations with the singing of hymns and popular songs. The program went on the road in 1933 when Lord purchased a schooner and, with a Frigidaire sponsorship, set out to sail around the world. NBC footed a bill for $12,000 worth of shortwave equipment so that Lord could broadcast from sea. When the yacht sank in 1935, Lord was accused of sending frantic SOS calls as a publicity stunt (Dunning 1998; Publicity Material 1935). This scandal led to the end of *Seth Parker* and almost ended Lord's career. He became convinced that a program about crime might reform his tarnished image and approached the FBI.[7]

Hoover was not initially interested in Lord's offer to produce a program about the work of the agency, but Attorney General Homer Cummings was, and it was his interest in the project that got Lord into the FBI offices in the Justice Department. Cummings might have said yes, but once it was agreed to, Lord was required to meet Hoover's conditions for cooperation, which included broadcasting only solved cases and adhering to the carefully nurtured G-man formula (Powers 1983). Working closely with Hoover

and crime reporters Rex Collier and Courtney Ryley Cooper, Lord and his
associate Helen Sioussat operated from within the FBI to produce the program.[8] As Powers argues, the thirteen episodes of *G-Men* primarily functioned as another space to sell the G-man formula to the American public.
The first episode dramatized the death of Dillinger, while successive episodes worked in chronological order to document the continued success of
the FBI.

The G-man formula, based on Hoover's own celebrity, was a public relations strategy to gain support for federal crime fighting efforts. As Powers
(1983) thoroughly details, a significant part of Hoover's efforts involved the
circulation of popular culture images of his carefully constructed G-man.
Efficient, strong, humble, educated, intelligent, and scientific, Hoover's
G-man was no brute but the symbol of a masculine, professional crime-
fighting force out of which only Hoover would be afforded individual
notice and merit. Hoover's vision of the racially and ethnically pure officers drew on the long-standing American pulp literature archetype of the
action hero. Onto this character were projected only the most favorable
attributes of the culture. No quirkiness of character was tolerated. The
actions of the villains in the story were concisely accounted for; the villain
had no motives—he was simply evil. Frequently very violent, the action
hero stories detailed battles of good versus evil. However, as much as classic and hard-boiled detective fiction and the confessional were changed in
their encounter with police reformers, so was the action hero archetype.
For Hoover, Americans needed to see the FBI as a scientific, professional
organization, and therefore, as much as he could, he worked to deemphasize the use of guns, violence, and automobile chases, precisely those elements central to the myth of the Depression-era social bandit.

Among the most important journalists involved in forming the G-men
in the action hero mold was Courtney Ryley Cooper, who also worked with
Lord in putting the program together. In 1933, Cooper, a reporter who had
written about crime, was sent to the bureau to see if he could find any
stories. He ended up making a career of writing about the FBI, and he was
key in developing the G-man formula and helping to create the sense that
the nation was facing a crime wave. One of his popular works included *Ten
Thousand Public Enemies* (1935b), which, as the title suggests, told tales of
a world filled with criminals at every turn, then advocated support of the

FBI as the agency most able to handle this "crisis." Central to the G-man formula, as developed by Cooper, was linking the various cases as part of a continuing story regarding the efforts of the agency rather than treating each story as a discrete case report. J. Edgar Hoover acted as the hero of the stories, even if it was his agents doing the work. This was significant in that Cooper turned the agents into action heroes but only up to a certain point. While the traditional action hero worked alone, it was important to Hoover that his agents not be understood as lone wolves but as part of a scientifically managed organization. The successes belonged to the agency as a whole, as represented in the person of Hoover, rather than to the efforts of any particular individual (Powers 1983). Hoover was willing to cooperate with Lord in dramatizing solved FBI cases but only to the extent that he adhered to the "G-man formula."

To radio's number-one "showman," the G-man formula proved stifling. For one thing, Lord and Hoover had very different conceptions of how to address the public. Hoover found in the public a feminine weakness for bandit heroes and a failure to support crime-fighting efforts and legislation. Hoover was often aggressively bombastic and accusatory when addressing the public. While the carefully constructed G-man formula represented an attempt to entertain as well as berate, any entertainment value was required to take a second seat to Hoover's desire to carefully control popular culture images of the FBI. Lord approached the program with a different conception of the audience. In an interview with Helen Mencken (1936) of *The New York American,* he explained his concept of the "average listener." Mencken explains, "When Mr. Lord plans a radio program, he invariably pictures an ordinary family sitting around a loud speaker. He asks himself what broadcast could be interesting enough to hold the attention of that average mother and father, of those average children." After the subject heading "Recipes for Successful Radio Programs," Mencken considers Lord's approach to radio entertainment: "'I've discovered that one dead sure formula is a story about treasure hunting and gold seeking,' Mr. Lord said to my amazement." Radio programs needed to attract listeners and to hold their attention throughout the span of the broadcast, a key condition of radio "realism" (Altman 1994; Russo 2004). For Lord, the programs had to be entertaining and exciting to attract and hold the attention of a dispersed domestic, middle-class audience.

In the end, neither Hoover nor Lord was able to abandon their conceptions of the public. The files regarding *G-Men* are filled with many examples of clashes between Hoover and Lord that frequently hinged on their different conceptions of the public and different motivations in creating a radio program. Working within the radio industry, Lord understood that the program must, first and foremost, attract an audience for sponsor Chevrolet's products. For this reason, he frequently attempted to change the stories as presented to him by Hoover and his staff. For example, in a letter to Hoover regarding the scripting of the capture of Machine Gun Kelly, infamous for the kidnapping of wealthy businessman Charles Urschel, Lord (1935) notes that while he appreciates the information provided by another one of the key architects of the G-man formula, Rex Collier, he finds it insufficient. He writes, "I have, however, done a good bit of research in connection with the Urschel script, for I felt that the material submitted to me was not sufficient to make a strong program." Later in the letter, he deals with Hoover's alarming suggestion that scripts be performed *exactly* as they were scripted. As one of radio's premiere showmen, Lord often tinkered with his programs during rehearsals. He writes, "It is going to hamper us quite a bit to not be allowed to make some changes in rehearsal, but I can appreciate your position in this matter, and so we will change nothing." But Lord continues to insist that this decision will mar the quality of the final broadcast. Hoover, however, wanting full control, was unwilling to allow Lord the kind of freedom he felt necessary to make his program entertaining.

A key example of the clash between Hoover's desire to adhere to a strict formula and Lord's desire to make a program engaging and entertaining is evident in the differences between Lord's dramatization of the "Eddie Doll" case on *G-Men* and later on *Gang Busters*. The *G-Men* episode concentrated on the careful, thorough, scientific, and often tedious work completed by FBI agents. The *Gang Busters* episode subordinated tedium to the excitement of the chase. In the *G-Men* ("Eddie Doll" 1935) version, fictional agents Haynes and Dennison demonstrate the use of the "modus operandi" in identifying Doll as the bank robber they are seeking. However, once the agents identify him, they still need to locate him. As with other episodes of *G-Men,* this one demonstrates that police officers are willing to endure a great deal of tedium in order to be thorough and methodical in their approach to apprehending criminals. In this case, the "Interpreter," the name given to the narrator, explains that the officers spend two tiresome months going through marriage certificates in New York City. Their attitude toward their work is expressed in a somewhat lengthy scene that uses dialogue to dramatize their final success in getting a possible address for Doll.

It begins with the two agents reiterating the exhaustive nature of their search, as Dennison tells Haynes, "I've got to rest a minute. Six weeks of this—seven days and nights a week is beginning to tell." Haynes, chuckling, echoes Hoover's emphasis on scientific detection, replying, "This is patience—this methodological part of our job nobody else ever stops to think about." After noting the "thousands" of marriage certificates they have examined, Haynes stops, telling Dennison, "Don't say anything. Don't even speak." From there, the two engage in a protracted discussion about the names on a particular license and a comparison of the handwriting on the certificate to a sample of Doll's. Haynes offers, "I think we've got our first clue here, Dennison" (14). While this revelation might have sufficed as an exciting close of the scene, instead the two continue talking about the address, exchanging several more lines of dialogue before determining where Doll might be hiding:

DENNISON: Foley there gives his address as the Barker Hotel, Dallas, Texas— that's a fictitious address all right.

HAYNES: Yes—but Doris Mathews gives her address as Danville, Vermont. Um—I think that's a correct address.

DENNISON: I wonder what Doll would say if he knew we were tracing him through this little clue.

HAYNES: He never had a suspicion in the world this license would ever give him away—changing his name and everything.

DENNISON: What's the next step?

HAYNES: The next step is to get to Danville, Vermont—and start tracing Doris Mathews. (15–16)[9]

This scene not only demonstrates the thoroughness of the police in following up on clues, even in the face of extreme tediousness, but in its drawn-out dialogue might also be experienced as tedious by the radio audience.

In the *Gang Busters* ("Eddie Doll" 1939) version, the use of sound effects, emphatic delivery, and more explicit expressions of excitement make the same scene crisper, more engaging, and more entertaining for radio audience. First, the sound effects crew is instructed to provide the sound of "TYPEWRITERS AND OFFICE HUM" (19) in the background. Rather than belaboring the tediousness of the process, Haynes reveals he has found a marriage certificate in the second line of dialogue in the scene, quickly pointing out that "this is worth our weeks of tiresome checking." After several lines of dialogue in which the two compare the handwriting samples, Haynes excitedly says, "Dennison, its our first clue!" (20). The exclamation point in this version renders the discovery a source of excitement for the listener rather than simply an illustration of the often tedious work done by the FBI. Rather than a protracted follow-up on the significance of this discovery, the scene quickly ends as the two discover the possible location of Doll:

DENNISON: Foley gives his address there as the Nemo Hotel, Dallas Texas— that's probably fictitious.

HAYNES: But Janet Galatin gives *her* address as Danville, Vermont. That's probably correct. Come on, Dennison. We're going to Danville, Vermont. (20)

The differences here are small but significant. In working with police cases, *Gang Busters* often dealt with the scientific aspects of criminal investigation. Yet, for Hoover, demonstrating the reasoning skills and mastery of details was a key to the G-man formula. For Hoover, although apprehension of criminals was a key goal, detailing the process of detection was one of the cornerstones of the G-man formula. For Lord, the radio program must also be entertaining. Although the discovery of the marriage certificate is a key moment in both versions, in *G-Men* it is handled as a muted moment that illustrates the scientific methodology of the FBI. In *Gang Busters,* it becomes an important discovery that must be mentioned but, in order to keep the attention of the radio listener, dispensed with as quickly as possible so that the key action of apprehending Doll can continue unabated.

As their relationship soured over these clashes, Lord (1935) expressed his dismay at Hoover's disapproval. He wrote, "You and your staff had been so very kind and cooperative, when, all of a sudden, the whole spirit of the Department seemed changed and I felt like a whipped dog.—I didn't know what I had done and was unable to determine what had occasioned this change."[10] After broadcasting thirteen episodes in the summer of 1935 for sponsor Chevrolet, *G-Men* went off the air. No longer having access to the FBI files, Lord retooled the *G-Men* program and based his new program, *Gang Busters,* on solved police cases from around the country. With free rein to make his programs as entertaining as possible, it is not surprising that this weekly half-hour program ran for almost twenty years, beginning on CBS in 1936, but switching sponsors and networks during its run, a practice not uncommon in radio programming. No longer constrained by the strictures of the G-man formula, Lord worked to make his program as entertaining as possible. The entertainment value of the developing crime docudrama was increasingly justified by the frequent claims that the programs were based on factual knowledge.

FACTUAL AUTHORITY VERSUS TRUTHFUL SENTIMENT

As MacDonald points out, the first radio crime docudrama was *True Detective Mysteries* based on Bernarr Macfadden's magazine *True Detective.* The *True Detective Mysteries* radio series, while never as popular as the magazine, began in May 1929 and was broadcast on CBS for a year. Absent for six years, it returned to radio in September 1936, this time airing on the Mutual network. Ernst (1991) notes that Macfadden's publication was a significant forerunner of the "factual crime magazines" (83). Macfadden and his associates attained their stories from newspaper reporters and police officers. The magazine expressed Macfadden's interest in crime control, which he linked to his physical culture empire by encouraging exercise for youth as an antidote to the seductions of crime. The magazine featured a "Line Up," which published information regarding wanted felons; sections on scientific crime detection; and stories taken from police cases in Europe and Russia. As much as Macfadden was willing to support the efforts of J. Edgar Hoover and other police reformers (Ernst 1991, 84), he was also willing to criticize police departments, especially local police forces, for failing to deal with political radicals. Despite Macfadden's support, however, the radio crime docudramas would make a key break from the confessional style. While confessionals worked with a commodified idea of "truth" as the guarantee of authenticity, it was an authenticity from the point of view of regular people. The docudramas would replace truth with "facts," which were more clearly tied to police authority and to the reform vision of police as a scientific profession.

While formulaic in its own right, *True Detective Mysteries* never achieved the longevity and success of *Calling All Cars* or *Gang Busters*. In part, this can be seen as stemming from the confessional tradition inspired by Macfadden and the way that truth functioned in his publications, especially *True Story*. Stott (1973) discusses the confessional publications produced by Bernarr Macfadden's publishing house, including *True Story, True Romance,* and *True Detective*. The stories in these magazines, heavily orchestrated by a team of professional writers, were designed to tell the "true" story from the point of view of one who was closely involved with the story. As Stott notes, "The strategy of the 'true confession' is exactly that of the vicarious method: 'I am the man, I suffer'd, I was there.' The pulps showed the formula to be so successful that genteel magazines picked it up" (40).[11] Confessionals tended to focus on human interest and issues of individual sentiment rather than on the larger social issues that documentary did.

In the world of *True Story*, truth was clearly gendered and was primarily defined by its relationship to women, who were largely disregarded by advertisers as fickle, overemotional, and lacking a strong sense of self (Marchand 1986, 66). Appealing to a working-class female audience, like other Macfadden publications, this one valued the voices of its readers over the voices of experts. If *Physical Culture* sold a conservative populist masculinity to male readers, eschewing the advice and knowledge of the medical profession, *True Story* used emotion to create "a working-class version of the bourgeois culture of consumption by hailing themselves as the 'authentic' voice of the people" (70). Fabian (1993) considers the way truth functions as a commodity in Macfadden's publications. To Macfadden, writes Fabian, truth "was everyone's experience: it required neither precise argument nor careful documentation" (71). The confessional version of truth was too feminine and populist to be consistent with reform ideas about police authority.

Even a cursory listen demonstrates that, coming out the confessional tradition, *True Detective Mysteries* is far more sentimental, verging on the maudlin, than any of the other semidocumentary crime series. Its appeal is to populist sentiment rather than to professional authority. Despite John Dunning's (1998) claim that, like *Gang Busters,* most of the programs were told from the point of view of the criminal in order to emphasize where he made his inevitable mistake, these programs often went to great lengths to dramatize the fate of their victims, thus adding an air of horror to the stories. While claiming to tell true stories of crime, *True Detective Mysteries* often featured a kind of emotionality and sentimentality that was largely missing from other docudramas. The anthology drama waxed especially maudlin during the broadcast of its dramatization of "Secrets Never Told Before" (1937). This episode tells the story of the murder of Charles Poole by a vigilante white supremacist group, the Black Legion. Most of the broadcast, however, is spent telling the story of Poole, an unemployed white man with an expectant wife, Alice, and young daughter, Mary.

Poole is dramatized as a proud man who, like many during the Depression, is unable to find work despite his best efforts. Worried about supporting his growing family, he nonetheless exhibits no temper and is always kind and gentle to his wife and daughter, who are both unquestionably devoted to him. The action of the episode begins when Alice accidentally burns her arm while cooking. In a montage sequence representing a gossip chain, this small event eventually gets passed along as a purposeful act committed by Poole against his wife. This is how the news reaches the Black Legion. When Alice goes to the hospital to have the baby, Charles is also excited that he is being asked to attend an unnamed company baseball game, a sure sign to him that he is about to be hired. When a stranger shows up and tells him to come for a meeting that evening, Charles quickly agrees even though it means he will have to forego visiting his wife and new child at the hospital.

The episode then dramatizes an inside meeting of the Black Legion, where a group of men discuss the punishments they will mete out. In this instance, a black man accused of "talking back" to a white man is judged to deserve a beating, while the innocent Poole, whom the group believes burned his wife, is judged to deserve death. Listeners next hear Alice trying to tell her daughter Mary that she does not know when her father is coming home. The episode quickly moves to a speech by the prosecuting attorney, given during trial, in which he tells the jurors (and the audience) that the Black Legion has committed fifty murders, leading to a stiff sentence for

Legion members. The end returns the listener to a sad Alice telling her daughter Mary that she wishes she could tell her when her father would come home. The maudlin dramatization of the plight of this one family no doubt elicited great sympathy from Depression-era audiences. Garnering sympathy for the victims of crime was an important element in efforts made by the producers of these programs to deglamorize criminals. The "truth" of the situation seems less guaranteed by police authority than by an emotional connection with the ill-fated Poole and his wife. The docudrama series developed during the 1930s avoided the confessional tone of *True Detective Mysteries* in favor of a documentary tone that more thoroughly dramatized the actions of police and criminals than the actions of victims.[12] Gone were all but the most occasional hints of any kind of feminine sentimentality.

Given the strongly masculine nature of the cultural construction of the G-man formula, Hoover was especially concerned that representations of the FBI not be tainted with any feminine sentiment. After all, he built his G-man image on the foundation of scientific, masculine rationality, and such a critique could not be tolerated. When the National Women's Radio Committee criticized the program for being too "sissy"-like, Hoover was quite upset. Lord tried to explain to Hoover that most radio programs met with criticism from the press because the radio industry had emerged as a significant rival for newspaper advertising dollars. In another instance, Lord saved correspondence from the American Legion that praised the program for providing "plenty of 'thrills' to hold" that audience. The writer noted that "there is no maudlin, misconstrued romance whatever connected with the lives of the gangster or his 'Moll,' and, for once, they are painted in their true colors."[13] A representative from the Parent Teacher Association praised the program for "the straight-forward virile manner in which the series is presented without over-dramatizing and without an overdose of shooting and shrieking." This was a world where no matter how "truthful," sentiment was not permitted.

Docudramas replaced confessional-style emotionality with a documentary style that purported to dramatize how the police and criminals "really" behaved, but this time clearly from the perspective of the police. Claims to being factual thus began to play an important role in establishing the authority of the police in the telling of these stories. Whereas "truth" resulted from the everyday experience of regular people, "facts" were verifiable pieces of information provided by professional experts. The emphasis on factualness in these programs can be traced to what William Stott (1973) called the "documentary imagination" of the 1930s. This imagination was characterized by a reliance on concrete, firsthand accounts of the events of the time. Unlike contemporary definitions of documentary that rest on some idea of neutrality, documentary in the 1930s was expected to be politically motivated and to provide some point of view. It pervaded all areas of expression and was used by both radicals and more conservative elements. Stott argues that radio was especially good at conveying a documentary feel and portraying this aura of truthfulness. He uses *War of the Worlds* and descriptions of FDR's use of the medium as evidence of radio's documentary quality. He sees *March of Time* as an example of documentary imagination of the period, and it is important to understand this program as a significant predecessor for programs such as *Calling All Cars* and *Gang Busters*. The *March of Time* radio program was remarkably similar in form (if not content) to the "Living Newspapers" produced by the Federal Theater Project of the Works Progress Administration, which were plays that dramatized for audiences important events and "current problems" (106). While Denning calls part of Stott's analysis into question, stating that "it tends to reinforce the sense that social realism was the dominant tendency, rather than seeing that the documentary impulse itself was less a triumph of realism than a sign of the failures of narrative imagination" (1996, 119), the radio crime docudramas nonetheless exhibited many of the characteristics discussed by Stott. The point is not that they represented some form of "truth"; they were, after all, constructions. Rather, it is that "facts" provided a sense of truthfulness compelling to Depression-era audiences. Moreover, the docudrama's confident march toward the narrative closure achieved by criminal apprehension further marked its break from cultural front populism.

The claims to factualness, especially by Lord, did not simply suggest that the stories were true but validated the authority of the version of the story being told. "Facts" functioned as the docudrama's counterpart of the "truth" in the confessional. But facts from police "case files" highlighted the professional and scientific nature of police work in the wake of the increasing adoption of progressive reform measures rather than populist claims over the validity of experience in the public sphere. As Lord commented in a column written for the *New York American*, "These programs could be presented in such a way that youngsters wouldn't sleep for weeks and the listeners' hair would stand on end, but if they were so presented it would have to be done without the consent of the Department of Justice and I feel the authenticity of the broadcasts more than make up for the cheap melodrama which is lost."[14] In its own promotional material, Chevrolet similarly stressed the factualness of the program it sponsored. Explaining the concept of the program in an advertisement, the copy read "In each broadcast, the listener will be taken behind the scenes, as if he were a 'G-man' himself, to learn how, step by step, the Federal operators work, both in the locality of the crime and in the Washington laboratories where the science of crime detection outdoes the feats of the most famous detectives of fiction" (1935).[15] Colgate-Palmolive, sponsor of *Gang Busters,* also associated itself with the claims to factualness, hailing its sponsorship of "an authentic dramatization of Police cases. . . . On this series we present many hither-to unpublished facts and these are taken right from the files of Police records, from Police Chiefs, from Detectives who worked on the cases and in many instances right from the criminals themselves."

Claims to possession and dissemination of the "inside" facts were a consistent element of the radio crime docudramas. For example, in the opening of the "Gray Anthony Gang" episode of *Gang Busters* (1936), listeners are reminded that "this dramatization is NOT A STORY, it is a series of TRUE FACTS taken right from the records of Police Departments, and the detectives who worked on the cases." The host continues to note that such factualness is a key part of the series, "On this series we present many hitherto unpublished inside facts of crimes in the hope of arousing American citizens to a closer cooperation with the law enforcement officers in smashing the underworld." Most episodes began with introductions that continually reminded the listeners that they were hearing such inside stories. The "Fats McCarthy" (1936) episode began in a similar way by informing the listener that "Every story is authentic . . . based on police records . . . or on the personal accounts of policemen and detectives in the case. Many facts will be revealed for the first time" (1). In this case, however, the program offered its audience more, promising to tell them who killed well-known gangster Legs Diamond. The introduction continued: "In tonight's case—the dramatic story of the capture of the Fats McCarthy Gang in New York—you will hear the *inside story* of who killed Legs Diamond—and why" (2). As it turns out, the killer is Fats McCarthy himself, who kills Diamond thinking he has tipped off the police. After dramatizing the meeting between Diamond and the two officers featured in the episode, the factualness is again highlighted in the following exchange between the host Lord and the guest "Chief:"

> SULLIVAN: The public has never been allowed to know who really shot Legs Diamond, but the inside facts are that Fats McCarthy heard of Diamond meeting Detective Mark and Biggs in the building, McCarthy thought that Diamond had tried to tip off the detective, shot Legs Diamond, and, because of that incident which I have just told you.
>
> LORD: That information *is* a scoop. (10)

The constant claim to the possession of such inside "facts" increased the authority of the versions of the stories told in these programs. Presented as "truth," they encouraged listeners to identify with the police point of view. Whereas *True Detective Mysteries* frequently invoked emotion and sentimentality, Lord's programs and the other radio crime docudramas only rarely did so. In this way, claims to factualness had less to do with connecting the truth of these stories to the daily lives of working-class readers by speaking *with* them and representing their concerns than with presenting the voice of police professionals. Factualness allowed listeners to enter the inside world of police knowledge but only for the police to speak at its audience. Facts were the nonsentimental, masculine, and scientific counterparts of truth.

The claim to factualness often had more to do with selling the program than with faithful adherence to the events as they transpired. Lord, as evidenced in his clashes with Hoover, and other writers were more than happy to stretch the facts to fit formulaic notions of entertainment. A key example of this is the "Livacoli Gang" (1936) episodes of *Gang Busters*. Adapted from a story in *True Detective,* this was one of the largest arrests made without the help of federal authorities. While the choice of case to dramatize is clearly meant to annoy Hoover, Lord further focused on aspects of the case that Hoover would certainly have found too maudlin and fantastic.

The program begins by promising its audience that "tonight's interview with Prosecuting Attorney Reams is going to be one of the most startling crime interviews ever heard over the radio" about the Livacoli gang, who "had high political connections" and had grown so powerful that "NO ONE dared oppose them" ("Livacoli Gang, Part 1" 1936, 2). With this promise of excitement, the two-part episode tells the story of one of Toledo, Ohio's most notorious gangs.

Adapted from a lengthier, serialized version, *Gang Busters* takes several small incidents from the magazine version of the story and exaggerates them for dramatic effect in a manner that drew the ire not only of Reams but of Livacoli himself.

The most blatant exaggeration, which amounts to a lie, is the program's dramatization of a courtroom scene in which the key witness for the prosecution is a parrot. Detectives discovered the parrot when they infiltrated the "hangout" for Livacoli's gang, a secret room in Livacoli's mansion.[16] While there, they are startled to hear "stick 'em up" behind them. Fearful, the officers turn around to face their enemy, a parrot mimicking what he has heard during conversations in the room. The police in the episode decide to take leave of the secret room, but leave the parrot behind, seeing him as a source of information. As the trial begins, the dramatized Reams grows increasingly frustrated as witness after witness reneges on testimony given to the police out of fear of retribution from Livacoli's gang. A dramatic decision is then made to bring the parrot onto the witness stand, as the parrot mimics the orders given by Livacoli.

While the parrot does appear in the *True Detective* version of the story, he does so only briefly, providing the police with a small bit of evidence but nothing more than that. The parrot, of course, never did appear in court. Reams responds to this part of the program in a letter to Lord's associate, John Ives, dated July 8, 1936: "The parrot incident I dislike very much because every lawyer in the courtroom knows that a parrot would not be tolerated in the courtroom and it would put me in a very asinine position, even through impersonation, to suggest that a parrot be brought into court for testimony." Not being unreasonable, Reams does not suggest dispensing with the parrot altogether. "It is my suggestion that the parrot be brought into this picture as giving clues to the detectives when they made the investigation. I think you can work this out very nicely." In this case, Reams's request is that it be more clearly indicated that he is being impersonated, a request that leads to the following disclaimer in the broadcast of part two: "And now visualize this scene at New York Police Headquarters. A special office given by Commissioner Louis J. Valentine to Mr. Lord and Prosecuting Attorney Reams, who is represented tonight by Gale Gordon" (1). This small concession proved especially important as the program ended with a special guest: the parrot it purported to have testified in court against Livacoli.

In correspondence with police officers and others, it is clear that while Lord, his sponsors, and the network reveled in the idea that they were presenting factual cases in the interest of the public, the makers of these programs were more likely to go for entertainment value than public edification. Lord (1936) clearly explains why he thinks entertainment is important in a letter to Lieutenant Ledbetter of the Los Angeles Police Department:

> Obviously when one is dramatizing events for the radio an entirely new technique has to be brought into play. We haven't got any eyes on the part of the audience to help us see what is going on. Everything must be done by description or scenes reproduced in sound in some fashion. This makes it necessary that some incidents be changed so that those actually taking part in the event they are hardly recognizable, but to the average listener who is not a detective, the main foundation of the capture and the apprehension of the criminals is clear.

This quote indicates that accuracy must give way to excitement and ease of comprehension for the listener. Clues are important merely as a source of interest for the listener and as one step in leading to criminal apprehension. For Lord and his sponsors, maintaining listener attention was, at the end of the day, the most important aspect of commercial broadcasting. If Hoover wanted the *G-Men* radio broadcasts to fit into the G-man formula, originally developed by print journalists, Lord understood how techniques of storytelling that worked in print would not work in radio.

In working with actual solved police cases, both *G-Men* and *Gang Busters* dramatized key elements of second-wave police reform. Both programs, in dramatizing solved police cases, were clearly centered on successful criminal apprehension. Both drew on claims to factualness to authorize their tellings. And both worked to put police at the center of crime narratives the primary dramatic focus of which was criminal apprehension. In this way, both programs contributed to the development of the crime docudrama. However, Lord's ideas about the radio audience as dispersed groups of listeners demanding excitement and comprehensibility in return for their attention would prove enduring to the ways police would be represented in broadcasting. As much as the police professionals who offered their cooperation with Lord did so out of a desire to control their public image, their vision would always be subordinated to the needs of commercial broadcasters. This is not to say that the reform vision disappeared. The more important point is that reformers' ideas and the public ideas about professional policing would be negotiated with broadcasting ideas of entertainment.

At the same time, even if the needs of different groups involved in the creation of the programs were not always consistent, claims to factualness guaranteed that the authority of the police, rather than criminals, victims, or even beat cops, would be represented. Police authority through the trope of factualness would become a key part of crime representations in the broadcasting industry. Confessionals and hard-boiled fiction were populist cultural forms, the former sometimes leaning to the right, the latter to the left, that spoke to varied working-class, ethnic, and immigrant audiences. Although formulaic, they spoke to the quotidian aspects of modernization for a great number of readers grappling with shifting ideas of gender, consumption, work, and family. The radio crime docudrama, while drawing from aspects of these forms, diminished the populist influence by using factualness to place police expertise at the center of the narrative. Feminine sentimentality and masculine aggression were both erased from these narratives in favor of an emphasis on the police as a modern professional force governed by a scientific methodology for performing their tasks. While these negotiations with generic precedents led to a story form that centered on the police, this did not mean that police would have full control over the stories or their meanings. After all, these stories were created for commercial broadcasters for a medium that was bound by federal legislation to operate in the public interest, an interest that came to be identified with securing the broadest audience. For commercial broadcasters, attracting an audience of potential consumers was key.

"BLOOD AND THUNDER" IN THE PUBLIC INTEREST: MEETING NEEDS OF PRODUCERS

The radio crime docudramas worked to establish the authority of the police when it came to defining issues of crime and policing. The programs were full of self-conscious attempts to construct policing as a scientific profession, and they worked to highlight the scientific and technological aspects of crime fighting. However, in the end, these commercial entertainment programs were designed to gain a following of loyal listeners. They featured plenty of violence and excitement, or what radio producers called "blood and thunder," precisely those elements that caused concern in Hollywood. More troublesome was that these programs both appealed to and sold themselves to juvenile audiences, the audiences the Motion Picture Association of America was trying to "protect" from the negative influence of the gangster picture.[17] While these radio programs inspired some resistance on the part of parents, moral reformers, and social scientists, for the most part they were able to escape censorship. To do this, they drew on the dominant institutional discourse of broadcasting as operating in the public interest (Hilmes 1997; McChesney 1990). When it came to justifying their appeals to juvenile listeners, the program producers and sponsors further drew on the idea of public interest to claim that their programs served an educational function.

The radio docudramas continually constructed themselves as operating in the interest of the public. These programs made it clear that they were providing a public service by bringing public attention to the "problem" of crime. In many ways, this discourse followed that of the FBI's war on crime. Lord insistently foregrounded public service as a key narrative element in *Gang Busters*. Throughout the materials for the program are handwritten and typed notes that lay out the key elements of each episode. While some of these elements had to do with the construction of policing, many had to do with the ways in which criminality was to be presented in the program. "Public service," such as educating the audience about criminal activity, was one such frequent element. For the two-part dramatization of the exploits and eventual slaughter of Bonnie and Clyde, notes regarding the preparation of the "Bonnie and Clyde" episodes (1936) indicate public service as "broadcasts are to *arouse* public to 'crush racketeer' and *prevent parole,* p. 2, p. 22."[18] In the dramatization of the criminal career of "Fats McCarthy" (1936), public service is noted as "make public conscious of dread disease called crime."[19] Claims that he was serving the public interest were further bolstered by the most memorable segments of the program, the broadcast of clues that came at the end of the episode. The clues regarded the police search for fugitives and usually provided physical descriptions and possible location of wanted felons. These broadcasts were presented to cooperating police departments and to the radio audience as a public service offered in the name of aiding the police.

These claims to public service were also used by commercial networks and sponsors to justify their domination of the airwaves. McChesney (1994) argues that even into the early 1930s, radio networks were pressured to serve the public, noting that "commercial broadcasters faced the considerable dissatisfaction with advertising over radio" (115). Commercial broadcasters worked to avoid any hint that "the sole purpose of broadcasting was to serve as an engine for profit-making" (115). Yet, Fones-Wolf and Godfried (2007) point out that "broadcasters proved much more accommodating to the use of radio to sell the political and economic agenda of business. This is not surprising given that the networks were corporations themselves and dependent on business support of their programming" (66). They argue that as public attitudes toward big business soured during the Depression, broadcasters advocated that corporations think of radio "as a pubic relations tool" (66). NBC sought out those companies whose reputations had been most damaged in order to use their sponsorship of programming as a way to extol their efforts on behalf of the public.

Sponsors reveled in claims to public service in their publicity for the programs and in sponsorship continuity. For example, Chevrolet boasted of its service in its publicity for *G-Men,* advertising that the "company is proud to announce tonight the opening of a series of broadcasts of vital interest and concern to every citizen of the United States." The copy continued to heap on praise, telling readers that Chevrolet was "setting out earnestly and resolutely to dissipate the false glamour that has surrounded enemies of the public, feels that it is performing a public service." The company claimed that it was doing so "to bring assurance to law-abiding citizens that the country is being made safe for them to live in." They were also pleased "to aid the Department of Justice, by letting the public know how it operates and how the public may co-operate with it in its war on crime." Ending with a crescendo, this ad informs readers, "And now—hear ye, hear ye— and learn how the 'G-Men' relentlessly, surely, inevitably, get their man" (1935).[20] Chevrolet is figured as a responsible corporate citizen, using its sponsorship not simply as a way to sell cars or, in this construction, even to gain the goodwill of consumers. Instead, the corporation is staking a claim as an entity that, like the FBI and the radio industry, serves the needs of the public. In dramatizing FBI cases, commercial interests could claim that they did so in the name of public service, thus playing on the commercial network's dominant justification for their virtual monopoly over national programming.

Rio Grande Gasoline likewise used its sponsorship of *Calling All Cars* to bolster its public image. William Robson, creator of *Calling All Cars*, recalls that Rio Grande was approached in the fall of 1933 by the sales department of the Don Lee Network. He stated that "they had just sold the Los Angeles Police Department a contract for gasoline for the police cars for a year. They wanted to tie up the fact with a dramatic radio program, and I was tagged" (Robson 1966, 4–5). The sponsor's copy for the program was filled with references to public service, and the opening lines of the program specifically connected the sponsor to the excitement of the program as the announcer promised that Rio Grande Cracked Gasoline would offer "police car performance for your vehicle." Rio Grande frequently reminded its audiences that it was sponsoring the program in the interest of the public. In "Fingerprints Don't Lie" (1934), the sponsor tells the audience that "if it has done nothing else, we are certain *Calling All Cars* has brought home to you, the average citizen, the hazards and dangers of police work. In their war against crime the police must be provided with equipment that is de- pendable." In "The Poisoning Jezebel" (1938), the announcer says he hopes the broadcasts have shown the audience "the unprofitable nature of crime."

By mobilizing the public interest discourse used by the dominant com- mercial interests in broadcasting, these fictionalized docudramas were fur- ther able to justify their appeal to juvenile audiences. This was important in the wake of the publication and popularization of the Payne Fund Stud- ies, which were used by moral reformers to argue that a direct connection existed between movie portrayals of crime and juvenile delinquency (Jowett, Jarvie, and Fuller 1996). Continually stating their concern over juvenile delinquency and actively presenting their programs as a source of education for the youth of America allowed the program creators to serve the additional *commercial* purpose of creating a set of narratives based on material that Hollywood was supposed to avoid. While the gangster film was perceived to miseducate juveniles about the consequences of crime, the radio docudramas constructed themselves as presenting the proper education by celebrating authority.

The specific attempts to deal with juvenile delinquency are found in the files for *G-Men,* where Lord self-consciously worked to construct his program as an educational forum for juveniles. In a letter to Jesse Sarber, the widow of one of the jail guards killed by the FBI's first Public Enemy, John Dillinger, Lord (1935) writes:

> I went to Washington, met Attorney General Cummings, had a long talk with Mr. J. Edgar Hoover, and the more I studied the Department of Justice, the more I realized that we could put on programs that would be vitally effective in teaching the youth of the nation that CRIME DOES NOT PAY! I have talked this matter over with ministers, boys' clubs workers, Y.M.C.A. men, and to a man they are all enthusiastic about the series—they believe it will be a genuine force to combat crime. . . . For years, as you know, the gangster has been made something of a hero in the moving pictures and in stories. This has been a very serious factor and influence on the boys of the country. They have played gangster games in their own backyards. This is now being slowly changed—with the coming of the "G-Men" and their popularization, law enforcement officials are now the heroes that boys worship and imitate— they are learning to take the gangster for what he is. In our radio series we hope to convince young and old that crime does not pay and in this way we may have a genuine influence for good on many young people in difficult circumstances who might otherwise have been tempted to take the "easier" path of the criminal.

In his effort to sell his reform-minded goals to program sponsor Chevrolet, as well as to the FBI and the network, Lord worked to get the approval of the leaders of various youth, religious, and civic groups from around the country, many of them the same groups involved in the Legion of Decency's crusade against movie depictions of crime that led to the 1934 ban on gangster films. Lord clearly sets himself up as a devoted public servant. While he might have clashed with Hoover over certain elements of the program, in this letter he constructs himself as concerned only with the future of America's youth rather than with his own career.

His efforts paid off in a series of letters praising the program for its efforts to educate youth about the futility of crime.[21] He even received a letter from George Harris, executive secretary of the Organized Bible Class Association, praising the program: "The programs are very interesting because they are taken from actual experiences and not the proverbial storybook make-ups and the great moral is brought home very forcibly to the parent and to the youth who listen in each Saturday night; that *crime never pays*" [emphasis in original]. F. Elton Rogers, president of the Washington Round Table, wrote to Lord that "a program such as this is bound to have a decided influence on the 'boy' of today when there is so much crime in our midst. He sees thru your fine portrayal just exactly what happens or what would happen to him 'IF' he wanted to try it too." Emphasizing his faith in the educational value of such a program, he continues, "A boy is growing for good or for bad and every boy if he is guided in the right way will stick to the good and we believe therefore that a program such as yours which is unique indeed, has a decided bearing for the side of good for the thousands of boys you reach every Saturday Evening throughout the land." On a similar bend, George Harris also expressed this belief: "We believe that this is one of the finest ways that has yet been devised to assist the 'Youth of America' to walk the right way."

Letters of this type came from the Boys Work director of the Central Branch of the Washington YMCA, as well as from the general secretary of the Washington YMCA. Letters came from the radio chairman of the National Congress, Parent Teacher Association, and the director of the Ohio School of the Air. Godfrey Hammond, editor of the *Christian Herald,* wrote, "Speaking as a father of four young boys whom I wake up to listen to your Saturday broadcasts, and speaking also as the Editor of the 'Christian Herald,' I hope you may continue your 'G-Men' series. . . . It is very important that criminals be pictured as mean outlaws instead of heroicized as they have been for so long a time in many newspapers." Letters came also from numerous other organizations, including the Women's National Radio Committee, the radio secretary of the Federal Council of

Churches of Christ in America, the National Congress of the Parent Teacher Association, the head of the Americanization Committee of the Lions Club, the head of the Boy Scouts of America, and the president of the National Education Association. These letters from various civic and moral reform groups expressed a strong commitment to the Progressive faith in education as a method of combating juvenile crime. For the writers of these letters, *G-Men's* dramatization of solved FBI cases not only demonstrated their moral, crime never pays, but also set up the G-man as a behavior model that young boys, especially, could emulate.[22]

What is significant about Lord's attempts to gain the support of these groups is that they were precisely those groups involved in the Motion Picture Production Code ban on movie gangsters. While *Gang Busters* and *G-Men* dealt with juvenile delinquency as part of their overall work at celebrating the efforts of the police and constructing a representation of policing that specifically countered the negative ones of the past, other programs sought to reach out specifically to juvenile audiences. For example, *Calling All Cars* intentionally hailed its child listeners to become junior partners in the war on crime by offering free junior police kits, available through magazines given out by the sponsor. While the main point of the advertisements was to get adults to purchase Rio Grande gasoline, the use of the children's junior police kit, complete with "real metal badge," indicates that the sponsor was well aware that children were a significant part of the program's audience.

CONCLUSION

In his exploration of NBC's *America's Town Meeting of the Air*, David Goodman (2007) argues that American radio programming never divided entertainment and educational programming in the ways that public service broadcasting systems, such as that of Great Britain, did. Instead, American broadcasters developed programming "that combined undeniable educational and civic value with entertainment. This was the distinctively American settlement of the struggle over radio: not the complete bifurcation between public service programming and commercial entertainment that appeared in many nations but rather the invention of a hybrid of the two" (45). While the radio crime docudramas never approached their topics with the same seriousness as *America's Town Meeting of the Air,* they nonetheless worked to merge an attempt to educate the public about policing with entertaining stories that would thrill radio listeners. When a representative of the advertising agency handling *Gang Busters* wrote to Lord, he expressed his delight in a "swell script too, for the blood and thunder thrill seeker. Exciting to the point of exhaustion as it reads. The guy was a fiend, and the dialogue shows it very clearly" (1936).

The creation of the radio crime docudrama emerged out of a key set of historical developments and tensions that linked police, broadcasters, and corporations together in ways that none of the groups could have fully predicted. The confluence of the second wave of police reform and the emergence of a new mass medium regulated by the principle of public interest created opportunities to tell new kinds of stories about crime that neither valorized criminality nor denigrated policing. Facing seemingly schizophrenic attitudes toward policing and criminality, reformers came to view image management as a significant cornerstone of their efforts to professionalize police. At the same time, the unique communicative challenges and seemingly endless need for content made radio a key site for reconstructing the crime drama. Police reformers, radio producers, and sponsors all wanted to use the radio to reach the public, but they conceived of the public in different ways and wished to address them for different ends.

For the police, reaching the public was a matter of education and readjustment of public attitudes toward criminality and policing. Professional reform would work only if citizens accepted the reform philosophy that increasingly marginalized citizen input in favor of submission to the professional expertise of the police. For those in the radio industry, especially program producers and sponsors, reaching the public was a matter of direct economic survival. For radio producers, entertaining audiences large enough to justify corporate investment in sponsorship and a time slot on a local station, regional network, or one of the national networks was a key goal. For sponsors, the motive for reaching the public was the profits to be gained through increased sales that would come not only from selling products directly to consumers in their homes but also from building goodwill by providing "free" programming to audiences and by being part of the show. At stake was the entire apparatus of radio itself.

The tensions between these groups collided with a wealth of existing generic models for telling stories about crime and policing. Placing police and their vaunted goal of scientifically and technologically enhanced apprehension at the center of these narratives demanded that program producers negotiate their way through existing generic templates, such as classic detective fiction, hard-boiled detective fiction, dime novels, confessional magazines, emerging documentary forms, and gangster films. As police reformers, radio showmen, advertisers, commercials sponsors, and broadcasters pursued their goals according to their different definitions of and relationships with the "public," they created a group of programs that dramatized the activities of the police in capturing criminals. If they come off as less than fully formed and contradictory, it is easy to see why. Meant to educate and entertain at the same time, the programs wavered between a sincerity in forwarding second-wave police reform discourse and cynical appeals to public service clearly meant to defend the programs' commercial function.

Bound by the federal requirement to operate in the public interest, broadcasters were able to justify the most sensational, or "blood and thunder," elements of the show through an appeal to public service. The trope of factualness guaranteed the involvement of police officials in a program form whose formulaic consistency had more to do with satisfying broadcasters' imagination of the radio than honestly dramatizing police work. For police reformers, broadcasters, and corporations, the radio crime drama was a site to shore up their public images. Is it any wonder the programs seem dated? Yet out of these tensions emerged a programming form that was among the first to imagine the police as the protagonists of crime dramas and to bolster the authority of police claims to exclusive, professional knowledge of policing and criminality. This professional authority was extended beyond the realm of politics and into the world of popular culture. While these tensions continue to shape broadcasting representations of policing, the enduring legacy of the relationship between broadcasting and police authority is the most significant result of this period.

chapter 2

The Sound of Intimate Authority

Professionalism and the Reformation of Police Officers

For the first time in my radio life I find myself hampered by facts. The average fictioner in approaching his subject has what he calls poetic license. He can create his hero with a deep voice, his villain with a high squeaky voice, or whatever he likes, so long as he adheres to the writer's first law—to be interesting. I cannot portray these people—I must photograph them in sound.

—PHILLIPS H. LORD

In publicity for his upcoming *G-Men* program, Phillips H. Lord emphasized one of the key concerns in the creation of radio dramas: how to represent events in the world through sound alone. While, as discussed in chapter 1, Lord clearly overstated his adherence to facts in an effort to publicize his programs, he nonetheless identified a problem many in radio faced during the first years of the Depression: How do you create meaning about the world through sound alone? Images already saturated culture. Photography, advertising, and cinema filled the United States with visual representations of many aspects of life. By the late 1920s, however, sound emerged as a cultural concern.[1] As radio became one of the dominant mediums to colonize leisure time, those in the industry grappled with how sound would work to convey meaning to audiences. While many of the markers of the police professionalization movement, such as uniforms, patrol cars, and the use of scientific equipment, were based on their visual impact, radio producers faced the problem of how police authority could be represented through sound alone. How could one sound authoritative?

This chapter argues that it was not simply didactic exposition but, more important, the expressive aspects of radio that constructed the meaning of policing in the radio crime docudramas. More significant than what was said was *how* radio actors spoke as police or criminals and *how* the stories were structured to accommodate the production of meaning through sound alone. Paddy Scannell (1991) argued that when thinking about broadcast talk, it is important to not only think about the content of speech but also to think of the ways that content is spoken. According to Scannell, "the expressive dimensions of communication, how things are said, why and for what possible effects" (11) are a key way to think about the meaning of broadcast talk. The more convincing representations of police authority came from these "expressive dimensions" of broadcasting. The "lessons" of these broadcasts were conveyed not necessarily in the stories or in their moralistic endings but in the structural choices broadcasters made to communicate in sound alone with their home audiences. Decisions about how actors would speak were important to the construction of the idealized police officer as a male, white, nonethnic, knowledge worker whose first loyalty was to the police force rather than private or individual interests.

Sound effects and other narrative devices used to convey meaning through sound were equally important. This is especially significant if we consider that during this period, radio professionals were still negotiating radio production practices. Developments in microphone technology, design of studio space, and a growing understanding of radio's sonic potential mark this as the era that radio communication moved "from an indexical system (where recorded and broadcast sound represent a faithful transcription of the actual spatial situation around the microphone) to a symbolic system (in which particular learned sound configurations take on meaning through their relationship to one another)" (Altman 1994, 11). In fact, as radio's premiere showman, Lord's efforts in the creation of sound dramas were frequently noted by those in the industry for their narrative efficiency, excitement, comprehensibility, and dynamism. Lord and his sponsors certainly regaled in their claims to factualness, but his decisions as an entertainer were just as important in constructing public ideas about policing. In developing the symbolic system of the radio crime docudramas, the writers developed a consistent set of devices that dovetailed with the increasingly bureaucraticized, rationalized, and hierarchal vision of modern policing. When combined with particular forms of address, the programs conveyed a form of authority that was comfortably intimate for home listeners.

This chapter examines the construction of authority through sound. First, it explores the reform discourse about police officers and the construction of the ideal officer and his place in a hierarchal chain of command. Second, the chapter considers the expressive elements of radio speech to examine how police authority was represented in a way consistent with the reform vision. In particular, it examines the strategies writers used to consistently convey meaning to radio audiences. The common understanding of those writing for radio was that radio drama required certain narrative strategies to help orient the listener. This was achieved by, first, an emphasis on clear characterization that helped create a remarkably consistent representation of police as deethnicized professional knowledge workers. It was further achieved through efforts to orient listeners that worked to reinforce the authority of the police to speak about matters of policing and criminality by positioning them as members of an organized, hierarchal organization. Finally, by adapting the content of the radio crime drama to the dominant understanding of the requirements for acceptable domestic reception, the radio dramas created a form of intimate authority between police and radio listeners. In these ways, citizens were positioned to relate to police as hierarchal authorities and to understand police power as penetrative of private spaces and concerned with the protection of private property and safety rather than with forms of social disorder, such as labor strikes. As the concerns of reformers met the representational strategies of radio writers, a particular idea of police officers and police authority was constructed that validated the authority of the police by constructing them as inside knowledge workers.

POLICE AS PROFESSIONAL KNOWLEDGE WORKERS

For police reformers, improving both the quality of police officers and the occupational prestige of policing were among the biggest obstacles to instituting changes in policing. In reality, the overall state of police personnel across the nation was quite dim. Compounding this problem, the overall social status of policing was so low that attracting better "qualified" candidates was difficult, and maintaining good relationships with the public seemed impossible unless citizens could muster even a modicum of respect for police officers. In the battle to depoliticize policing by wresting it from the machinations of urban ward politics, the definition of what constituted a quality police officer and what that police officer should spend his time doing were central concerns. Professionalization efforts aimed at improving the quality of police officers were a key part of reform efforts to separate policing from forms of social mobility and ethnic political power centered in urban wards. Police jobs were no longer to be viewed as a way for immigrants, ethnic groups, or the working classes to improve their lots in life or as a form of political influence available to ward politicians.

Reform groups, including the Wickersham Commission, posited that a key hindrance to improving the police was the status of the rank and file despite earlier efforts at improvement. Second-wave reformers were in agreement that a key problem with police officers resulted from the relationship between ward politics and police personnel. In cities across the United States, local politicians were inclined to treat police officers as extensions of their personal and highly localized authority. Police officers engaged in such questionable activities as pursuing extralegal solutions to politician's problems, using intimidation and violence to guarantee election outcomes, and improving the financial situations of their ward bosses. Police jobs were granted as a form of political influence and had little to do with the qualifications or abilities of those hired, leading to a general lack of professionalism and training. Moreover, with little attention to the qualifications of the men hired, the overall intellectual and physical fitness of the existing officers serving in police departments across the country suffered.[2]

Reformers noted that in addition to being underpaid, policemen were often lazy, inattentive, and frequently violent and abusive. Put succinctly:

> As the patrolmen are directly selected by favoritism because of their partisan political activities or by civil service examinations, which can only remotely make certain of their qualifications for the discharge of their duties, since they have no practical experience, have as a rule had nothing more than elementary schooling, are usually without cultural background and without an adequate set of qualifications for the discharge of their duties, it follows that a large part of them are not likely to be and are not competent patrolmen. They all have political backing to get their positions and look to it for retention and promotion in the services. And from that source must come the

commanding officers and nearly always the chief. ("Wickersham Report" 1931, 339–40)

Discussions about officer fitness and politics were greatly informed by the reformers' concern with the control of social mobility and its relationship to race and class in American cities. As Fogelson (1977) argued, the often first- or second-generation immigrant police officers viewed their jobs as a form of social mobility and were quite willing to pad their incomes by profiting from and participating in vice activities such as drinking and gambling.

The relationship among policing, ethnicity, and class further complicated both reform and citizen attitudes about the rank and file. Police officers most often came from those newly arrived immigrant groups most targeted by white middle-class anxiety and hostility. Since the turn of the century, reform efforts had attempted to control movements of new immigrants into police jobs through tactics like civil service examinations, which gave an overwhelming advantage to those literate in English and led to an over-representation of Irish officers in a number of cities throughout the United States (Fogelson 1977; Wilson 2000). Compounding these problems, officers were often implicated in street conflicts between various ethnic groups through their efforts at strike control, vice law enforcement, and political work on behalf of their bosses. Given this situation, police were little re-spected by the public, a situation that threatened the workings of the justice system.[3]

In addition to addressing the problems with the status and fitness of the rank and file, reformers worked to determine precisely what role officers should play in their local communities. As a number of historians point out, police have been responsible for an array of functions in urban communities. In urban areas throughout the nineteenth and early twentieth centuries, police performed a number of what Monkkonen (1981) calls "catchall and responsiveness" functions, including finding lost children, checking boilers, providing lodging for the homeless, and fighting fires, that, as far as reformers were concerned, had little to do with policing. Progressive police reform involved narrowing the function of policing to criminal apprehension. Police should engage only in activities related to upholding the law. On this point, reformers met a great deal of resistance from police officers,[4] who did not always feel compelled to enforce vice laws; from citizens, who continued to treat urban police forces as general urban functionaries; and from ward bosses, who used police to enforce their own political influence. In general, reformers could count on very few among the rank and file who might be willing to change.

In keeping with moves toward professionalization of policing, reformers imagined police as professional knowledge workers, firmly situated within and controlled by a hierarchal, bureaucratic apparatus. Reformers encouraged police to work in a scientific, standardized, and efficient manner. Various reform efforts centered on educating and recruiting quality officers, donning official uniforms, standardizing investigative procedures, creating and maintaining criminal records, using forensic science, fostering expertise in particular areas of law enforcement, and adopting a hierarchal organizational structure to oversee beat cops.[5] Police would work like other modern professionals, such as doctors and lawyers. They would produce their own specialized knowledge, organize themselves as a hierarchy like other modern organizations, and provide professional, scientific training for officers. Because Progressive reform involved the creation and professionalization of a number of urban social services, second-wave reformers were in a position to aggressively pursue the narrowing of the police function. Increasingly, effectiveness in police work was measured by the success in identifying and capturing criminals (Kelling and Moore 1996; Walker 1998; Wilson 2000). Police should be modern, educated, specialized knowledge workers serving as the ideal public representatives of professional police bureaucracies.

THE SOUND OF PROFESSIONALISM

While the reform perspective was never fully articulated in the radio crime docudramas, when it came to representing the actual police officers, the decisions radio professionals made to convey meaning through sound created consistent characterizations that strongly conveyed an aura of professional authority. These programs often emphasized the ideal police officer as defined by police reformers. These men were consistently and clearly represented as educated, in possession of a technical knowledge, and dedicated to professional norms and public service rather than personal interest or local politics. While this ideal image could be described to listeners either specifically through didactic intent or through plot elements, there were also ways that writers, in representing these characters through sound alone in order to make them recognizable, created a model of the ideal police officer.

Radio Voices

Most writers for radio agreed that voice characterization was a crucial aspect of radio production. Early debates about the voice in broadcasting led to the diminished role of women as announcers on radio and to the development of standardization in the speech patterns of radio announcers (Douglas 1999; Hilmes 1997). Standardized performances through voice type, dialect, and patterns of speaking became key to marking the identity of characters that radio listeners could not see. Voice performances were highly varied and offered Depression-era radio listeners a cacophony of difference. From the coded blackness of *Amos 'n' Andy,* the parade of ethnic characters that populated *Allen's Alley,* the comic appearances of ethnic characters such as Schleperman on Jack Benny's program and Nick Depopulous on *Fibber McGee and Molly,* to the urban spun tales of making it in America as dramatized by Gertrude Berg in *The Goldbergs,* ethnic and racial difference was not only a theme of old-time radio but a central organizing practice for differentiating characters in a medium that communicated by sound alone.[6] It is important to realize that these differences represented not just individual differences between characters but the standardization of different character types. This emphasis on difference resulted from the practices of radio professionals, who generally recommended that the number of characters in any radio drama be kept to a minimum and clearly differentiated through voice and accents so that the radio listener, always in danger of distraction and disruption, could easily distinguish each voice from the others.

One of the key problems in writing for radio was that all the action of the narrative needed to be verbalized. While sound effects could punctuate scenes or create imaginary space and movement for the listener, and while narrators could set up scenes, the burden of narrative cohesion rested on the speakers. But hearing speakers without visual confirmation of identity posed additional challenges. How could listeners distinguish among voices in a narrative? The solution to this dilemma was an extreme emphasis on differentiating characters inside a narrative through voice tones and speech patterns. Firth and Erskine (1934), instructing future radio drama-tists, note that

> the playwright must take every precaution against listeners being unable to know, at once, which character is speaking; contrast between characters must be more extreme than on the stage, because of the possible confusion of voices. The characters should address each other by name far more often than they would in everyday life—and violence, as a rule, should be replaced with intensity.
>
> Writers should unblushingly give each character mannerisms of speech, so that each will be known by his vocal "trade mark"—which may be a spe-cial laugh. (66)

Later in the same volume, they exhort that "extreme voice contrast is essen-tial to the understanding of a radio play, and this can be aided to a great extent by the author's exaggerating this contrast by the individual manner of speaking, and the choice of words each character uses" (82). As Rick Altman (1994) argues, the goal of making dialogue intelligible in a medium communicating by sound alone was a constant concern of radio profes-sionals. The strategies of clear differentiation among actor voices to assure correct character identification and "theatrical voice modulation as the major form of volume and tone variation (as opposed to variations involv-ing spatial or transmission concerns)" (9) were key to commercial radio's dramatic economy.

In choosing how radio actors would represent their characters through speech, writers entered a high-stakes world of speaking. Cmiel (1991) details the cultural debates surrounding the move away from formal to more in-formal modes of speaking during the nineteenth century. As the century wore on, speech became a less reliable marker of class identity as these informal modes of speaking invaded more areas of life. However, Cmiel also argues that by the end of the century, under the influence of the Pro-gressive movement, technical forms of language developed. Once reviled for alienating or tricking audiences, by the end of the nineteenth century and into the twentieth century, technical talk rooted in the embrace of science and professionalization became a key part of public culture. Its effect was to distance the public from an emerging world of experts. Radio was able to combine this technical language with its own authority. As Scannell (1991) notes, "Broadcasting is an institution—a power, an authority—and talk on radio . . . is public, institutional talk, an object of intense scrutiny, that gives rise to political, social, cultural, and moral concerns" (7). Who was able to deploy technical language and who was not said a great deal about where groups were arranged on the U.S. cultural hierarchy. In an aural medium, differences in accent, dialogue, and manner of speaking carried extra weight because the voice was the key sign of the body on radio. As Russo (2004) observes of his review of radio production practices, "Dialect could add culturally defined layers of meaning to speech. Within practices of radio drama construction, details like noun/verb agreements, improperly pronounced r's, or subject/verb inversion called forth a whole host of cultural values" (258).

The two most frequent characters in the radio crime drama that needed such exaggeration for identification purposes were the police and the criminals. In choosing the vocal patterns that distinguished these characters from each other, these programs furthered progressive police reform definitions of criminality and policing. In these dramas, police deployed the technical language of police reform, separating them from any ethnic stereotypes associated with police inferiority. It is significant that the radio drama policeman, unlike his Irish-accented screen or pulp-fiction cousin, spoke in a clear, professional tone marked by a mastery of the emerging technical discourse of professional policing. The radio policeman could be tough, but he was, above all, professional. The educated radio policeman spoke in unaccented "American" speech. Even if his name marked him as ethnically other, his voice indicated his inherent whiteness during an era when the ethnic working classes were often not considered part of "white" America.[7] The police rarely used slang or contractions beyond the need for maintaining some level of naturalness in radio dialogue. They referred to themselves as police, beat cops, or detectives. Unlike the criminals, they had command of both the technical, professional language of policing and the language of the underworld, thus wielding a great deal of authority.

For example, both *G-Men* and *Calling All Cars* feature descriptions of the modus operandi process of identifying criminals. Both go to some length to explain this technical concept to radio listeners. In the "Eddie Doll"

(1935) episode of *G-Men*, FBI agents are left without a tangible clue to a bank robbery. The fictional inspector Haynes carefully details to his men, and hence to the listening audience, the process of developing a modus operandi: "Every musician has a definite individual musical touch, every painter has a style all his own, every criminal has his own individual approach to a crime." He explains that the crime currently under investigation "may have been committed by a leader who had his schooling from some gang that's already been caught. If we can find that one of the middle western gangs which operates similar to the procedure used in this robbery, it'll be a nail to hang our hat on" (8). The scene continues as the officers discuss how the robbery was committed and compare the records of other bank robberies to determine the methods that were used. Through this patient comparison, the FBI finally identifies Doll as the robber in question.

In *Calling All Cars* episode "Fingerprints Don't Lie" (1934), the police officer guest-hosting the program explains with even more detail not only how the process works but also how the scientific collection of data allows the police greater knowledge about criminals and their activities:

> Good evening friends. The modus operandi, which is known in police par-
> lance as the method of operation of criminals, is one of the most recent police
> systems for running down criminals. It is a highly efficient [muffled] Depart-
> ment of the Bureau of Records and Identification, your police department
> maintains files on every type of crime and every type of criminal, so that even
> the most inexperienced can quickly and effectively go through the catalogued
> files and determine what criminal or gang of criminals may be playing in a
> particular part of the city and committing particular crimes. This system
> went into effect in the Los Angeles Police Department eleven years ago. It is
> rapidly reaching a state of—uh—profession.

Written a full year before the *G-Men* episode, this episode of *Calling All Cars* dramatizes an important element of both national-level and local-level police reform: the adoption of scientific methods and scientific record-keeping to help ensure the apprehension of criminals. While this point is demonstrated through the story, the deployment of the specialized vocabulary of police professionalization is significant. The police alone had access to such specialized and intelligent ways of speaking.

Scripting police officers to speak without slang becomes particularly apparent when compared to the *written* version of *Gang Busters,* published as juvenile pulp fiction. The juvenile books, featuring stories from the radio program, made frequent use of the visual signifiers of professional police authority, such as uniforms, badges, and square-jawed, masculine officers. In this visual world of police authority, slang was permissible. For example, "The Phantom Bandit," one of the two stories in the pulp publication *Gang Busters In Action* (McAnally 1938), tells the story of police captain Jim Olsen, who was assigned to the case by Chief Foster. The chief assures him that he is right for the case: "Listen, Jim . . . I believe you and your men will get this bandit. And I have never believed anything else. There never was a clever crook who was more clever than a clever copper. And you, Jim, are a clever copper" (28). The term "copper" was associated with criminal slang, a reference to the copper badges carried by police officers. Criminal use of such slang in *Gang Busters* led to complaints that the program was corrupting children (Razlogova 2006). However, for the most part, police officers in the program did not use slang.

Impersonality and the Character Type

While the use of a technical language of professional policing marked the difference between the criminals and police as individual characters within a specific narrative, these programs faced the longer-term problem of how listeners could clearly identify criminal and police characters each week. In other words, even in an anthology style drama, the building of consistent characterizations was still important to orient listeners. While criminals and police were to be clearly distinguished from each other in specific narratives, over time, programs like *Gang Busters* worked to build clear criminal and police types, marked by their internal similarity to each other. As much as the demands of vocal characterization demanded a certain infusion of "personality" to mark individual characters, the burden of producing a weekly program dramatizing different real-life stories led to the simultaneous impersonalization of the two main characters: the police and the criminal. As recognizable types, criminals and police came to represent broader cultural categories.

The radio crime docudramas achieved a careful balance of creating a recognizable police type while sufficiently downplaying the personality of individual officers. The docudramas served, in some ways, as ideal places to do this. The time compression required forcing complex real-life events into carefully scripted and timed half-hour stories with an easily identifiable beginning, middle, and end and a clear narrative chain of cause-and-effect events. Characters were important only in as much as they forwarded the development of the plot. In addition, the documentary emphasis on "real-life" solved police cases, culled from an ever-wider geographical terrain, meant that, beyond the host, individual police "characters" would not reappear. The anthology-style dramas, then, lent themselves more to the creation of character "types" than to types of "character."[8]

Deethnicized impersonality of the police was achieved on *Gang Busters* by the scripting of specific narrative "slots" that were to be filled in with the names of specific police officers involved in the case being dramatized. In an effort to achieve narrative consistency, *Gang Busters* episodes regularly figured two officers who were the main investigators of the case. In a letter dated January 27, 1936, Phillips Lord wrote to the chief of police in Salt Lake City to explain why only two main police characters could be used:

> On most of these criminal cases the criminals go from one section of the country to another and different police units have charge of different parts of the search but this is almost an impossible situation to dramatize over the air. For instance, if we start dramatizing a Boston Scene and crime and then the criminal goes to Chicago and we have the Louisiana State Police and then he goes to Texas and the F.B.I. works on him there, the radio audience would be so confused after a few minutes that they would not be able to follow the plot. It has therefore been necessary for me to select one locale such as the Sacramento Mail Robbery and then appoint two fictitious inspectors or detectives to follow the case through from start to finish. *In this way the radio audience becomes accustomed to the voices of the detectives and can follow the plot* [emphasis added].

Lord and the people who wrote for him were well aware of the narrative devices necessary to ensure dramatic consistency in the program and thus to keep the action easily recognizable to listeners. The two officers in the program "appeared" only in relation to their work. The use of fictional detectives also indicated that their personalities mattered less than their function in forwarding the story of apprehension. Unless there was some important detail about the officers' family that might build sympathy and support for the police, dramatized officers were not represented with reference to any kind of community life outside of the force. Even *Police Headquarters,* which did feature the same police department in each episode, nonetheless often featured a variety of officers. Richard Gid Powers (1983) argues that such impersonality was an important element of the "G-man formula." Hoover made sure that any success in crime fighting was attributed to the power of the FBI as a whole rather than to any individual. The impersonality of these programs worked in a similar way, suggesting that the power of the police emanated from its organizational structure rather than from any individual leader or officer. The protagonists of these programs were the "police," in a general sense, rather than individual police departments or officers. This meant that listeners from across the nation could identify with their local police forces as part of the general "police." With the docudramas' emphasis on criminal apprehension, police officers appeared only in regard to their efforts in this endeavor. This consistent representation of dedicated officers, beholden to the law, worked to effectively sever these represented police from any specific ethnic or communal ties or from any political allegiance beyond their professional code. These were men dedicated to the goal of serving the public rather than any individual interests, including their own.

Police as Knowledge Workers

While the use of language and the use of standardized narrative slots affectively indicated that the police were professional knowledge workers beholden to a professional goal rather than to ethnic, political, or communal ties, this was further enforced by the consistent emphasis on police training and knowledge of procedures and scientific methods. The special knowledge that police possessed was not simply a matter of innate intelligence. While it is true that the overall quality of police recruits needed improvement, professionalism involved the formation of a specialized body of knowledge. In addition to using specialized vocabulary, the radio crime docudramas often emphasized police knowledge either through specific reference to police training or by explicitly noting how current police methods differed from those critiqued by the Wickersham Commission, especially with regard to the use of procedure and science rather than brutality or arbitrary enforcement of laws.

Police training was one of the key tenets of the police reform movement. Policing was not simply a matter of patrolling and of using strong-arm tactics; it was a matter of careful education in professional methods for identifying and apprehending criminals. Police officers, in contrast with more typical representation on film and in detective fiction, were intelligent. But unlike the individual genius of the classic detective fiction detective, this intelligence was a specific result of police training and thus also prevented the radio police officer from relying on the force of the hardboiled detective. The intelligence of police officers was one of the most consistent themes in the characterization of the police on radio. In direct contradiction to other popular imagery that represented the police as stupid, oafish, and incompetent, these programs presented listeners with a cadre of well-trained men steeped in a professional methodology. While their intelligence harkened to the classic detective, the emphasis on their training marked a significant departure. Just as Foucault (1979) argues about mid-eighteenth-century soldiers, the modern police officer was made, not born. Such training was also significant in demonstrating police were professional knowledge workers whose efforts were performed on behalf of the public rather than special, political interests. Education was a further step in depoliticizing and deethnicizing police officers.

Unlike the classic detective, who is gifted with a special intelligence, the intelligence of the police is a result of their training in scientific methods. Several episodes of *Gang Busters* worked to demonstrate the kind of training policemen went through to become qualified for their jobs. For example, the "Edward Metelski" (1936) episode was originally scripted to feature an entire opening exchange instructing listeners in the rigorous training provided by professional police academies. The episode starts with Lord introducing Colonel Schwarzkopf and asking him to explain to listeners "some of the things officers are taught in Police School." Schwarzkopf replies, "How to draw their guns quickly, how to use the butt of their gun to stun a man and not kill him. They're taught legal angles, laws, how to question a suspect, observation, ju-jitso." At this point, Lord presses him to explain how to "teach observation in a police school." Schwarzkopf invites the listeners to hear what happens in a "typical class."

MURMUR OF MEN

TEACHER: Attention gentlemen.

MEN QUIET

TEACHER: Now you did very well on that instance—but that's where you
have time to observe a suspect over a period of time. Now that door to
the left is going to open—a man is going to walk across this platform
and out the door to the right. I don't know who this man is going to
be any more than you do. After he passes I want you to tell me about
him. (9)

After the students deliver a basic description of the man, their instructor
stuns them with the amount of detail he is able to add. His powers of observation are not innate, however, but a result of his training, and we are
assured that his students soon will be able to do the same.

The "Chicago Kid" (1937) episode of *Gang Busters* returns to the idea of
the police officer's training, which gives him exceptional powers of observation. This episode features a number of short segments designed to highlight the work of the police. The segment about the Chicago Kid begins
with the "guest," Inspector Coglin, discussing the police officer's powers of
observation. He tells Lord, "In this country there are some one hundred
seventy thousand law enforcement officers walking the streets tonight to
protect us. We see them as we pass them, but how are they different than
we are? What are they thinking?" He continues, "Mr. Lord, citizens don't
stop to realize, but practically all of those police officers have been through
a very severe training. For instance, their observation powers have been
developed to a very high degree" (5). The scene shifts to the backroom of
a bar, where the police question a friend of the Chicago Kid, something
they routinely do. They find the man playing cards alone, but one of the
officers notices that the deck seems a little thin. He counts the cards, and
as suspected, there are only forty-seven out of the fifty-two that make a full
deck. The officers then know that the Chicago Kid must have hidden when
he heard them approaching. Sure enough, the officers open a closet door,
and the Chicago Kid, hiding inside, fires his gun at the officers. They fire
back, killing him. This incident, and others like it, reminds listeners that
successful criminal apprehension is not a matter of mere luck or happen-
stance but of carefully developed professional methods.

Another consistent theme that emphasized the professional authority of the police was the focus on scientific knowledge, which further emphasized the ways that modern police operated differently than those in the past. The programs took on one of the most significant critiques of police officers, their use of the third degree. While the emphasis on hierarchy and professional training indicated that these officers would not employ such questionable tactics, *Calling All Cars,* a show tied to dramatizing the activities of a large municipal police department—precisely the type most castigated for their brutality—specifically compared these new professional methods with those of the past. In "Crooks Are Human" (1934), Los Angeles police officers refuse to resort to the third degree even when dealing with a man suspected of murdering a fellow officer.

In "The Murder Quartet" (1934), a group of four people conspire to murder their elderly landlady. Los Angeles Chief of Police James E. Davis invites the radio audience to listen about their thwarted plan to "commit cold-blooded murder." He asks that "particular attention" be paid by "those listening in tonight to the splendid work done by the police officers in wringing from the group of conspirators and would-be murderers whose story this is, the true confession concerning one of the most barbaric killings in police annals." While listeners might well wonder what brutal tactics were used to secure such a confession, instead Davis assures them, "This splendid piece of detective work was done without resorting to the antiquated, so-called third-degree." When the four suspects refuse either to confess to the crimes or to implicate each other, the police notice during questioning that one of them seems more nervous than the others. When the captain tells the nervous man he is free to go, he offers to shake hands in order to apologize for holding him so long. When the nervous man winces in pain, he confirms what the captain already knew: he was the one who delivered the deadly blow, injuring his hand in the process. Chief Davis instructs his listeners to note "the psychology used by the police officers in this story to break down the resistance of these clever criminals." This episode not only demonstrates that the police rely on intelligence and psychology rather than on strong-arm tactics like the third degree, but in presenting four obviously guilty and morally reprehensible people as the object of the police investigation, it also suggests that even if the police have been criticized in the past, only the guilty have suffered from police brutality.

The emphasis on officers possessing specialized, professional knowledge was achieved through ways of talking, including being scripted to speak without accents and possessing technical vocabularies, and through frequent specific reference to police training. Possession of a professional knowledge that guided the relationships between police and criminals and police and citizens was further emphasized through the frequent mention of forensic science. As discussed in chapter 1, in many ways, these programs tended to deemphasize procedure and technical knowledge in favor of the excitement of the chase, but this is not to say that science disappeared altogether. In representing police as professional knowledge workers, reference to science remained a consistent part of these programs. If not belabored in detail, as Hoover might have preferred, and if subordinated to the chase, reference to fingerprinting, blood types, and other forms of scientific knowledge were common. Like the specific attempts to demonstrate that police officers were not wantonly cruel and abusive, science was a way to depoliticize the relationships between police and criminals and between police and citizens.

Given the intensive drive by the FBI to form a national fingerprint database, it is not surprising that it features prominently in all of these programs. In "The Fleagle Brothers" (1935) episode of *G-Men*, fingerprinting helps not only to identify the bank robbers but also to free four innocent men who are mistakenly captured by local police forces in Kansas. The script reads like a primer on the FBI's advocacy of fingerprinting, describing its effectiveness in both identifying the guilty and protecting the innocent, thus circumventing criticisms that the collection of fingerprints violated civil liberties. In this case, while the Fleagle brothers are robbing a bank, one of their gang is wounded by police fire during their escape. The brothers find a doctor to treat the member, and while he is driving his truck, he asks one of the brothers to put the window down. This simple act allows for the retrieval of the fingerprint. After the doctor treats their wounded companion, the brothers decide they must murder him lest he reveal to the police what he has seen. They drive near a cliff and rig the car so that it appears the doctor drove himself off of it. On examining the evidence, the FBI agents realize that the doctor was murdered. Fortunately, they are able to collect that single smeared fingerprint from the window.

The fictional Haynes is concerned that they have only a very "fragmentary" print from the Lamar Bank robbery. Weaver responds by emphasizing the potential benefits of fingerprint collection, stating that "Mr. Hoover is planning on a new single fingerprint file, and in it will be the prints of all the more desperate criminals. If that file were existing today, we'd have a good chance of knowing whose fingerprint this was." As Dennison and Haynes continue their conversation with Weaver, they point to the twin-pronged benefits of fingerprinting:

DENNISON: *Have the fingerprints of the four suspects they're holding* been compared with this one?

HAYNES: Yes—none of their fingerprints matches this one. This is fragmentary—but it was taken off the glass of the right handle front window of the doctor's car.

WEAVER: But *the suspects* have been identified by eye-witnesses *from* the bank.

HAYNES: *I know,* but any ordinary person in a robbery of that kind becomes hysterical. Feeling has been running high out there—the people who identified these men are sincere, but there's *a possibility they're mistaken.*

WEAVER: That would be terrible. (14–15)

The possibility of mistaken identification by unreliable witnesses is a frequent theme in the discourse of police science. Such unreliability itself serves as the warrant for the continued development of scientific methods of policing. Yet, as Haynes continues, he notes that there is a greater danger than the apprehension of the innocent. The fictional officer tells Dennison and Weaver, "If those four men should be executed—and it is later found out that they were innocent—it would affect every court of law in this country. Every jury would be so afraid to convict men—they'd lean over backwards. Crime would increase—nobody knows to what extent" ("The Fleagle Brothers" 1935, 15). Here, fingerprinting not only secures the identities of the guilty and innocent but guarantees the public faith necessary for the functioning of the justice system. This episode also demonstrates how increasingly sophisticated the FBI's collection and identification of fingerprints had become.

Fingerprinting, however, was just one aspect of forensic science that was used as an important weapon in bringing criminals to justice. A number of episodes demonstrated that no matter how perfect a criminal perceived his crime to be, the police would discover him. Several episodes of *Calling All*

Cars point to the use of scientific evidence to prove guilt. In "Stop That Car" (1934), while out selling magazines two days after Christmas, a young boy is struck by a hit-and-run driver. When police take a suspect into custody, they are unable to prove conclusively that he is the driver until the scientists in the police laboratory match yarn fibers off the smashed fender of the suspect's car to those in the sweater the boy was wearing. Several episodes highlight the use of different kinds of cameras in solving crimes. In "The Poisoning Jezebel" (1938), a woman has been poisoning her stepdaughters with arsenic, which eventually leads to their deaths. Although the woman consistently demonstrates concern for the girls and vows to help police find the source of the arsenic, the police remain suspicious of her. A search of local farm supply stores leads to the knowledge that the woman recently purchased arsenic. When the police question her, she admits that she purchased the poison as an insecticide but tells them it is in the cellar, unopened. The box they find in the cellar is half empty, at which point the "Jezebel" recalls having dropped it. However, microphotography reveals that the box does not have any indentations, which clearly would indicate that it had fallen—thus proving this "Jezebel" poisoned her own stepchildren.

The power of the police laboratory takes center stage in the episode "The Bloodstained Shoe" (1938). Chief Davis begins the episode by succinctly stating, "Science is putting crime on the spot." Davis explains the ways that "new scientific weapons of defense are constantly being placed at the disposal of the police. Today, few major crimes remain unsolved or their perpetrators un-captured. Law and chemistry have combined in the laboratory to make it impossible for even the cleverest criminal to get away with murder." In this particular case, the police laboratory proves instrumental in bringing a black man to justice for murdering an old woman during a robbery. Science is instrumental in identifying blood on the shoe of the man's heel as human blood, thus proving he used his shoe to kill her. However, the use of science does not stop here. In this particular episode, as Davis explains to listeners that "one of the most advanced and at the same time most certain, means of bringing criminals to justice," the "motion picture camera," is used to record the man's confession. Excited about the prospect of appearing in a motion picture, the man freely confesses to the murder. The camera thus allows "the police to build an airtight case against the defendant."

As the suspect confesses, the police continually ask him if he is in any way being coerced into giving his testimony. The man continually denies that he is. During trial, the man's lawyer attempts to get him off by suggesting that the police used brutal tactics to secure a confession; however, the film clearly proves that this is not the case, and the man is sentenced to prison. Davis ends the episode by telling the audience that "Wesley Jackson was convicted by his own testimony. The irrefutable testimony was recorded on the sound film. No longer could he claim that his confession was obtained by the third degree. The picture clearly showed his willingness, even eagerness to talk. This same willingness sent him to prison for life." Science trumps violence in professional policing.

Playing on the discourse surrounding police science, *G-Men*, by heralding the efforts of the FBI, paid particular attention to the FBI laboratories in its efforts at criminal identification and apprehension. The investigation of "invisible clues" and "silent witnesses" frequently helped the FBI solve its cases. For example, the "Cannon Case" (1935) is solved by the identification of the type of ink used in a ransom letter that leads the FBI agents to the kidnapper. In addition to featuring science as a key to solving its cases, *Gang Busters* featured occasional episodes titled "Scientific Cases" (1937, 1942). These episodes would follow several cases, rather than a single one, to demonstrate to home listeners how the smallest possible clue could ruin the best-laid plans of a criminal. In one of the earliest episodes, the host, Dr. Simon, tells the audience that "no matter how carefully a crime is planned, the criminal will always make some slip, or some unforeseen clue will give him away. The perfect crime has never been committed and never will be" ("Scientific Cases" 1937, 4). In this case, a woman and her husband are arrested for murdering their boarder, after the woman claims that the dead man is her husband, a victim of suicide. The two were attempting to collect insurance money. Hair fibers lead to the correct identification of the body as that of the boarder.

In addition to drawing on the discourse about proceduralism and science among police, the police were frequently represented with complete focus on criminal apprehension. Unlike the stupid, bumbling, or blatantly corrupt police of film and fiction, police in these dramas were honest, thoroughly committed to their jobs of upholding the law, and ready to serve the public. For example, the "Skid Row Dope Ring" (1934) episode of *Calling All Cars* presents listeners with indefatigable narcotics traffic agent O'Farrell, who, despite a consistent lack of funding and manpower, works diligently and single-mindedly to stop the flow of narcotics into the Bay Area. When investigating a woman selling narcotics out of her supposed treatment center, O'Farrell runs up against a number of obstacles, as this woman cleverly works to distance herself from any evidence of her illegal activities. When O'Farrell and his partner question a suspect who can lead them to the woman, his partner suggests they give up after hours of getting nowhere. O'Farrell, however, keeps up his line of questioning until the suspect eventually cooperates. Later in the episode, his partner praises O'Farrell for this diligence.

These qualities became especially poignant as episodes highlighted the special dangers that awaited these committed officers. While post–Hays code films were not allowed to show police officers as victims of criminal violence (Doherty 1999), the radio docudramas positively regaled in these representations. Officers in these episodes are frequent victims of criminal violence, often leading to their deaths. "The Phantom Killer" (1936) episode of *Gang Busters* tells the story of Paul Hilton, radio thief, a murderer who wantonly kills police officers through the use of a trick device, which pulls the trigger of a hidden pistol when any police officer requests that he raise his arms. After several murders occur, Chief Sullivan, the host of the program, tells the listener that he "assigned Detective James A. Pyke and Detective Sergeant William Jackson to twenty-four hours service—to get this killer" (7). As detectives look over photographs from the "rogues gallery," they discuss their desire to identify the phantom killer and bring him to justice:

PYKE: You ought to go out and get something to eat Kenney. You've been sitting there going over those pictures about eight hours.

MCCARTHY: (OUT) I'm not going to stop looking Lawton, till I've looked at every rogues gallery picture in our files. (8)[9]

The commitment of the police is continually stressed despite the dangers of their jobs. Their commitment is further highlighted when the programs deal with what police reformers view as the problem of public apathy and lack of support for the police. While police officers bravely faced death at the hands of vicious criminals, their situation was made especially bitter by the lack of public sympathy. *Calling All Cars,* in particular, frequently dealt with the issue of murdered officers.

The representation of professional police officers was achieved by using both the expressive and narrative elements of radio broadcasting to construct the ideal, depoliticized, deethnicized police officer. As intelligence workers par excellence, the police officers of the radio crime docudrama were educated, intelligent, and found their identity in adherence to a professional code of conduct. These officers were not ethnic or political operatives; they did not operate in the realm of personal gain. Neither fear of death nor lack of public appreciation could mitigate their dedication to criminal apprehension. They were beholden first and foremost to a professional code, which they mastered through training in method and science. These were not the hoi polloi polluting the rank and file of police forces that reformers so often bemoaned. Through radio voices emerged the ideal officer imagined by reformers: white by virtue of the absence of any ethnic marker beyond his name, intelligent, capable, diligent, responsible, masculine, honest, fearless, and dedicated to public service.

THE INTIMACY OF ADMINISTRATIVE AUTHORITY

As important as the ideal officer was to the reform vision, clear leadership was also necessary to spearhead the development of professional police forces. Reformers were clear that police authority needed to be depoliticized by removing the position of the head of police departments from civilian or political influence. As the writers of the Wickersham Commission Report argued, "The chief evil, in our opinion, lies in the insecure, short term of service of the chief or executive head of the police force and his being subject while in office to the control of politicians in the discharge of his duties." ("Wickersham Report" 1931, 337). In keeping with the idea of professionalizing the police, they continued to argue that such short terms of service would be entirely unacceptable in the corporate world, leading to poor organizational structure and sure bankruptcy. Not only did this state of affairs stand in the way of professionalization, it further threatened the already tenuous relationship between the police and public as each change in government administration led to new appointments and new pressures on police forces. The fear was that such appointments, based on politics rather than ability, would put in charge of the police those least likely to understand or manage police efforts.

The decision to use "chiefs" as hosts of the radio crime docudramas was therefore significant at this moment. Regardless of their location or size, police forces were constructed as organized and hierarchal and as having a clear and professional chain of command. This gave the impression that beat cops were under the firm control of an authority figure. In *Police Headquarters,* this was demonstrated by having each "call" initiating the program sent to a captain or lieutenant of the department. In *Calling All Cars,* the voice of authority was most frequently that of Los Angeles Police Department Chief James E. Davis. Davis's weekly introductions highlighted his knowledge of the case in question and suggested his close supervision of the activities of the Los Angeles police officers. In most episodes of *G-Men,* the investigations were run by the fictional inspector Haynes, a clear stand-in for Hoover himself. Inspector Haynes's high position and coordination of the FBI officers assigned to the case demonstrated the way that the organization ran smoothly. *Gang Busters'* deployment of a police chief as a guest on each episode symbolized the hierarchal structure of police organizations, indicating that beat officers were not rogue agents, wielding authority arbitrarily, possibly to the point of violence. Beat cops were neither agents of political ward bosses nor engaged in pursuing some individual interests. Instead, they were part of a hierarchal organization.

The importance of clear leadership found its way into the crime drama through the structure of the program itself. The decision to make the radio program more comprehensible to listeners and to fill each half-hour segment with as much narrative action as possible authorized the police to speak on matters of policing both at the level of narrative action and in affective ways whose influence would last beyond the specific historic moment. First, the importance of the chief figures in these programs spoke directly to the emphasis on hierarchy and organization that was a touchstone of progressive police reform movement by emphasizing the authorial power of the police. The organized criminality of the Prohibition era demanded an organized police force to combat its methods. Hierarchy was a symbol of the attempt to remove policing from the machinations of local politics and of effective control, discipline, and organization of police officers. Second, the use of police chiefs as a narrative device to orient transitions through the fast-moving plots effectively allowed the police interpretation of events to control the telling of these stories or at least to provide the appearance of doing so. In this way, not only did the police match wits with criminals, they effectively controlled the understanding and definition of criminality. Third, in its most expressive dimensions, these scripted speeches and conversations by those high up in police hierarchies were delivered in intimate terms, thus extending a form of intimate authority directly into the living home of radio listeners.

Hierarchal Authority

While perhaps not directly intended, decisions that writers of these programs made to render their programs comprehensible to listeners represented the police as hierarchal and organized. This was especially true when it came to the use of narrators and hosts. Writing a professional manual for those involved in the radio industry, Eric Barnouw (1939) notes the advantages of the narrative transition as a way to guide the listener through the events]of the story, pointing to *Gang Busters* as an exemplary illustration of such transitions. Barnouw argues that "if skillfully handled," narrative transitions "need involve no cessation of the story. The pauses between dialogue and narration can be short, almost negligible" (82). A narrator proved especially useful as a device to keep the program moving with only "an instant's lag" (82). Thus, "causing no delay" that might "bog down the script," narration was considered particularly effective at forwarding action. As Barnouw notes, "In *Gang Busters,* a narrator can introduce a dialogue of four short speeches between two policemen, shift us somewhere else for another six speeches, and so on. Great rapidity is possible" (82). In an anthology drama where individual characters and settings shifted each week, the narrator served an important role in guiding the listener through the course of events. The narrator also offered structural consistency that listeners could depend on and allowed for the rapid verbalization of important plot information. Such a guide was even more necessary because the radio crime dramas often compacted lengthy, complex stories of apprehension into standardized half-hour-long programs.

Makers of the documentary crime dramas used the idea of the narrator as a way to establish the authority of the version of the story being told and to give it a documentary quality by scripting an "actual" officer into the role of program host. The presence of the host lent an air of authenticity to the dramatizations. At the same time, this host confirmed the authority of the police to understand and make sense of the events that would transpire. The regional program *Calling All Cars* was the first to achieve this by featuring the chief of the Los Angeles Police Department, James E. Davis, presenting a short speech before the narrative started and a short speech near the program end to highlight whatever lessons listeners were supposed to take from the episode. For the most part, Davis highlighted the modernization of police work in an attempt to improve the public image of the police and, as chapter 1 discussed, to marshal public support for reform efforts. Occasionally, another officer would introduce the program, usually someone closely involved in the case. In all instances, it was a chief or captain, again stressing the authority of the host to present the dramatized case while at the same time emphasizing to audiences the important role a professional police chief played in reform efforts.

Lord mimicked this idea but gave it a different twist. Rather than having a police authority appear at the beginning and end of the program, so that the police voice book-ended the dramatic action of the program, in *Gang Busters*, Lord expanded the authoritative voice of the police by extending his voice more fully into the narrator function. In his first foray into police dramas, the FBI drama *G-Men*, Lord scripted a "Translator" to effect narrative transitions between scenes. While useful in guiding the listener, it was not necessarily effective in engaging listener attention or interest. Perhaps reflecting his rift with Hoover, Lord tried something different with his spin-off program. While the program would feature a recurring narrator figure, the narration would be scripted not as a straightforward didactic chat between the authority figure and the radio listeners but as an "interview" between a program host and a guest chief.

Lord himself assumed hosting duties for the program for one year until the end of 1937, at which point Colonel Norman Schwarzkopf of the New Jersey State Militia took over as host.[10] Schwarzkopf was already well known to radio audiences for leading the search for the Lindberg baby. The addition of Schwarzkopf and, later, of former captain of the New York City Police Lewis J. Valentine (an important figure in the police reform movement as well),[11] contributed to the program's authority in a way analogous to the use of Chief Davis in *Calling All Cars*. The interviewee was always scripted as a chief or some high-level officer involved in some way, however incidentally, with the case being dramatized. For example, in the "Dago Paretti" (1936) episode, the chief is Chief of Detectives of Chicago, even though most of the action took place in a nearby small town. All episodes were written with the "Chief" character, regardless of whether or not the producers had secured someone to fill the slot. The chief provided a voice of authority and support to the program's claim that it gave listeners the "inside facts" of the cases. This "interview" took place in the offices of New York City Chief of Police Lewis J. Valentine, thus ostensibly taking place from right inside a police station. In addition to authorizing the dramas' claims to factualness, such representations also emphasized to the public the importance, or at least the givenness, of clear, professional leadership. As the one in command of the knowledge regarding policing and criminality, the chief was focused on overseeing and coordinating efforts at criminal apprehension, not serving political whims.

The authoritative power of police chief hosts was further emphasized through the structural peculiarities of commercial broadcast radio. Whether positioned at the beginning and end of the program, as in *Calling All Cars,* or positioned throughout the program, as in *Gang Busters,* the use of chiefs created distinctive moments by mixing the discursive and narrative elements of radio. Altman (1994) argues that commercial radio was conceived in fifteen-minute increments that had "two main gears: discursive framing (references to program name, time slot, place in radio flow, sponsorship, audience, next appearance, and so forth) and narrative material (series, serial, news, sporting event, personality, performance, and the like)" (7). However, these two functions often intermixed throughout the program. He argues that all programs on commercial radio had a double discursivity, authored once by the network originating the program and once more by the commercial sponsor.[12] Consequently, all sound potentially had a dual function of marking both discursive and narrative aspects of the program. The use of chiefs in the radio crime docudramas likewise confused the separation of the two elements. On the one hand, through sound differentiation and placement in the text, chiefs seemed to serve a discursive function by bookmarking the narrative story of criminal apprehension. On the other hand, these "speeches" were clearly scripted elements of a narrative story meant to entertain and edify radio listeners. The speeches of narrating "host chiefs" were part of the overall diegetic space of the "documentary" about apprehending the criminal.

It is in their potential discursive function that these speeches bolstered the authority of the police. Each program worked in different ways to mark these speeches as a separate space within the broadcast. In *Calling All Cars,* addresses by Chief Davis or other guest hosts acted as clear bookends of the overall narrative rendering of the case of the week. This chief host was placed at both the beginning and end of each episode between the network/ sponsor introduction and narrative kernel. In *Gang Busters,* the interview segments were placed similarly to the placement used in *Calling All Cars* and further throughout the program to bookend each moment of narrative representation of the case of the week. These moments were marked sonically by an absence of background sound effects and by a manner of speech more measured than that of the commercial sponsor. The effect was to give the programs a triple discursivity. The placement of these speeches created the effect that the stories were authored not only by the network and the sponsor but, further, by the police authorities themselves.

As the ones firmly in control of the narrative, the police host, narrator, and/or interviewee had a great deal of power in framing the understanding of events for listeners. They used this power to specifically discredit the populist interpretations of criminal behavior that reformers saw as rampant in mass culture (the more specific constructions of criminality are discussed in chapter 3). Public sympathy for criminals was redirected to police forces. That a narrator was necessary to orient listeners was clear to those writing radio dramas during the 1930s. The use of the narrator became even more important in anthology-style narratives that did not feature recurring characters whose voices listeners grew accustomed to through weekly programming. However, by choosing to have police associated in some way with the narrator function, the radio crime docudramas proved especially successful at forwarding progressive definitions of the crime and policing, because the police themselves were given the power to frame and interpret events of the narrative. Significantly, the dramatized criminals rarely occupied this discursive space, giving them no authority or authorship in the story told about them.

Intimate Authority

This emphasis on narrative comprehensibility created the conditions for figuring the authority of the police in a particularly intimate way. A key concern of radio writers was the privatized reception of radio that created an emphasis on, or belief in the success of, particular forms of address. Cantril and Allport (1935) explored this topic in their study of audiences listening to a preacher. They were taken by the ways that forms of public address aimed at a copresent audience were not as effective on an audience listening through radio.[13] As radio crooners early on discovered, a more intimate mode of address worked especially well on the radio (McCracken 1999). Debates over the nature of radio address were central in determining the meaning of radio. As Jason Loviglio (2005) argues, the "tension between intimacy (interpersonal communication) and publicity (mass communication) was the defining feature of early network radio, its central problem and its greatest appeal" (xvi). Those in the industry were especially aware of the privatized nature of radio reception. As Russo (2004) notes, the "radio industry felt sound enabled it to affect the audience directly. Radio's advantage, it was widely held, was that it potentially possessed a special form of address. American commercial radio aspired to produce an intimate relationship between broadcaster and receiver" (249). At a time when mobility and the growing use of motor patrols seemed to be creating more distance between police officers and citizens, radio's form of address offered a way to develop an intimate relationship with radio listeners.

On *Calling All Cars,* this is evident in the ways that James E. Davis addressed radio listeners in his weekly scripted address. Although known for his aggressive personality, on the radio, Davis used a quiet, even manner of speaking that in many ways recalled the radio addresses of Roosevelt in his Fireside Chats. Each of Davis's scripted speeches begins with "Good evening, friends," addressing his listeners in a respectful manner. Like Roosevelt, Davis frequently invokes his listeners as a public willing to support his view of policing. *Gang Busters* achieves its intimate effect by simulating the private space of reception through its "interviews" set in the office of Lewis J. Valentine of the New York City Police Department. For example, the dramatic action of an episode from 1936, when Lord was still hosting, begins with the announcer telling the radio audience, "And now visualize this comfortable private office at Police Headquarters in New York which Commissioner Valentine has so kindly given to Phillips H. Lord for his interview with Commissioner Higgens of the Buffalo Police Department. The two gentlemen are seated opposite each other across the desk" ("Alex Bogdanoff" 1936, 2). The interview thus becomes doubly intimate. Listeners are positioned as eavesdroppers to the private interior space of police authority. At the same time, these authority figures, through the institution of broadcasting, gain access into the private reaches of family homes.

The intimate forms of address, both through styles of speaking and narrative structure, allowed the programs to address listeners both as members of a larger community and as private individuals. In many ways, they drew from the successful use of radio by the Roosevelt administration during the Depression years. The effect was twofold. First, addressing radio listeners in such intimate tones was an effective way to explain police reform and convince the public that the police were capable agents rather than bumbling fools and, in doing so, to argue for a relationship of reciprocity. In exchange for public support, police departments would provide excellent public service. In examining the power of Roosevelt's radio speeches, Loviglio (2005) argues that his "broadcasts were an apt medium through which to explain the New Deal's unprecedented expansion of the state's regulatory and administrative authority, in the 'private' economic spheres of industry, agriculture, labor, and the family" (8–9). In a similar way, police forces turned to radio to expand their own shifting use of power, one that involved a use of power to protect middle-class citizens as private individuals and property owners. Their access to knowledge about policing and crime allowed the hosts to act like reporters imparting exclusive information. Miller (2003) makes a similar observation about Roosevelt: he argues that during his Fireside Chats, Roosevelt acted like a reporter, possessing specialized access to and understanding of world events, then sharing that knowledge with his listeners. By linking their authority to the radio medium and continually reminding their audiences of that fact, the police on these programs further suggest their capabilities. As Loviglio (2005) notes about the Fireside Chats, "Understanding and helping to solve a national crisis, Roosevelt assures his audience, depends on the public's confidence in the 'machinery' of government—in particular the apparatus that enables Roosevelt to 'talk for a few minutes with the people of the United States'" (11). The intimacy accomplished through radio crime docudramas promoted a relationship, built on confidence in police forces, between police hosts and radio listeners. Hayes (2000a) argues that the intimacy of the Fireside Chats positioned the federal government in just such a relationship with citizens, thus lessening anxieties about both the Depression and the expansion of federal powers. While citizens traditionally looked with disdain at police interference in private life as being specifically directed against particular ethnic and racial communities, such as in the case of Prohibition, this intimate address delivered by deethnicized police officers suggested that any anxiety about the police was unfounded.

Second, this form of address allowed for the imagination of the police as linked to everyday, private life rather than to public forms of disorder. As definitions of policing shifted to a focus on apprehension of criminals engaged in attacks on private property and persons, this form of boundary crossing encouraged listeners to identify with a model that asked them to think of the police as a daily presence. This was achieved by the ways that these intimate ways of speaking forged a nonthreatening link between the private sphere of the home and the broader concerns of the public sphere. Hayes (2000a) argues that "Roosevelt personalized both himself and his audience and directly engaged each listener in a dialectic of intimacy and national community. In this way, Roosevelt's Fireside Chats made the nation part of the personal experience of a majority of Americans" (87). In a similar way, the structure of radio crime docudramas, which encouraged individual identification and familiarity with policing, also worked to make the police part of everyday experience. This is significant because the emphasis on bureaucracy and efficiency, and the removal of policing from local politics and thus community discussions, had the potential to make policing seem more removed from everyday life. Yet, as Scannell (1996) argues, broadcasting has the power to personalize bureaucratic life: "It does so because it exists in two worlds of concerns: the great world and everyone's my-world. If as an institution, it stands in the former, it speaks (as it well knows) to listeners and viewers who live in the latter and who they judge what they see and hear by the norms of social, sociable daily life" (172). Encouraging people to identify with the police as "public" servants entrusted with the responsibility of protecting "private" persons and property gained affective power through this articulation of intimate authority. Listeners were not addressed as members of particular communities or ethnic groups, or as possessing any political ties, but as a group of dispersed private families. They were encouraged not only to think of the police as separate from political and ethnic conflict but also to think of their own relationship with the police as an individual one tied to crime rather than to forms of public disorder.

THE SOUND OF AUTHORITY

In many ways, the radio crime docudrama is a clear relic of the past. To contemporary listeners, they sound clunky, didactic, and sometimes just plain silly. For audiences of the Depression era, however, the radio crime docudrama offered something new to listeners: it offered the voice of police authority. It was in this sound of authority that listeners began to understand the shift in the discourses of policing. In particular, the programs aimed to shift citizen attitudes toward the police from one of disrespect and ridicule to one of, if not respect, then at least deference to their professional authority. The new police were an educated, expert class who served the public and knew how best to deal with urban and rural criminality. The narrative tales of these dramas might have been overly didactic, occasionally unbelievable, simplified, and concretely stereotypical to such an extent that listeners need not have taken them seriously. However, it was not in the narrative elements alone that these programs constructed the police as authority.

In telling new tales about a redefined police force, radio crime dramas developed a consistent set of narrative strategies based on the sonic limitations and possibilities of radio to represent the police. From the ideal G-man at the federal level to the representation of city, county, and state policemen from across the country, police were constructed in ways that progressive police reformers imagined. Working with ways of speaking and representation through technical forms of language, the police of the radio crime docudramas were professional, trained, and intelligent, bound to the force rather than political bosses, and they found their identity in their profession rather than in their ethnic background or community. To say that these dramas celebrated the work of the police is to assume that what constituted a good police officer was recognizably evident. As reformers worked to re-define what or who an officer was, the radio crime docudramas entered the terrain representing police officers in ways that were often at odds with the dominant representations of the police in popular culture or as represented in the findings of the government-sponsored Wickersham Commission. These were neither the bumbling fools of the film world nor the stereo-typical Irish flatfoot of popular lore. They were not wanton law breakers, violent strike breakers, graft-seeking agents out for their own gain, or bru-tal men wielding their power arbitrarily. Instead, these shows presented a professional, educated, deethnicized, specialized, and hierarchal organized force of men devoted to apprehending criminals on behalf the public. The radio crime docudramas developed a set of strategies to guarantee that their radio policemen would be perceived not simply as born cultural heroes but as men whose training, intelligence, and commitment to their profession made them ideal foils to what many perceived as an increasingly organized, mobile, and intelligent criminal population.

This professional training was transmitted over the airwaves into the in-timate settings of people's homes. The aural presence of the police assured the public that they were safer than they had been in the past. Within the domestic comfort of listeners' homes, these disembodied sonic voices cre-ated an intimate authority. In doing so, the programs encouraged listeners to imagine themselves as privatized individuals rather than as members of an ethnic or class community. Police work tied to the private space of the home was not an activity involved in the controversial control of public disorder but a public service providing private individuals with safety and security in a complex and increasingly unsteady world. Instead of being objects of ridicule, police were positioned, through radio narrative and dis-course, as professional agents of public service and safety untethered from conflicts surrounding class and ethnicity.

It is tempting to end with a discussion of Adorno (1994), who found radio authoritative, and never more so than when attempting to "educate," as he especially considers in his examination of the *NBC Music Apprecia-tion Hour.*[14] In the many strategies for representing police discussed in this chapter, there appears to be a perfect union of the rationalization of broad-casting with the rationalization of policing. Inherent in all representations of police are questions about the state of the social order and the kinds of threats it encounters. The answer is found in perfected bureaucratic rationalization through the trope professionalism. Rendered thoroughly familiar through intimacy, the reactions to police authority are determined by the structure of the program. But as much as this idealized construction of bureaucratic rationalization shaped both police and citizen understandings of policing, they also provided the grounds on which citizens would come to expect certain things from the police. As police presented themselves as offering a public service, the public increasingly made demands of the police, ones that reformers never imagined.

chapter 3

Gang Busting

Criminals and Citizens in a
Professional World

VERY ANXIOUS TO STATE CAPTAIN HAMER IN LINE OF DUTY FACING OUTLAWS
BEAT THEM ALL TO THE DRAW AND KILLED SIXTY THREE stop THIS IS VERY
PICTURESQUE AND SHOWS HIM FAR SUPERIOR TO BARROW stop AM VERY
ANXIOUS TO MAKE THIS STATEMENT SO THAT ALL BOYS LISTENING WILL IDEALIZE
FRANK HAMER INSTEAD OF BARROW stop

—Telegram from PHILLIPS H. LORD to the
Superintendent of Texas Prisons

Reformers found public attitudes toward criminals particularly troubling. They marveled at public interest, sympathy, admiration, and seeming desire for criminality. The public devoured newspapers with famous gangsters and desperados on their covers or paid hard-earned money for a glimpse into the glamorous world of the screen gangster. Citizens seemed far more attracted and reverent toward criminals than toward police. Clyde Barrow, boyfriend of and partner in crime with Bonnie Parker, was certainly one of the most romantic of these criminal figures. Newspapers and magazines treated the couple's life of crime as resulting more from romantic desperation than from any inborn tendency toward violence. The grisly murder of the couple at the hands of Texas police, who riddled the pair's car with machine-gun fire, only furthered popular interpretations of Bonnie and Clyde as romantic desperados. Dramatizing the tale of such popular icons would require an almost total reversal of public understanding of and sympathy for the criminal stars of the Depression era.

Representing the activities of criminals, including some of the most famous Depression-era celebrity bandits, necessitated a direct encounter with a range of negotiations regarding gender, ethnicity, class, social mobility, consumerism, and institutional authority. Stories about crime during this period are notable for the ways they critiqued power institutions of big business and government, calling into question the presumed fairness and equality of the American dream.[1] On the one hand, in the world of the police-centered radio crime docudrama, such social critique did not have a place. On the other hand, as discussed in chapter 1, the people who made these programs understood that criminals had a tremendous appeal for audiences. No matter how carefully they were presented, populist interpretations of criminal activity might not only inform listeners' enjoyment but also attract listeners to the programs.

Given the complex reasons that citizens were attracted to figures like Bonnie and Clyde, simply stating that they were bad would not suffice. If populist fascination with and sympathy for criminals represented a more generalized dissatisfaction with social and state institutions, and if, on the opposite side, fear of crime led to a strong criticism of the police, reformers and radio professionals had to find somewhere else to place the blame. The docudramas relentlessly insisted that while blame certainly lay with criminals themselves, it even more so lay with the public that valorized criminals and failed to support the police. The programs worked in four key ways to redefine criminality and shift blame for the "crime problem" from the police to criminals and, most surprisingly, to citizens themselves. First, the programs went head to head with populist interpretations of gangsters and bandits in order to deglamorize them. Dramatizing the eventual deaths of Bonnie and Clyde and John Dillinger, the programs were relentless in their attempts to shift blame for their criminal careers from social institutions and police incompetence to citizens themselves. Second, in the intersection of shifting definitions of crime and the needs of radio producers to produce recognizable character types in an anthology drama, the programs created a recognizable criminal type. Just as the programs worked to make police officers instantly recognizable to audiences, so they worked to achieve the same with representations of criminals. No matter the particulars of any individual criminal career, criminals were increasingly made to fit a set of generic categories that spoke more to reform definitions of crime than populist understandings. Third, the programs negotiated the complex social debates over the meaning of crime. If the FBI attributed crime to individual pathology, local police and the makers of the crime dramas themselves were more receptive to Progressive theories of delinquency that posited environmental factors as a cause of crime. Finally, the programs worked to not only blame the public for crime but also to directly suggest the ways that they could properly support the police. The programs railed against vigilantism, instead arguing that citizens could best improve the crime problem by submitting to the professional authority and expertise of the police.

DEGLAMORIZING CRIME

When it came to representing criminals, the writers of the crime dramas entered a terrain already filled with many existing images of criminals. In film, pulp novels, and the press, criminals emerged as sources of public fascination, if not popular heroes. As police reformers concerned themselves with questions of social mobility during a time of tremendous social change, they encountered stories that seemed to normalize criminality as a legitimate path to upward mobility for those groups who had been ill served by the existing social structure. From the ethnic heroes of Hollywood gangster films and the hard-boiled heroes of detective fiction to the rural bandits of both the news and tabloid presses, crime stories were a key site for articulating a range of responses to economic change, consumerism, ethnic strife, and changing gender norms. Public fascination with criminal exploits practically guaranteed an audience for the radio crime dramas, which, as discussed in chapter 1, happily offered the excitement and adventure of these criminal figures to radio audiences in exchange for their attention. At the same time, while delighting in the exploits of criminals, these radio professionals nonetheless worked to deglamorize criminal heroes and to shift identification and blame for crime from the state to the entertainment industry intent on perverting normative ideas of class movement and the American dream.

Gangster Films

Gangster films, as discussed in the introduction, were a key source of worry among police reformers and middle-class reformers in general. Their celebration of ethnic achievement, glamorization of criminal exploits, and voyeuristic glimpse into the world of urban amusements rendered the content of the films decidedly troublesome. Of special concern was the belief that these movies were turning children into criminals. In the early 1930s, the efforts of two groups coalesced to create a national movement to create better films for youth. The Payne Fund supported a series of studies on behalf of the activist Motion Picture Research Council. Although the studies conducted by academic researchers were moderate in their assessment of the relationship between juvenile delinquency and film viewing, a popular summarization by Henry James Forman, tellingly titled *Our Movie Made Children* (1933), sensationalized the results. Written with the express intention of effecting public opinion, the book culled only select facts from the academic studies to argue that movies were in fact a cause of juvenile delinquency[2] (Forman 1934; Jowett, Jarvie, and Fuller 1996). The other group involved in trying to improve film content was the Catholic-led Legion of Decency, which, by cooperating with civic and religious groups, led a campaign to boycott certain films unless the movie industry rendered its content more moral (Jowett et al. 1996).

Concerns about juvenile delinquency were heightened by the Depression. Among the first victims of the massive unemployment were the young and inexperienced, and it was likewise the very young whose future employment prospects looked bleakest. This fear, combined with Progressive reformers' concern about urban juvenile delinquency, led to efforts to combat youthful criminal activities. Following Progressive efforts at juvenile reform, including the formation of a separate juvenile court system and separate juvenile prisons (Walker 1998), education emerged as a key way to combat juvenile crime. For example, a speaker before the Interstate Commission on Crime (1936) informed members that a "project which has had the close attention of the Commission" was "a general educational program as to crime, education throughout our homes, our schools, our churches and elsewhere, and education particularly of our youth. We must remember the somewhat startling fact that more criminals are sentenced at age 19 than at any other age" (8). It was therefore important that anticrime education efforts begin during childhood and include the coordinated cooperation of schools and families. Moral and police reformers of the time were also quick to point the finger at popular cultural representations of crime and policing as a source of miseducation about crime.[3]

While gangster films often began with warnings from the filmmakers, those both inside and outside of Hollywood were quick to see through the publicity ploy. Controversy surrounding the film *Scarface* led to a tacit stop to the production of gangster films in 1932, which was enshrined as an official addendum to the official Motion Picture Production Code of 1934 (Doherty 1999). The addendum specifically stated that "crime stories are not acceptable when they portray the activities of American gangsters, armed in violent conflict with the law or law-enforcing officers" (quoted in Doherty 1999, 366). The sight of ethnic urban criminals asserting their own interests against official forces of law and order must have been considered especially incendiary. The specific ban on one kind of crime film was therefore also followed by a host of regulations regarding the more general appearance of crime in motion pictures, including specific bans against showing "the details of crime," "wholesale slaughter of human beings," "excessive brutality," too much or unnecessary murder or suicide "unless absolutely necessary for the development of the plot," the use of machine guns or other illegal weapons, the "flaunting" or "hiding" or weapons, murder of law enforcement officials, and specific regulations about how kidnapping could be represented (Doherty 1999, 361–62). While the gangster film gave ethnic, urban, working-class men an opportunity to speak and offer alternative interpretations of the story of success in the United States, the specific ban against these actions took away much of the kinetic verve that made him such an attractive figure to many. Yet the ban did not mean that the screen gangster completely disappeared; he simply reemerged in ways that accommodated the code, appeased moral reform groups, and prevented outside censorship.[4]

Romantic Bandits

While gangsters emerged as popular icons in both the press and film, rural banditry also was celebrated in the popular press. There was a strong tendency to treat these figures as a version of what Eric Hobsbawm (1959) called "social bandits." Bandits such as John Dillinger, Bonnie Parker, and Clyde Barrow were treated as romantic heroes who bravely flaunted their ability to escape the power of the law. In a time when faith in government and business institutions was perilously low, the bandit emerged as a populist hero who refused to submit to the authority of such institutions. Unlike the ethnic working-class gangster of cinema, the bandit was rural and white and was frequently discussed in ways that highlighted his or her affinity with the "average folk" left destitute by the Depression.

Powers (1983) argues that such favorable coverage was common while a bandit was still alive and free from police custody. For example, before his death at the hands of the FBI outside the Biograph Theater in Chicago, John Dillinger was continually treated in the mainstream press as a popular hero whose daring and cunning rejection of authority made him a folk hero to a wary public. Powers explains how the story of Dillinger drew on the ritual appeal of trickster heroes in Western culture, stating that "audiences identify with trickster heroes because they are, like all popular heroes, winners, but also because they beat enemies who are stronger, richer, and more respectable, humiliating them and their pretensions to social and moral superiority" (123). Audiences enjoyed the way bandits outwitted authority figures while battling those social institutions that seemed so little concerned with the lives and concerns of rural citizens. Powers cites a letter published in an Indiana newspaper in which the reader writes, "I am for Dillinger. . . . Why should the law have wanted Dillinger for bank robbery? He wasn't any worse than banks and politicians who took the poor people's money. Dillinger did not rob poor people. He robbed those who became rich by robbing the poor. I am for Johnnie" (quoted in Powers 1983, 123). When Warner Brothers screened a newsreel featuring Dillinger's father, "reports came from around the nation that audiences had cheered the bandit's photograph and catcalled footage of the G-Men" (Potter 1998, 148).

The romanticization of bandits drew on the long history of social banditry in defining them as folk heroes rather than potential enemies. Hobsbawm (1959) defines social banditry as a primitive type of social rebellion, primarily occurring in rural areas. Regarded as heroes by the poor, social bandits, as in the case of Robin Hood, are mythologized. Because they see them as champions of the poor, rural dwellers are likely to support and champion the bandits and protect them from the state, provided they do not become unnecessarily violent. While bandits do not advocate any specific political agenda, Hobsbawm argues that banditry tends to occur during times of social dislocation, "or at moments when the jaws of the dynamic world seize the static [rural] communities in order to destroy them," such as the years of the Great Depression (24). Although bandits like Dillinger no doubt found a great deal of popular support, it is important to note that in the U.S. context, the national character of the mass media effectively sundered such bandits from any specific social and political context so that banditry emerged as a more generic mythology (Slotkin 1992, 128). Yet as Potter (1998) argues, in the context of the Great Depression, the rural bandit was a pointedly political character. If the ethnic gangster offered urban working classes a figure of alternative social mobility to identify with, the rural gangster generated a critique from within, providing evidence that it was not only immigrants who were prevented from moving up the social ladder. While social bandit mythology might be tied to both, their different origins permitted them to speak to a broad range of interests and raise a variety of concerns about the possibilities for social mobility in a nation that seemed so structured around social and cultural hierarchies. The bandit and gangster spoke to these concerns in both specific and general ways.

Confronting the Romance of the Criminal Desperado

When it came to constructing criminality, the radio crime docudramas were relentless in their attempts to deglamorize criminals in order to prohibit any hope of audience identification with or sympathy for them. Taking on populist interpretations of real-life criminals necessitated a direct encounter with a range of existing interpretations. Few bandits were as romanticized as that trickster hero John Dillinger or Texas bank robbers–turned-fugitives Bonnie Parker and Clyde Barrow. Stripping such figures of their hero status required more than simply negating their actions. The crime docudramas turned the finger of blame away from existing social relations and police incompetence and pointed instead to criminal violence, to an inadequate legal system, and to citizens themselves. Whether being blamed for overromanticizing psychopathic violence or failing to support stronger crime legislation, when told from the perspective of the police reform movement, the public bore the brunt of blame for placing the police in an impossible position. Instead of stories that featured the perspective of and sympathy for ethnic immigrant and native white working classes, radio crime docudramas featured stories in which police were featured as the victims of weak laws and aberrant public attitudes.

Dramatizing the demise of Dillinger must have been seen as particularly dangerous. Hollywood was forbidden to make specific references to the actual Dillinger case because of fears of popular fascination with and attraction to his personality. Radio, however, did not suffer such similar sanctions. Both *G-Men* and *Calling All Cars* dramatized the Dillinger case in ways that worked not only to deglamorize him but also to deny that he had been a folk hero in the first place. *Calling All Cars* did this first by rewriting Dillinger's popularity and influence as terror and violence. As this regional program concentrated on crimes he committed in the West and Southwest, his capture by the Tucson, Arizona, police was dramatized in the March 21, 1934, episode "The Dillinger Case." From the beginning, we are told that the "lesson" of the episode is that the United States needs trained law enforcement officers, but even more important, citizens who support them. The episode opens with a sonic montage of sirens, newspaper barkers, and simulated police communications telling of Dillinger's 1933 escape from the Indiana State Penitentiary. What is significant is that the program compares Dillinger to another popular outlaw of the American West, Jesse James; only in this case, the connection is based, according to the program, on shared fear rather than admiration. Dillinger's activities are named by the program as a "reign of terror" that paralyzed citizens of the Midwest. As the montage continues, the voice of the narrator grows increasingly agitated while detailing Dillinger's activities, including the killing of a police officer.

After casting him as a public menace terrorizing innocent citizens of the nation, the first episode of the Dillinger case moves into the fairly standard *Calling All Cars* treatment and documents the careful and detailed work of the Tucson police in apprehending Dillinger and his associates, Pierpoint and Clark. Among the methods showcased are the use of fingerprints to secure the identity of Clark, who gives an alias when the police question him after a drunken encounter with two salesmen pretending to be gangsters at a local bar. Dillinger is captured when Officer Jimmy Heron approaches him from behind while staking out the house where Dillinger, Clark, and Pierpoint are staying. Dillinger goes quietly with Heron but boasts that he won't be in jail for long. Telling the listeners about the extradition of Clark and Pierpoint to Ohio and Dillinger to Indiana, the narrator continues to suggest that as news of Dillinger's capture is "flashed" across the country, the citizens are relieved. Then, in a rare instance of leaving a case open ended, the episode tells of Dillinger's escape from the Crown Point, Indiana, prison. The narrator, again in an excited voice, tells the radio listener, "Dillinger made good on his promise, once more peaceful citizens cringe in terror, once more the cry goes out, Dillinger is loose." Here again, citizen support for Dillinger is rewritten as fear. Gone is any reference to Dillinger as a trickster hero, and the representation of the public becomes more prescriptive than descriptive. The program ends by suggesting that mandated state violence is the only way to deal with a fearsome criminal such as Dillinger: the guest host tells listeners, "Any man who elects to declare his own personal war against society, has all society against him." If Dillinger meets a violent end the "next time he runs up against police officers," it is only because "he asked for it." In fact, should an officer choose to "shoot first and talk afterwards," the host assures the audience that "in the case of men like Dillinger [this] is the most efficient way to operate."

Through the suggestion that violence is an efficient method for dealing with Dillinger, this episode clearly echoes the discourse of the FBI in its attempts to deal with Dillinger. As Potter (1998) argues, the Dillinger case was important to the FBI, and as the case was worked, "the new cultural politics of centralized federal policing would replace 'cooperation and coordination' with Homer Cummings's famous edict: 'Shoot first—then count to ten'" (141). Like police reformers from across the nation, the FBI similarly worked to symbolically sever crime from its social contexts. Potter notes that "in this process, state violence was not constructed against a set of social practices or an illegal market that implicated citizen constituencies and class domination, but against a psychopathic fugitive, who was unique in his viciousness even among criminals" (141). What marks this statement even further is how it justifies violence as part of the Progressive goal of achieving efficiency in police operations. In these police-centered versions, violence begets violence not as simple revenge but as a plan to use state-sanctioned violence as the most rational use of resources for combating crime.

The second episode of *Calling All Cars,* which aired on July 7, 1934, focused on the "Execution of Dillinger" by federal agents in Chicago. In his introduction, Chief Davis harkens to the end of the previous dramatization of Dillinger's arrest by telling listeners that the next time Dillinger met with any law officer, the officer would shoot first and ask questions later. Davis says that this is what happened seventy-two hours earlier. The episode then proceeds exactly as the first one by telling about the terror caused by Dillinger and by briefly retelling parts of the previous tale of his capture in Tucson. Again, Dillinger is cast as a source of terror rather than as a popular trickster hero. The final confrontation between Dillinger and the G-men is dramatized as a tense waiting game for the police, who identify Dillinger as he goes into the theater, then must endure two hours before he emerges again. Although Dillinger has dyed his hair and is wearing gold-rimmed glasses, G-man Purvis confidently identifies him, telling the agents that they should try to take him alive but should also shoot if necessary. Then the program dramatizes the death of Dillinger outside of the theater at the hands of federal agents.

Despite rewriting the popular sentimental story about Dillinger as a story about widespread terror, the program ends by addressing the listeners as a public that too easily glamorizes criminals, turning them into celebrities. The host warns the public against this course of action by treating Dillinger as an unintelligent man. James E. Davis tells radio listeners that Dillinger was not a brave trickster but simply stupid:

> John Dillinger died on the way to the hospital. The post-mortem of rumors and sob sister conjecture is now taking place. The king is dead and already the public are crowing the new king. Already the crown of fame as public enemy number one rests on the head of "Babyface" Nelson, a henchman of Dillinger. Stripped of all of this dime novel romanticism, of this crime publicity which is only possible in this publicity conscious nation of ours, stripped of all of the glamour, John Dillinger was just a hoodlum—a cheap criminal, whose stupidity made him appear a daring outlaw. ("The Execution of John Dillinger" 1934)

Here the press is blamed for the valorization of Dillinger, and this favorable treatment is summarily dismissed as misguided. It was the police alone who understood the danger posed by Dillinger, and it was incumbent upon the public to support their efforts to improve policing, even as reform efforts called for violence.

While the public is carefully chided in these dramatizations of Dillinger, in *Gang Busters'* treatment of the criminal career and death of Bonnie and Clyde, they are treated to a far more sustained drubbing. The couple's violent escapades across the South and Midwest were combined with a romantic love story between the charismatic poor farm-boy and the young middle-class girl-turned-wrong. Beginning their careers as small-time bank robbers, they quickly became celebrity bandits and suffered under intense police pressure. Few stories illustrate so well the struggles involved in defining the motivations, actions, and demise of criminals. As the battle over how the pair's career and violent deaths at the hands of Texas authorities should be interpreted raged, *Gang Busters* weighed in with a two-part episode, originally aired February 12 and 19, 1936. Many popular accounts celebrated the two as romantic folk heroes, but the narrative conventions of the program reduced Bonnie and Clyde to violent bandits who pursued their careers by choice and met a violent outcome that was a product of their own making. For many, the story of Bonnie and Clyde was one about too much police pressure, which drove the increasingly desperate criminals to commit ever-greater violence (Potter 1998). *Gang Busters* turned the story of Bonnie and Clyde into one about too little police pressure, focusing on how futile, outdated laws hampered the police in dealing with these mobile criminals.

Two lessons were driven home in the *Gang Busters* dramatization. The first was the necessity of putting a stop to the practice of paroles.[5] A handwritten note detailing the elements of the dramatization pointedly stated that the program's "public service" element was to be found in its strong avocation to "prevent parole." The second, related lesson was that citizens should support laws that would not "hinder" the police in their efforts at catching criminals.[6] At the beginning of the program, the chief (the "chief" slot had not yet been filled) tells the audience how it is supposed to interpret the events that unfold:

I refuse to mince any words. The story of these crimes will shock the radio audience, but if these facts are too terrible to hear—just how terrible do you think they were for the folks who experienced them . . . and the point I want to bring out is this: Many of these atrocious killings would never have happened if the Police had had a freer hand. Now, is it better to soft-pedal those facts in presenting them and have a recurrence of them or is it better to present them honestly in hope of arousing the public to action so it won't happen in the future? (2)[7]

Gone are any references to police misconduct, excessive use of force, or the desperate social conditions of rural Texas. Instead, weaknesses in the legal system and citizen support are posited as the source of blame for the events that unfold.

From the beginning of the episode, Bonnie and Clyde are stripped of all possible romantic associations with folk heroes. Clyde is introduced as a most unattractive figure: "Clyde was rat-like . . . had a weak chin, and looked anemic" (3). The weakness in his appearance is clearly meant to represent the weakness of his character, marking him as feminine and hence deviant. Bonnie, on the other hand, is masculinized. She is not a young, romantic girl but is portrayed as being tougher than Clyde. The chief introduces her as "an attractive girl . . . with flaming yellow hair . . . who liked masculine attire and had a passion for smoking big black cigars" (3). This gender reversal was significant, because as Potter (1998) argues, "Romance confirmed the bandit's masculinity, refiguring him as the engine of someone else's fate rather than the victim of his own" (143). Rendered so utterly deviant, there is little room to read the relationship between Bonnie and Clyde as anything other than one of convenience rather than romance. Their very deviance likewise secures the inevitability of their deaths and justifies the excessive force used to bring them to their ends.

When the two first encounter each other in a speakeasy, their conversation immediately turns to crime, and the twin themes of the episode are introduced. When Bonnie expresses her concern about the police, Clyde tells her that she does not need to worry. Even if she were caught, parole would limit any actual time she spent in jail. "Just as soon as the public forgets your case, you get out" (5). Bonnie presses him, asking him how they "can keep out of the way of the police" (5). Clyde tells her all they need to do is "pull a job . . . scram . . . across the state line" (5). Clyde continues, introducing what the episode posits as the reasoning behind their violent behavior: "There's just one secret to it, Bonnie. Don't give the other guy a chance. Kill him . . . bump him off before he knows what's happened to him" (6). As they continue to talk, Bonnie and Clyde agree that they must remain continually on the move, never pausing to stop. Thus, their first meeting, rather than being a romantic encounter between a charismatic stranger and an attractive young woman, is reduced to this simplistic violent plan. There is no reference to Barrow's background in poverty or Parker's middle-class upbringing, a key source of public fascination with their romance. Their "plan" is referred to as the "origin" of the "bloody Barrow gang," suggesting that these two had an organized and coherent set of intentions, thus necessitating special police effort and calls for preventing paroles.

Part 1 continues to characterize Bonnie and Clyde as needlessly violent and heartless criminals. They murder a number of police officers. One pair of officers meets their ends at the hands of the criminal couple simply because they pulled next to them at a dance in Oklahoma. When officers find the bodies of two Missouri state patrol officers Bonnie and Clyde have murdered, they also find the parole slip for Clyde's brother. Just in case the irony is lost on the audience, the investigating officers make it explicit, "Look at this . . . Irony. Here's the official pardon of Buck Barrows . . . given to him three weeks ago . . . and down there in the yard are our pals . . . officers . . . murdered by this gang of paroled killers" (11). Although they acknowledge the discovery of Bonnie's famous poem, "Suicide Sal," they do not discuss it. This omission is significant, because as Potter (1998) observes, this poem constructed its main character as a passionate heroine driven by love rather than criminal pathology. Bonnie and Clyde also kill average citizens, honest businessmen trying to support their families. They murder a sixty-seven-year-old butcher and his young assistant while they are closing the shop, but not before the audience learns that the butcher is supporting nine people and that the assistant has loving parents anxiously awaiting his arrival for dinner. Left without any hint of redeeming human qualities, Bonnie and Clyde are completely deromanticized.

As the first episode works to break all possible audience identification with and sympathy for Bonnie and Clyde, the clear hero of this version of the story emerges by the end. Weighted with the heritage of the Old West and its more individualistic ideals of law and order, the episode presents us with the character of Frank Hamer. To introduce him, the program dramatizes a conversation between Superintendent Lee Simmons, warden of the East Texas State Prison, and the governor of Texas, in which they discuss the problems with the existing state of the law and a possible solution:

WARDEN: I'll tell you, every officer we send out after them has a millstone tied around his neck—laws, useless, worn-out laws that he must observe. Our police force is a courageous group of men—a dozen have already given their lives needlessly—they've been sacrificed in the altar of red tape. They can't shoot until they've warned the criminals—they can't cross the state borders—they can't do fifty things that these murderers do. We've sent enough of our men to their death. We've stood by—hampered by red tape while this gang has murdered, plundered and laughed at us. I beg you, Governor, by the law of God—and the law of justice to assume responsibility of sending one man out to face these killers. Relieve him of all these hindering, useless laws—let him get out and meet these killers at their own game. I realize what I'm asking—its outside of what you have the right to do according to the law—but I beg you governor, to assume this responsibility. It means saving the lives of other innocent victims. (21)

It is significant here that Hamer is needed not to correct the failures of his fellow law enforcement officers. Rather, the fault for the violent actions of the pair rests firmly on the shoulders of an ineffective legal apparatus. As the provenance of local and state governments, the inference here is that citizens have not provided the necessary support for improving this situation, and they are thus reminded of one of the key lessons of the episode. Any possible critique of police violence is placed on the failures of the legal system rather than on police corruption or incompetence.

The warden asks the governor to appoint Frank Hamer, a former Texas Ranger, as an "execution squad" to "get this gang." The governor grants permission, thus ending the episode with the chief telling the audience, "Frank Hamer oiled up his old six-shooter, Mr. Lord, and the way he went after that gang was one of the most thrilling manhunts ever conducted in this country" (23). As in the ending of all episodes, the moral of the episode again is communicated to listeners, who are reminded of the second lesson of the episode. The chief tells Lord, "Thus far I've only had time to give you a picture of the hideous crimes this Bloody Barrow gang committed—[in order]—to show what *has* happened in this country—what *is* happening and what will happen again if the citizens don't relieve the police of old useless, encumbering laws—and give them new laws with teeth in them." Lord replies simply, "And stop wholesale Paroles" (23). While Bonnie and Clyde's deviance clearly warrants extreme measures by the police, the episode further works to argue that a public too sympathetic to criminals, as evidenced in their weak support for effective crime legislation, is equally culpable for the pair's killing spree. In this case, the violence resulting from this legal nightmare warrants a return to "Old West" methods of law enforcement. Part 2 reminds the listener of the appointment of Hamer, who will be their new hero. The episode dramatizes the hunt for Bonnie and Clyde and their eventual deaths at the hands of Hamer and his men. The description of the heroic Hamer is the exact opposite of the description of Clyde in the first episode. Rather than small and weak, Hamer "stands six feet three, a power in himself." Rather than unintelligent, "He's shrewd," possessing "the coolest hand, the best shot the rangers ever had." The heroic Hamer is further described as "a man with a nerve of steel—a fighter," who "has faced the toughest gangs that ever came into this state." Quickly linking this second part to the first, the Warden pleads with the governor to "relieve Capt. Hamer of all hindering laws under which the Police work—I beg you to appoint him an execution squad to get this gang" (2). The masculine allure of bandits like Dillinger is stripped from Barrow and conferred upon Hamer. More than a competent police officer, he is a pinnacle of masculine virtue.

Hamer's determination is clear from the beginning; his goal is not to capture Bonnie and Clyde but to kill them. As he and his men study maps, they begin to discern a pattern in the crimes the "gang" commits. Bonnie and Clyde commit a robbery, then head five hundred miles to the east. Eventually, Hamer and his men locate the father of one of the Barrow gang members in Louisiana, and Hamer sends a detective there to eavesdrop. When Bonnie and Clyde arrive, they make a plan to meet another gang member, Wass, the next day on the road, but they do not specify the exact location in case he decides to tell the police. The episode then dramatizes Hamer's efforts to calculate the exact spot where Barrow and Parker are likely to meet Wass. When Hamer and his men finally spot Bonnie and Clyde, they see Bonnie reaching for a gun, and they riddle the pair with gunfire.

After the shootout, the officers find a number of weapons in the trunk of the car that Bonnie and Clyde were using, a fact the chief repeats in his closing statements, telling the radio audience, "In the back of the car, Mr. Lord, were three rifles . . . ten automatics . . . a revolver, all loaded . . . in addition to over two thousand rounds of ammunition. There were ten extra sets of license plates" (20). Lord responds by complimenting the efforts of the Texas authorities on their "excellent work" and reiterating the claim that "the Barrow Gang got what was coming to them . . . but that doesn't help the families of the twelve men who were murdered by them." After dismissing any possible criticism of the extremely violent end of Bonnie and Clyde, the chief makes sure to remind listeners where any logical criticism should lie, telling Lord that he is "right," and the way to prevent these things from happening is to "give the Police Laws with teeth in them—so they can act—quick and sure—and another thing—stop this paroling of criminals. Over half these killers you meet are convicts who have been paroled from prisons" (21). While Bonnie and Clyde are marked as sufficiently deviant to deserve death, the closing of the episode acts as further justification for the grisly killing of the pair by the police. State violence is the only recourse left to the authorities. Bonnie and Clyde were free to go on violent crime sprees because outdated laws and overly sympathetic parole boards hamper the police in their efforts to stop them. Criminal deviance and citizen weakness are equally blamed for the violent actions of the pair.

The romantic desperado is dramatically redefined in the radio crime docudrama. Criminals like John Dillinger, Clyde Barrow, and Bonnie Parker are not products of unequal social relations, a crumbling economy, or failed social institutions. Dillinger is not a bold trickster hero but a callow, nervous, unintelligent figure undeserving of public worship. Rather than a romantic pair engaged in a desperate struggle to escape police pressure, Bonnie and Clyde are stripped of all glamour and reduced to individual psychopaths whose gender reversals, bloodthirsty violence, and wanton mobility mark them as objects who necessitate increasing state authority, including the use of violence as a way to manage social order. Drawing on reform-centered interpretations of banditry, police failures in apprehending these figures and their use of violence is not the fault of police incompetence but of public support for criminals rather than for police. Had the public sympathized with the police and supported stronger laws, such violent outcomes, leading to the deaths of citizens, criminals, and police officers, might have been prevented.

DEFINING CRIME AND CRIMINAL TYPES

In dramatizing the exploits of men and women who many saw as populist heroes rather than criminals, these tales of solved police cases entered a terrain fraught with multiple meanings. No matter the devices used to deglamorize the most notorious of these figures, the programs could never fully contain the populist identification with their heroes. After all, sponsors and radio professionals wanted to attract and keep audiences, and what better draw than the exploits of these criminal heroes? As Razlogova (2006) argues, dramatization of criminal exploits was a key source of *Gang Busters'* appeal to its working-class audiences as the populist meaning of the stories spilled over attempts to contain it. In drawing on the conventions of populist confessionals, which, as discussed in chapter 1, emphasized the experiences of average people over and against the power of professional authority, dramatizations of criminals were likely to be understood as symbols of social critique. Yet, in working with police files to tell these stories from the point of view of the police, the programs began to create a recognizable criminal "type" who reflected reform ideas about crime and criminality. As police reformers worked to define policing as a scientific profession and to manage public perception, ideas about what counted as crime shifted, leading to an emphasis on crimes against personal properties or persons. The emphasis on rationality in crime fighting led to a consistent set of ideas about how criminals behaved. These beliefs intersected with the needs of radio professionals, burdened with producing weekly anthology dramas. The necessity for differentiating radio characters from each other through voice, language, and personality led radio professionals to create a consistent criminal type as a counterpoint to the police type.

Constituting Crime

Definitions of policing and criminality are inherently intertwined, each operating in reference to the other. As reformers worked to define policing as a modern profession centered on criminal apprehension, they began to focus their efforts on property crime rather than on urban racket crime or on the provision of social service to their communities. In seeking to improve policing through the development of a procedural apparatus, crimes committed against private persons or property, such as robbery, kidnapping, murder, rape, and confidence games, gained the most attention by police. This was particularly true at the federal level. As Potter (1998) notes, police work emerged as a career with clear rules and paths for promotion, making corruption a less stable path for social mobility. The investigation of vice crimes was considered both tedious and dangerous. Instead, the "best route to status was breaking major cases—mainly bank robberies, fraud, and confidence rackets. . . . Investigating crimes against property also conferred status, reflecting advanced knowledge of techniques for collecting, understanding, and analyzing evidence and a detailed knowledge of the criminal underworld" (44). These activities proved far more quantifiable, thus ensuring that they could be more easily counted and collated to signify the success not only of individual officers but also of police departments at large.

In the efforts to define crime through the trope of scientific rationality, the Uniform Crime Reports (UCR) were key. In many ways, the development of the UCR grew out of public complaints that crime was on the rise with the police little able to stop it. While newspapers routinely published tales of criminal exploits, lacking any coherent figures on the actual number of crimes, police forces were unable to counter public fears (Wilson 2000). A universal, systemized measure for reporting crime seemed an ideal solution to the problem. While initiated by local reformers, the responsibility for overseeing the reports was handed over to J. Edgar Hoover at the Bureau of Justice, and later FBI.[8] Because the UCRs reported a narrow range of crime, and because they measured success solely by the response of police to such crimes, they aided in the strong crime control orientation of police reformers and in the effort to narrow the functions of policing. Potter (1998) persuasively argues that federal crime laws focused on only specific types of crimes—those that could garner the most public support for the growth of a federal crime-fighting force. Therefore, urban gang crimes, political rackets, and the rash of lynching in the South were largely ignored by the FBI in favor of intense hunts for rural bandits labeled Public Enemies. Local police forces were likewise interested in more narrow definitions of crime. As police moved out of social service–type activities, sought to serve their middle-class critics, and worked to separate themselves from local political entanglements, a focus on property and personal crimes offered them the ability to "prove" their efficiency in order to herald the success of their professionalization efforts.

From Criminal Definitions to Criminal Types

Radio professionals needed a consistent set of strategies to mark the criminal and his or her clear difference from the police. Drawing on the reform definitions of crime and criminality and combining those definitions with the demands of weekly radio production, the radio crime dramas, especially *Gang Busters,* worked to develop a criminal type. By dealing with questions of criminal organization, intelligence, bravery, and origins, the programs consistently insisted that crime not be viewed as a viable path to upward social mobility. However, the radio crime docudramas met with a series of contradictions within the reform discourse itself. In attempts to deglamorize criminals, like the gangster, it made sense to cast aspersions on any notion of criminal intelligence. However, criminals could not simply be dismissed as unintelligent. A key justification for the expansion of police forces, the purchase of scientific and technical equipment to aid in criminal identification and apprehension, and investment in police education and training was that criminals were, in fact, quite intelligent and growing more sophisticated in their methods.

While reformers drew attention to the increasing brazenness of criminals and their infringement on the property and lives of middle-class citizens, they also knew that such bravado was precisely the reason audiences seemed so inclined to idolize criminals. Whether using crime as a form of social mobility and enjoying the material delights that their activities allowed them to afford, or boldly challenging the very institutions that people blamed for their plights during the Depression, criminals emerged as populist heroes who routinely defied state authority. To break this spell, criminals were portrayed by radio crime docudramas as cowardly rather than brave. As criminals were already framed within a narrative that structured police interpretation of the events as dominant, criminals would come to be identified as cowardly and acts of bravery reinterpreted as acts of desperation from fear. In this way, a criminal type emerged.

Criminal Organizations

Whether criminals were urban gangsters or rural bandits, the radio crime docudramas frequently portrayed them as being in organizations that had clearly marked leaders. The programs made little distinction between urban gangs and rural bandit groups, though, as Potter (1998) demonstrates, there were significant differences in how these criminals were organized. In general, rural bandits were represented as belonging to criminal organizations that had leaders, though in reality, many operated in loose groups, often based on kinship ties. Radio producers, whose main goal was simply to demonstrate that criminals were organized, largely ignored these differences. Given the title of the program, this was especially important to the producers of *Gang Busters*. In notes regarding the preparation of the scripts, frequent reference is made to "TALK OF HIGHER UPS OR BOSSES (organized gang)," "BASED ON RACKET" (1936),[9] "One crime boss over others" (1936),[10] and "Getting at higher ups" (1936).[11] Even romantic desperados Bonnie and Clyde were to be represented as gang heads: "Organized gang. Bonnie Parker and Barrow = heads" (1936).[12] While it is true that most of the criminals were involved in some kind of group, *Gang Busters* and the other radio crime docudramas pointed out that regardless of where a criminal operated or of his ethnic background, he was part of some kind of hierarchal organization.

The portrayal of criminals as part of an organized gang sometimes ran counter to actual events. In the "Jessie Wendell" (1942) episode of *Gang Busters,* a group of five men shoot and kill two police officers during a gun battle, leading a dedicated pair of detectives to track the group down. After tracing them to a bungalow, they install a Dictaphone so that they may eavesdrop on what the group intends to do. They eventually capture four of the men as they try to flee the bungalow, suspecting the police know where they are. Missing is the "leader" of the gang, Jessie Wendell. An anonymous tip leads police to Wendell's possible location in Arizona. After an exciting chase with an Arizona sheriff, who hops aboard a speeding freight train to catch up with Wendell after he escapes in his car, Wendell commits suicide. What is interesting about this episode is the program's insistence on naming Wendell as the leader of the gang. A letter from an Arizona official notes that the details of the capture of the gang are incorrect: "The gang were captured singly, at gun point, in various spots of Los Angeles." While the dramatization of separate captures would undoubtedly take too much time in a half hour radio production, the decision to represent the group as being captured together has the effect of making the gang seem more strongly organized than they might actually have been. More significantly, this writer informs Lord that "Jessie Wendell was not actually the leader; just one of the gang" ("Jessie Wendell" 1942). The producers of *Gang Busters* drew on the police reform discourse regarding criminal organization and professionalization in order to represent criminality in its program.[13] This was done to highlight the exceptional organizational power of the police and their more thoroughly professional hierarchal ranking system. Thus, it was more important that each "gang" have some sort of "leader" than it was to faithfully represent the actual situation.

This emphasis on gangs might seem to represent a break from Hoover's desire to individualize criminality through his well-publicized campaigns against Public Enemy Number Ones. This tactic might also have been influenced by the breakdown of relations between Lord and Hoover. While Hoover emphasized the pathology of individual public enemies, Lord, in the very title of his program, emphasized criminals as belonging to groups. Still, in working with solved police cases that detailed the work of criminal apprehension, it is significant that these were not complicated rackets or gangs engaging in complex activities that simulated those of modern businesses, such as those in the gangster films. These were ragtag groups of individuals whose relationship was tenuously centered on the perpetration of property crimes. In addition, whereas urban rackets were seen as particularly tied to local political corruption, representing gangs in this fashion further sidestepped questions regarding their relationship with the police. Neither the gangs nor individual members were tied to any ethnic or community group. A key part of the justification of police reform was the modern, organized nature of criminality, which reformers claimed needed to be matched by modern, organized law enforcement agencies.

Criminal "Intelligence"

When it came to representing criminal intelligence, these programs walked a fine line. On the one hand, part of the justification for the increasing use of invasive methods and increased funding for police departments was the frequently lauded claim that criminals had grown more intelligent. On the other hand, representing criminals as rational and intelligent risked furthering the very identification with criminals that these programs sought to break. The programs negotiated this tension in several ways. One way was to simply name the actions of the criminal as stupid and suggest that any belief to the contrary was an incorrect interpretation of events. By simply stating that a criminal was unintelligent and by rejecting any populist interpretations, these programs worked to strip any glamour or bravado from the public image of the criminal. This proved especially important when dramatizing events surrounding the cases of most populist criminals of the era, including, as discussed earlier, John Dillinger. The label "stupid" was applied to counter any idea that a criminal was glamorous and brave. Sometimes the police deployed the same tactic in the reconstruction of their own cases. For example, George Matowitz, the chief of police in Cleveland, sent a letter, dated March 9, 1936, to J. T. Vorpe, the production manager of the local Cleveland radio station, providing background for the episode that dramatized the capture of Joe Filkowski. He notes that "considered exceptionally clever by his associates, Joe had no difficulty in forming a gang and became bolder and bolder. . . . The newspapers publicized his slightest move with headlines and called him 'Cleveland's Public Enemy #1,' and this fired Smiling Joe's egotism and he goaded the police, boasting that he would never be taken alive." Having gained local celebrity status, the police made the mistake of overestimating him. As the host chief tells Lord:

> It is apparent that the members of the police department credited him with too much intelligence, for as we look back, each depredation and every depredation, screams with stupidity and yet Joe always kept one step ahead of the police. The newspapers squirmed in delight; Joe boosted circulation and the police department became the target for almost daily editorials.

In this case, the denial of Filkowski's intelligence curiously allows the police to account for the amount of time it took them to identify a criminal who operated within their city. For the producers, it allows them to posit "Joe" as unintelligent from the outset rather than in the hindsight of the Cleveland police.

While directly referring to criminals as stupid was fraught with complication, a more consistent way to clearly mark criminals as less intelligent was through their speech. Consistent with the construction of policing, the educated radio policeman spoke in unaccented "American" speech, even when his name marked him ethnically. The police rarely used slang or contractions. They referred to themselves as police, beat cops, or detectives. And unlike the criminals, they had command of the technical and professional language of policing. The police not only could understand the language of the "underworld," they also could understand the methods of modern policing, and hence they wielded a great deal of authority. From the moment the criminal spoke, he was marked as inferior. But it would not suffice to make the criminal simply inferior to the police. In comparison to police, criminal speech was marked both by its absence of any technical knowledge and by its "generic" accent. Criminal speech borrowed the speaking style of the tough-talking urban gangster of the movies, as discussed by Jonathan Munby (1999), and combined it with a sort of uneducated Midwestern-style expression. Radio criminals thus spoke with a lower-class accent, which was sometimes tied more specifically to the urban ethnic underclasses. Unless otherwise marked as educated or upper class, they spoke in a broken, ungrammatical English, punctuated by a great deal of slang. For example, criminal characters frequently were scripted to say "yer" instead of "you" or "your" and made frequent use of contractions such as "can't" instead of "cannot." When referring to the police, they frequently said "coppers" or "dick" rather than "police" or "detective." From the moment they entered the narrative through their speech, the criminals in the radio docudramas were immediately marked as less intelligent when they spoke. Such forms of nongrammatical dialogue and slang had long been associated with representations of groups of people as less intelligent, as Denning (1998) argues about dime novels and Hilmes (1997) argues about the production of speech patterns in *Amos 'n' Andy*. As Razlogova (2006) notes, scriptwriters for *Gang Busters* were instructed to give criminals standard verbal characterizations.

For example, in the script for the "Tony, the Stinger" (1936) episode of *Gang Busters,* the Stinger, under fear of police pressure, engages in a killing spree. When a woman he is about to murder "screams in stark terror," the Stinger responds, "Shut up, you, do ya want the coppers down on us? Yollin for the law, yollin for the law. Everybody I know yollin for the law" (9). In "The Blonde Tigress, Part 2" (1939) episode of *Gang Busters,* criminal Eleanor Jarman's associate is scripted to frequently speak with slang. When they are under pressure from the police, he tells Jarman "We got to stay hid out, Blondie. In a week or two, the excitement'll die down; then we can slip outta this burg," and later, "Blondie—you're letting yer nerves get the best of you" (25–26). In each of these cases, criminals speak in a generic "criminal accent," which includes the frequent use of grammatical imprecision and slang that clearly mark their difference from the police.

Moreover, while the scripting of police speech has the effect of deethnicizing them, criminal speech vaguely gives its characters an ethnic identity, but not strongly enough to encourage any specific ethnic identification. If criminals were simply stupid, there would be no apparent reason to develop increasingly complex scientific methods to apprehend them. Thus, the other tactic these programs used was to portray the criminals as intelligent but, due to the scientific power of the police, incapable of planning a perfect crime. These programs told listeners, no matter how smart, the criminal would always be caught. Some episodes actually stressed the intelligence of the criminal. The two-part "Willie 'The Actor' Sutton" (1936) episode of *Gang Busters* tells of a jewel thief who carefully plans his crimes by first seeking work in a variety of trades, including gunsmith, locksmith, and bank guard. He finds work in a contractor's office to learn about blueprinting and teaches himself about precious stones and makeup for disguises. Despite all his precise planning, his tendency to brag leaves a trail of persons able to provide information to the police. "The Phantom Radio" (1937) episode of *Calling All Cars* features a burglar who erases all traces of his identity, cleverly taking precautions not to leave any fingerprints behind. However, when this burglar discovers a broken radio during a burglary, he can't help but stop to fix it. It is from the radio that police get the fingerprints they need to identify and thus bring him to justice. The special skills needed to crack a variety of ever-improving safes are detailed in several episodes of *Gang Busters,* including "The Seattle Safecrackers" (1937) and "Safecrackers vs. Vault Makers" (1937). Here the program demonstrates that criminal intelligence accounts for the constant battle to develop burglarproof safes.

The producers occasionally emphasized the cleverness of a particular criminal but only to highlight the keen intelligence of the police. For example, the script résumé for "The Gray Anthony Gang" (1936) explains that it is an "unusual case" because it involves a group of men who plan on robbing a bank by coming through the sewer system.[14] As notes regarding the episode indicate, the episode was designed to highlight the "unusual clues" that demonstrated the cleverness of the detectives. For example, when searching the sewer after hearing strange noises, an officer finds some candles. Detectives determine where the candles were purchased, then discover that the purchaser was in a recent auto accident with a trolley. From the trolley company records they find the address of one of the gang members and use a skeleton key to get into his apartment. Finding evidence that he has been in the sewers, they arrest him, and through him are able to find the rest of the gang. In each of these stories, the episodes clearly demonstrate that the criminals in question are intelligent and clever, thus necessitating the growing array of police procedures and scientific methods to apprehend them.

Criminal "Bravery"

Radio crime docudramas used the common tactic of presenting criminals as needlessly vicious to deglamorize them. Depression-era Americans exhibited a remarkable capacity for identification with bank robbers and others who evaded the powers of institutions and the state, which had so bitterly failed them. These programs consistently worked not only to deglamorize but also to depoliticize the actions of their criminals. Social bandits garnered public support, provided they did not commit violence so excessive that it violated community norms. The radio crime docudramas worked to identify criminals as just that. Over and over again, these episodes present the audience with criminals who wantonly and needlessly kill police officers and innocent citizens. They are pathologically cruel, and nothing checks their capacity for violence.

Yet again, such violence might be interpreted as bravery. To be certain that this did not happen, the final move to deglamorize the criminal was to construct him as cowardly despite his propensity for violence. Whereas the police were honest and brave in the face of danger, criminals were often portrayed as lacking courage—"yellow"—especially when the odds were not in their favor. In the "Slot Machine Murders" episode of *Gang Busters* (1939), the police search for the O'Donnell brothers, Joe and Jack, and their accomplice, Rorick. This "gang" has been safecracking, but when two of Seattle's best detectives, Mahoney and Kuehl, are assigned to investigate these crimes, Rorick calls Joe nervously to tell him this information. The script specifically instructs the actor to speak as if he were afraid: "RORICK: (YELLOW CROOK. EXCITED . . . ON FILTER) Joe?" When Joe hears the news, even he is impressed: "Mahoney and Kuehl, eh? Much as I hate 'em, I gotta admit they're two smart dicks" (7). It is their fear of these two officers that leads them to join a slot machine racket outside of the Seattle city limits, thus, to their minds, rendering them safe from these two detectives. But when the gang shoots two police officers who catch them stealing a slot machine, Mahoney and Kuehl are called to investigate, leading to the gang's eventual capture. In the "Jessie Wendell" episode of *Gang Busters,* a group of four bandits armed with machine guns easily and fearfully give themselves up when cornered by two police officers carrying nothing by revolvers. Cop killer Edward Metelski, when finally cornered by two officers, falls to his knees in fear, leaving the cops to tell him smugly to get up and run because they can't shoot him on his knees ("Edward Metelski" 1936). Whereas criminals might be needlessly violent, that did not necessarily mark them as being brave. By stripping criminals of any glamour, the radio docudrama effectively instructed its listeners about the futility of sympathizing or identifying with criminals.

CAUSES OF CRIME

The development of criminal types resulted from the negotiation between reform definitions of crime and the needs of radio professionals to create a series of recognizable traits for a set of characters in an anthology drama. Yet the dramas further intersected with competing ideas about the causes of crime. The ultraviolent bandits of the radio crime docudramas clearly reflected the dominant discourse of bandit crime during the 1930s as individual pathology, which stripped any possible political meaning away from the criminals' actions and justified state violence[15] (Potter 1998, 84–90). However, the individual pathology explanation was limited when applied to localized forms of policing, where the complex interaction between crime and specific social conditions could not be entirely ignored. Moreover, the often-repeated lesson of radio crime dramas, "crime never pays," suggested that the propensity toward crime was, at least partly, a rational choice. If pathology was used too often to account for criminal actions, then it is unlikely that any "average," nonpathological citizen figured as the radio listener would rationally choose a life of crime. The idea of individual pathology was thus tempered by drawing on the Progressive theory of juvenile delinquency as stemming from environmental causes.[16] As argued in chapter 1, the radio crime docudramas drew on the public interest discourse of the radio networks to argue that although these programs were violent, they had the educational value of teaching young listeners that crime did not pay. By suggesting that crime was the result of environment, the programs could sustain the idea that no matter how tempered by circumstances, crime was the result of choice. This choice resulted from both negative social circumstances and the improper knowledge gleaned from films and the press that crime could somehow lead to success in life. Thus, even though the programs suggested that crime stemmed from social causes beyond the control of individuals, their overall message, "crime never pays," consistently treated crime as either a moral or rational choice. To suggest otherwise might have created too much sympathy for criminals.

The "Two-Gun Crowley" (1936) episode of *Gang Busters* offers a particularly vivid example of the Progressive view of juvenile crime as stemming from environmental causes and of the need for better ways to deal with juvenile offenders. The episode dramatizes the career of a small-time but very violent criminal, Crowley, who especially hates police officers and willfully sets out to murder them. What is interesting about the episode is that Lord, instead of interviewing a police authority, interviews "Mike," a convict in prison. He begins the episode by telling the audience that rather than doing the show in "police headquarters," as they usually did, they will host tonight's program from "the studio."[17] Whereas Crowley is portrayed throughout the episode as a vicious cop-hater, Mike is portrayed as nervous and naïve, a man forced into a life of crime by circumstance rather than character.

He begins, at Lord's request, by telling the audience of how he and Crowley grew up in the same neighborhood. Mike emphatically states that neither of them had a chance, growing up as they did, in the slums. He tells Lord, "Sure—and what chance did I have? A bad lung—sleeping in sewers—in the coal yard—eating out a garbage cans. Crowley was born on a dump" (2). The episode reenacts Crowley's traumatic experience, when he was just a baby, of his father tossing him out of the house for crying. He lands in a garbage can. Although he eventually is rescued, his penchant for crime has been set. As a young child, Mike tells the audience, Crowley began his career stealing peanuts from stands. His propensity for crime leads to a stint in a juvenile reformatory, but it is here, Mike tells us, that the youthful Crowley developed his hatred of police officers. Mike details how reformatories operate as places for learning more about crime. Incarcerated juveniles hear stories from other children about the terrible things cops have done, including throwing a child off a rooftop and dragging another child behind a car with a rope before eventually running him over. Crowley left the reformatory having learned "Kill 'em before they kill you" (11).

Without commenting on whether the stories Crowley heard might or might not be true, the program details how Crowley's hatred of the police was manifested. Showing a particular penchant for shooting at police officers, Crowley shoots down an officer who approaches him at a dance hall. After killing another policeman, Crowley goes into hiding with his girl-friend. When the police eventually locate him, Crowley, realizing his situation is desperate, resolves to kill as many officers as possible before his eventual capture, thus leading to a final, violent confrontation. As the episode closes, Lord and Mike complete their "interview" and in one short exchange careen between positing individual pathology and social conditions as the source of Crowley's criminal tendencies. The dialogue begins by emphasizing Crowley's mental deficiencies:

> LORD: (FADE IN) Mike, that's a powerful story you've told us tonight. I under-
> stand that Two-Gun Crowley kept up his bragging to the last. That he cut
> out of a magazine a picture of the electric chair and kept it pasted to the
> wall in his cell in the death house.
>
> MIKE: Yeah. The guy was a rat, Mr. Lord—but he never had no chance. His
> brains was like the brains of a guy ten or twelve years old. Even on his way
> to the electric chair he said he was glad he was going to be electrocuted
> because "Only big guys boin in the electric chair." He was nuts. (31)

Because Crowley is dismissed as pathologically "nuts," listeners might have been free to think no more of their own responsibilities in the creation of criminal figures such as Crowley. Yet the program makes the case that social environment played some role in his behavior. As soon as Crowley's mental capacities are called into question, the program instantly turns around to consider the social milieu that surely contributed to his activities.

> LORD: You've given us a very interesting angle tonight Mike—something
> to think over. We spend some fourteen billions of dollars every year on
> criminals—it might be a good investment to take care of our slums and
> prevent boys from being born criminals.

MIKE: Now yer talking—give them something ter eat—a place ter play—a swimming pool—a decent place ter sleep. Yer can't sleep in a sewer and get up feeling like a man.

LORD: That remark may hit a few people who are listening tonight, Mike. In the morning let's hope that certain calls are made to mayors of cities about the slums of their city. And Mike I want to thank you for being here with us—and I know that everyone listening thanks you too. Nobody knows how many boys in the slums may get a better chance because of your story tonight. (31–32)

In this rare instance, the program advocated that listeners could prevent crime if they acted to alleviate the social conditions that caused it. Usually, the program more simply suggested it was providing listeners with an "education" regarding the cost of crime and that this education provided a useful social function. Listeners were blamed for not supporting the police but rarely asked to see the relationship between social conditions and crime. Here they are asked not simply to support the police but to act to improve those conditions that may breed crime.

The Progressive view of juvenile delinquency was used specifically to tell young boys about the danger of crime in *Calling All Cars'* grisly dramatization of activities of the Blood Oath Gang ("Youth Rides Tough" 1935), in which a group of "young killers" commits a series of robberies in Missouri and Kansas. The gang leader's life in crime originates in his taking dope when he was only ten years old, leading to his involvement in gang life. After his teenage gang is arrested because one member "squeals" on the other, he makes the members of his new gang take a blood oath that they will never do the same. When one of the gang members is injured during a robbery attempt, forcing the gang to leave him behind, the police question him, only to meet with his firm refusal to identify the other members. It is only by questioning his girlfriend that the police learn the identities of the gang members, which leads to a drawn-out manhunt and a violent jail break before the last two members finally are caught. At the end of the episode, the host tells the audience that this was another gang of young men who thought they were smarter than the police but who learned that crime does not pay. The episode tries to appeal specifically to juvenile boys by discussing the importance of the Boy Scouts in "training our boys."

Then there is an announcement that the Scouts will camp for ten days in Washington State. The regional airing of the program made it likely that listeners could imagine attending this camp. The potential appeal that boys might feel for becoming part of a tight-knit group such as a gang is countered by suggesting the Boy Scouts as an alternative.

At the end of the "Akron Cop Murders" (1937) episode of *Gang Busters,* a Mrs. Langley of the National Congress of Parents and Teachers gives a short talk to the audience, telling them that criminals are made, not born. And what makes a criminal? Mrs. Langley notes that he is made by bad influences in the community and at home. Children need to learn to adhere to the law so that they will obey state and federal laws. Gangsters always will be on the lookout for new recruits, she tells the audience, and while crime never wins, the home can win. Listeners need to make their homes exciting, good, and lawful places to ensure that the young won't turn to crime, and "in many instances, crime is merely misdirected play or misuse of leisure." She praises the program for the way it routinely "strips the false glamour from the criminal. People who once felt they could find thrills in a criminal life are now realizing that being on the side of Society offers greater opportunities for self-expression, achievement and adventure." As discussed in chapter 1, Lord made a special effort to gain support from religious, moral, and civic groups to publicly support *G-Men.* In the case of *Gang Busters,* Lord incorporates this effort into the broadcast itself as a way to explore the reasons that crime exists.

As the programs sat at the intersection of tensions over defining the causes of crime, they nonetheless continued to suggest that education and guidance might still prevent criminal tendencies from being actualized. Yet this emphasis on guidance began to fade when the programs dealt with women criminals. As Potter (1998) argues, female bandits who exhibited a capacity for violence traditionally associated with men were especially confusing to Depression-era ideas about gender. For example, the first of the two-part "The Blonde Tigress" (1939) episodes of *Gang Busters* opens with Colonel Schwarzkopf telling listeners that "while Eleanor Jarman showed certain bad characteristics in her youth, proper guidance and correct influences could have curbed these tendencies and developed her into a character worthy of her beauty and ability" (2). Despite this caveat, Jarman is portrayed as being particularly vicious, manipulating men and murdering for sport. And though Schwarzkopf insists that "crime turned her into a vicious savage," by tracing her viciousness back to early childhood, the program suggests Jarman was born bad. For example, the first episode begins with a scene of Jarman as a young child, brutally torturing a puppy for fun. When a neighbor, an old woman, tries to stop the child, Jarman mocks her, demonstrating she has no respect for authority. When the police return to the Iowa town where Jarman was raised, they knock on the old woman's door. She tells them she is glad that Jarman finally is getting her due. While the program ends with the typical *Gang Busters* lesson, arguing that even though she might have been born bad, a more proper upbringing and a better understanding of the cost of crime might have tempered Jarman's criminal tendencies, after detailing her pathological cruelty for the entire episode, this last statement suggests more unease with female criminality than possible softening toward her.

When it came to constructing criminality, the radio crime docudramas negotiated a number of dilemmas. To counter what police and moral reformers saw as the glamorization of crime by Hollywood and the nation's newspapers, criminals were constructed as relentlessly and needlessly violent. Such a characterization, however, suggested that criminality was born out of some sort of individual pathology. If this were the case, however, then the claim made by the program that "crime never pays" would be futile. After all, if crime results from individual pathology, it is unlikely that any "normal" person would choose a life of crime on the assumption that it paid. The compromise was to temper the program's emphasis on the pathological elements of criminal behavior and focus on the social causes of crime, especially in the case of juvenile delinquents and those who began criminal careers while they were young. This allowed the programs to maintain, contrary to films and newspapers, that they were providing an education on the wages of crime.

THE PLIABLE PUBLIC

Reconstructing popular images of criminals put radio professionals and police reformers at odds with popular imagery but nonetheless was considered necessary in order to break the public's sympathy for and fascination with criminals and to encourage them to place their faith in the police. As has been discussed, as much as criminal pathology, violence, immorality, and irrationality was used to account for crimes against persons and personal property, the public was also held accountable. While segments of the public delighted in criminal exploits, by the Depression, citizens of the Midwest began to put pressure on the Roosevelt administration to improve efforts at combating property crime. Potter (1998) points out that this call for help was "generated from two basic political stances, neither of which were antistatist. One valorized criminal laws and police power as expressions of national will that were necessary to the public good," while the other played on the idea of social banditry "that drew its moral vision from the bandit's imagined commitment to the people and promoted national well-being by regulating corruption" (151). In some aspects, second-wave police reformers fell into both camps. A key part of the reform movement involved removing policing from local politics and hence from local political corruption. Equally important was the creation of a professional police force granted the authority to operate without citizen interference. Yet in the reformers' emphasis on controlling social mobility through the maintenance of a hierarchal structure of differences, professionalization focused most often on authority rather than community. Therefore, when it came to representing the ideal public attitude, the radio crime dramas by and large focused on questions of power rather than on any "moral vision."

Gone were the days of populist crime fighting, as epitomized by such things as posses organized and directed by citizens. Citizens were supposed to defer to police authority. As police reformers worked to create a scientific profession, the police became the creators and keepers of knowledge about crime and policing. If citizens were to agree to cooperate with the efforts of the police, they would have to be persuaded to switch from identifying with criminals to identifying with the police and to realize that crime was not a cinematic event to which they were simple spectators but an event in which they were potential victims. Yet professionalism demanded subordination to expertise rather than direct involvement. No matter how threatening crime might seem, the programs continued to insist that citizens not take the law into their own hands. Crime fighting was to be left to the professionals: the police. Citizen cooperation involved deference to the authority of the police, cooperation, and support of crime legislation. It did not involve vigilantism.

The Cost of Crime

In the radio crime docudramas, crime was represented differently than in other popular discourse. It was not the whodunit parlor game of classic detective fiction. Nor was it the politically, economically, or romantically motivated crime of gangster films or press accounts of bandits. Instead, the programs dramatized most often the exploits of roaming criminals who devoted their lives to crime and were not the least bit discriminating in their choice of victims. Kidnappings, bank robberies, home invasions, and the robbing and killing of small business owners were among the crimes designed to highlight for the listener that crime cost the average citizen.[18] *Police Headquarters* often told stories of crime that directly impacted "average" citizens, including the snatching of a businessman's son in the "Laundry Truck Kidnappings" (1932), the attempted kidnapping and injury of a young dance hall employee in the "Williams Brothers" (1932), and the robbery of a local employer's payroll checks in the "$40,000 Payroll Shipment" (1932). Not surprisingly, one of the earliest episodes of *G-Men* dramatized the capture of Machine Gun Kelly for the kidnapping of businessman Charles Urschel ("Urschel Kidnapping" 1935) and the kidnapping of "Edward Bremer" (1935) by Ma Barker.

Descriptions of the possible threat of crime waxed colorful. The second episode of *Gang Busters,* which dramatized the capture of the Fats McCarthy gang ("The Fats McCarthy Gang" 1936) opens with the following speech by Lewis Valentine, the New York City Police Commissioner:

> We of the police profession are grateful for the apparent signs of public awakening. We have criminals called mad dogs. We have heard them called human vultures, and we well know these appellations are not misnomers. The time is at hand when we must frankly admit that the menace of these mad dogs and human vultures, preying upon the honest, hard-working, sincere people of the United States, is a major problem—an infamous, vicious, cancerous growth, the roots of which must be torn out and completely destroyed. (2)

Any possible public sympathy with criminals and any suggestion that criminal behavior preyed upon institutions that were responsible for the miserable situations of listeners was quickly turned around. Here the blame is placed squarely on the shoulders of pathological "mad dog" criminals who prey on average citizens without provocation or reason.

Issuing the second part of a double-pronged assault on public celebration of criminal exploit, Valentine argues that the costs of crime are borne by all: "It has been said, and can be reasonably believed, that crime, with its by-products, cost us twelve billion dollars a year. It is truly a staggering amount. Twelve dollars for every minute since Christ was born . . . every sixty seconds for more than nineteen centuries, twelve dollars thrown into the gassy, belching maw of crime" (2). It is doubtful that Depression-era audiences wanted to throw their money into the "belching maw" of anything. As the repeated lesson "crime does not pay" suggested to listeners contemplating a life of crime that the cost was too high, so the radio crime docudramas told citizens busy enjoying the exploits of movie and newspaper criminals that the cost of crime was paid from their own pockets. The emphasis on the innocent victims of merciless criminals suggested that anyone might become a victim of crime. The frequent recitation of FBI statistics regarding the costs of crimes suggested that individual citizens shared the price. Populist interpretations of crime during the Depression suggested that crime was directed against the State or the institutions of capital that had caused the crisis. The radio docudramas drew on the discourse of suffering but suggested that the cause of suffering was those who preyed on or subverted social institutions rather than those institutions themselves.

Antivigilantism

That citizens should be concerned with crime was without question. However, it was important that their concern did not lead them to take the law into their own hands. Particularly worrisome to police was the potential for citizen concern to lead to mob violence. The "Unwritten Law" (1934) episode of *Calling All Cars* dramatizes the search for two criminals responsible for murdering a police officer. When a group of citizens learns that the killer is finally in jail, they gather there to seek retribution. The prison warden, Black, goes to the door and tells the crowd to step back, questioning their faith in the police. When they ask for access to the criminals in order to exact revenge, Chief Black retorts, "And to do that you would set aside the authority vested in the police department?" When the ring leader states that this is indeed the case, Black presses him, "Now look here (angry sounding) you're not very consistent. In demanding the right to lynch this man you infer no confidence in the police department, a member of which you are trying to avenge. Now that doesn't make sense does it?" After getting the crowd to acknowledge that their actions demonstrate a profound lack of respect, Black assures the crowd that the police will handle the situation, even if that requires action against the assembled avengers:

> BLACK: Okay, then this is all I've got to say to you. Go home and cool off. You say you have faith in the police department. Very well. There are six officers in here armed with sub machine guns, they are pledged to keep the peace even at the cost of human lives. You say you have faith in your police, well, let me assure you that these men will turn these machine guns on you as the law-breakers and offenders to the police that you now are unless you disperse at once and go to your homes.

At the end, the announcer states that Black's unflinching attitude averted a breach of peace. Black's threat of violence against those who were gathered clearly indicates that vigilante behavior on the part of citizens would not be tolerated. The continued lack of intelligence of the ring leader stands in contrast to Black's professional authority, knowledge, and control over the situation. As suggested by Black, vigilantism is predicated on both a lack of faith in the police and a disregard for the forces of law and order. At the same time, the very existence of mob violence is depoliticized. That police must deal with mobs results from their impartial support of the law rather than from political affiliations. It was up to the police and the courts, not citizens, to mete out not only justice but violence as well.

This antivigilante stance extends to groups and individuals, who take the law into their own hands to further their own definitions of justice. This is evident in the "Secrets Never Told Before" (1937) episode of *True Detective Mysteries*. As discussed in chapter 1, this episode tells the story of the murder of the innocent Charles Poole by a vigilante white supremacist group known as the Black Legion. It becomes evident during this episode that the group has no right to take the law into its own hands. Listeners might sympathize with the group's actions—the vigilantes, after all, are meting out justice to a man who is suspected of injuring his wife—but there is no room for sympathy in the narrative. First, the group mistakenly kills an innocent man. Not only is Poole innocent, but the episode also goes to great lengths to let the audience know that he is a good, decent man who loves his wife and child and who would do nothing to harm them. Second, this innocent man died because the Black Legion simply declares judgment on those deemed guilty without giving them the benefit of a trial or any chance to prove their innocence. The prosecuting attorney emphasizes these points during the dramatized presentation of the case to a jury.[19] During the trial, the jury, and by extension the audience, is specifically told that the actions of the group are not in keeping with the spirit of the laws of the nation. The prosecutor tells the jury:

> Gentleman of the jury we have laid before you fifty murders for which the Black Legion is responsible. The horrible, heartless murder of the innocent Charles Poole was not their first murder, but it must be their last [Murmur—noises in assent of this statement. Knocking of gavel.] No man, woman, or child is safe from the murder madmen, the Black Legion, one hundred and thirty five thousand members in Michigan alone, and the goal of six million throughout the United States, setting family against family, tearing down the stars and stripes and running up the yellow flag of cowardice. Gentleman of the jury, the eyes of America are upon you.

The group's actions are portrayed at once as heinous and unpatriotic. The vigilantes do not abide by the spirit of the law as interpreted by these radio programs. Justice and policing are scientific endeavors that are best left to professionals, and patriotism is best exhibited by deference to professional authority.

"Support Your Local Sheriff"

The radio crime docudramas worked to tell audiences that they should not take the matter of crime fighting into their own hands. It was the job of the police and the legal system to deal with criminals. This did not mean that citizens did not have a role in fighting crime. These programs offered some clear guidelines on what kinds of actions citizens should take to support the efforts of the police. Of course, for police reformers and radio producers, the repeated message of these programs, that crime never pays, was meant to be a deterrent. Thus, it was ultimately important for citizens to stop glamorizing and sympathizing with criminals. But other themes were stressed continually. Citizens were encouraged to support tougher crime legislation, call the police should they be either victims of or witness to a crime, provide any information they had regarding crime, and, when called upon, offer their service or expertise.

One of the most frequent forms of citizen involvement advocated by these programs was public support of tougher crime legislation. For example, the opening of the *Gang Busters* dramatization of the capture of Fats McCarthy ("Fats McCarthy Gang" 1936) admonishes listeners to support tougher crime legislation, telling them that with a "public militantly interested—a public who will join in providing us with up-to-date criminal laws—laws with teeth in them, and in addition support us, we can, in a reasonable time, curb the activities of the criminal and his crimes—we can weight the scales of Justice in favor of the people instead of as they now swing—in favor of the criminal" (2).[20] The call for support of such legislation is a frequent invocation of the program. But in keeping with the importance of establishing the professional authority of the police, citizen support had to be clearly and unequivocally defined. After all, according to this logic, if the police could not do their job, it was clearly not their own fault. Professional police forces knew what they needed; that citizens did not provide it made the crime problem not only a burden on them but also a result of citizens' own actions.

Another way that citizens were asked to cooperate was to call the police. Citizens were asked not to face potentially dangerous criminals on their own or to take the law into their own hands. The narrative structure of *Police Headquarters,* which initiated each episode with a telephone call reporting a crime, stressed this idea. In an entire episode devoted to extolling the merits of the police radio, *Calling All Cars* also stressed the importance of calling the police. Every radio call the officers responded to resulted from a citizen calling the police to report some kind of trouble. The suggestion that citizens should call the police was most famously stressed in one of the most remembered features of *Gang Busters:* the broadcast of clues at the end of each episode, which included information about criminals that citizens should be on the lookout for. Lord wrote to police chiefs across the country, especially those with whom he had had some involvement in putting his episodes together. For example, in preparing the "Scarnini Case, Episode 1" (1936) for broadcast, he wrote to Lawrence Mould, Rensselaer, New York, Chief of Police, and included an invitation to use the program as a source of information:

> One of the features of our program is the broadcasting over some sixty odd stations on the Columbia Network of police clues. We have done this for the past several weeks, and from letters which have come in to us from various police chiefs and others connected with law enforcement, it appears that in a minor fashion we may be of extremely important assistance on certain types of clues. If you have any special fugitive descriptions, with identifying characteristics which might easily be noticed by the average person walking down the street, we should be very happy to hear from you. Also, if you have any puzzling situations with regard to ownership of clues left behind at the scene of a crime and if you think that nation-wide broadcasting of these details would not hamper your work, we would be very happy to extend you the use of our facilities in this matter.

This same invitation, with almost exactly the same wording, appears throughout much of Lord's early correspondence with police chiefs. Although these announcements were made to aid police in their search for criminals, the audience for these "clues" was clearly the radio listeners. These announcements called on citizens to act, but not to act directly.

Gang Busters occasionally highlighted how its clues led to the capture of criminals. In these episodes, listening to the clues was constructed as a kind of civic responsibility. During the war, this kind of cooperation was even more specifically defined as part of the patriotic duty of all citizens. The opening of the "Jessie Wendell" (1942) case demonstrates this connection as the announcer tells the audience, "Today a criminal is a greater enemy of this country than ever before. He's stabbing us in the back while our boys are at the front" (2). Audiences are told that it is their patriotic duty to "listen to the clues carefully in the hope you may aid us in placing these traitors behind bars where they belong" (2). This particular episode highlights the cooperation of a citizen who allows police to use his home as a site from which to listen in on Wendell and his gang. This kind of cooperation, involving subordinating individual concerns to the professional authority and expertise of the police, was consistently valued.

The "Busche Brothers" episode of *Gang Busters* (1936) demonstrates the proper form of deference and cooperation expected of citizens through the young character Luther, an eighteen-year-old boy who witnesses a murder committed by the Busche brothers. In this case, Luther and his girlfriend, Maryann, have a personal connection to the murder. While at a dance, the Busche brothers barge in and begin shooting, killing Maryann's uncle and another man, who Maryann sadly informs the audience is the father of four young children. As the brothers escape, they are aware that Luther and Maryann recognize them and the vehicle they are driving, and they threaten the couple. Concerned for Maryann's safety, Luther vows to help capture the brothers. His desire does not lead Luther to act on his own but instead to cooperate with the police and inform them. When he sees the brothers' car heading down a local road, he instantly phones the police, which leads to a manhunt through the woods. While correspondence in the file indicates that the young boy (who is given a fake name in the episode) followed the Busche brothers on his own, *Gang Busters* has Luther follow Detective Russell into the woods and participate in the manhunt. Luther follows but does not act. He shows due deference to Russell both as an authority figure and as an expert on crime and criminals. By focusing on Luther, this episode gives young listeners a character model and shows them the brutal cost of crime from the perspective of the young. More important, it demonstrates to them their proper place with respect to the police and points out the appropriate role all citizens should occupy in the war on crime.[21]

Citizens were also encouraged to offer their expertise to assist the police. In the *Gang Busters* episode of vignettes titled "The Chicago Kid" (1937), the final case profiled involves the murder of an elderly Russian couple who owned a shoe store. This segment is prefaced by host Lord's inquiry to the guest host, Chief Coglin, about what citizens can do. Lord inquires, "Now, Chief Coglin, we've been conducting this Crusade against Crime for a year-and-a-half, and every week we get letters from citizens wanting to know how they can cooperate even more with the police" (19). In this case, expertise is offered by a local cobbler. When the killer leaves the scene, he replaces his old shoes with a pair of stolen new ones. The old shoes yield a great deal of information that leads the police to the killer, but only with the willing cooperation of the cobbler, who is an expert on shoes. When the segment ends, Lord asks if the man that police caught "was really the murderer of the old Russian couple. . . ." Coglin replies: "Beyond a shadow of a doubt, Mr. Lord—now you asked how citizens could effectively cooperate with the police. Obviously, the police of every city can't have in their department the best shoe expert, the best clothing expert, the outstanding electrician and so on. If citizens would offer their services to the police—it would be a great aid" (27). Then Lord introduces a group of citizen crime fighters for interview.

The suggestion that citizen crime-fighting groups should work in cooperation with the police is significant. Powers (1983) and Potter (1998) both discuss the formation of vigilante crime-fighting groups by citizens attempting to fill the void they felt was left by corrupt police departments during the early years of the Depression. Discouraging such action required that radio crime docudramas needed to prove to listeners that the police were supremely competent and honest in their dealings with crime and that citizen groups work best when they operate in cooperation with the police rather than supplant the role of the police.

CONCLUSION

As Razlogova (2006) argues, the appeal of these programs was the criminals whose apprehension was dramatized. In the complicated racial, class, ethnic, and gender politics of the Depression era, discourses about criminality represented an important site of resistance to forms of institutional authority and to existing cultural hierarchies. Inherent in many stories of crime was a critique of ways that avenues to social mobility seemed open to so few in a society based on equality for all. The excitement, glamour, and desperation of these real-life criminals was a strong draw for Depression-era audiences, especially those from the classes from which so many of the represented criminals came. It would be impossible to sidestep this appeal, and as chapter 1 argued, radio professionals and sponsors did not exactly want to do so. In many ways, the programs reveled in the illuminating the lives of criminals, pouring over the details of criminal activities, and providing them with the opportunity to speak.

Yet, however much draw the criminal might have had, the radio crime dramas represented a key step toward the creation of a police-centered drama. Constructing criminality involved a careful negotiation of public sympathy for urban gangsters and rural bandits that was tied to a mythology of social banditry, a populist distrust of the state in the wake of the failure of Prohibition and the calamitous Great Depression, and a vocal coalition that had already pressured the film industry into altering its depictions of crime. Doing so from the viewpoint of the police helped in these negotiations. Criminals were constructed as violent to the point of breaking from the social bandit mythology, yet not so hopelessly pathological that proper education and guidance could not have stopped, or at least tempered, their criminal behavior. From the perspective of the police, these constructions of criminality were sure to guarantee that the public would no longer sympathize with criminal behavior or glamorize it. The programs attempted to shift public distrust and lack of support for the police onto criminals themselves. Criminals were severed from the volatile political and economic context of the Depression, leaving little room for sympathy, understanding, or recognition.

Yet criminals alone were not to be blamed for any increases in criminal behavior. The public called into being by the program's discourse was also culpable. If police were constrained in stemming the tide of crime, it was not due to corruption or their own inadequacies. Instead, the blame lay squarely on weak crime laws, an appalling lack of citizen support, and public sympathy with criminals and fear of taking a stand against criminals. The proper role of the public was support of tough crime legislation, deference to the professional authority of the police, and a willingness to cooperate with the police in bringing criminals to justice. Vigilantism was not to be tolerated. These programs were able to use the authority they achieved to persuade listeners to see the world from the police perspective.

The results of these efforts were often contradictory and never achieved the stability that the representations of the police did. As Razlogova (2006) discusses, and as is considered in chapter 5, listeners and those whose lives were subjected to such dramatizations did not always agree with the police-centered nature of these representations. While taking on negative representations of the police posed its own set of problems, it was in some ways less fraught with potential danger than was taking on popular attitudes about criminality during the turbulent years of the Depression. As the radio crime docudramas entered this terrain, they found a way to balance the popular appeal of criminals in a way that left them open to more populist interpretations but at the same time set significant precedents for placing the police perspective at the center of public discourses about criminality.

chapter 4

The Dragnet Effect

Space, Time, and Police Presence

The Kalava Michigan State Bank was robbed, the cashier murdered by four men on Jan. 5, 1933. The headquarters of the Michigan State Police was immediately notified and WRDS was put into operation. Cars were dispatched to the vicinity of the crime, and a blockade laid down along the Muskegon River. City police, sheriffs departments and State police cars were all directed by use of radio. . . . The hunt was successfully concluded on the evening of the 6th of January when the robbers were apprehended, bringing to close the most spectacular example of radio effectiveness.

—Records of DONALD S. LEONARD

Donald S. Leonard, a key figure in supporting radio in police work during the 1930s, was justifiably proud of the accomplishments of his force, the Michigan State Police. In this short description of a "spectacular example" of the power of police radio is condensed many of the issues key in the adaptation of two-way radio to police work. Few crimes better symbolized the hard times of the Depression and public distrust of its capitalist institutions than bank robbery. Yet, in this statement, there is no populist celebration of a modern-day Robin Hood. Instead, there is a bold endorsement and celebration of the Michigan State Police as a modernized agency of social control. Here is a coordinated police force complete with a centralized location from which to organize its operations. This instantaneous dispatch of cars speaks to the ways that radio could be used to swiftly deploy resources over large geographical areas. That the state police used their radio to call not only their own officers but also officers of other Michigan police forces speaks to what many felt was a necessary cooperation between forces to deal with criminal mobility. The use of radio to ensure the robbers' apprehension speaks to the general shift in the definition of policing, to an endeavor largely centered on speed and efficiency in the goal of criminal arrest. As police reformers sought to close off policing and criminality as sources of upward mobility, control of social mobility was connected to the control of physical mobility. The quick movement from call to capture speaks to the increasing speed with which a properly equipped police force could act. Finally, the very act of extolling police success speaks to the ways that police forces used their radio sets as a form of public relations to effectively gain citizen support for police reform efforts. From today's perspective of a technologically enhanced police force, such an endeavor might seem mundane. In the 1930s, the spectacle of technological prowess spoke to the most fantastic possibilities of the application of modern technologies to police work. Here was the raison d'être of this most "spectacular" organization: the successful control of criminal mobility.

In an array of publications aimed at police, city managers, and middle and working classes, police radio was universally heralded as a modern miracle. However, there was no guarantee that the excitement generated by this sort of "spectacular" use of police radio would make its way into the radio crime docudramas. In a medium suited to intimacy and the conveyance of meaning through speech and dialogue, the management and coordination of resources across vast tracts of physical space might have seemed an odd fit. Yet these radio crime dramas drew on the chase as one of the key elements of drama and excitement. As much as the voices of police and criminals filled these dramas, equally important "characters" in the crime dramas were the increasingly sophisticated police technologies of communication and transportation, especially the police radio and automobile. As police reformers worked to redefine policing, attempts to conquer social mobility became increasingly intertwined with the growing problem of controlling physical mobility. The American landscape was reformed to make room for the automobile, and as mobility became a key feature of modern life, broadcasting, as Williams (1974) argues, emerged as a key solution to the gap between increasing mobilization and privatization that marked the development of twentieth-century life in the United States. While bridging the gap between public and private spaces allowed for the construction of a form of intimate authority, the radio's properties of simultaneous address across space further allowed for imagining the meaning of police radio and its relationship to control of mobility.

As police forces worked to modernize policing and focus police efforts on criminal arrest, both mobility and privatization caused problems. In keeping with the move toward quantifiable criminal apprehension as the goal of policing and with the growth of communication and transportation technologies, call-and-response became a dominant model of policing. As communities dispersed and populations expanded over greater geographical areas, as the automobile and then the two-way radio became necessities, and as police moved from catchall functions to focus more on crime control, call-and-response emerged as a way to manage the relationship between police and citizens. Call-and-response represented a different use of radio to respond to the social phenomenon of mobile privatization. This model of policing hailed citizens not only to support policy change and offer cooperation but also to call the police and trust them in matters involving personal property and self.

This chapter argues that radio crime dramas, by dramatizing the unique properties of the radio medium, played an important role in naturalizing the police's new focus on apprehension and aiding in the cultural construction of the call-and-response model of policing. The changing relationship between time and space in police work found its way into the narrative structure of the docudramas as they spun their tales of criminal apprehension. Yet it was the blending of radio's content with radio's technological and industrial form that intensified the impact of these dramas. Able to extend into the private spaces of its listeners' homes, networked radio could penetrate all spaces. This understanding of radio as an omnipresent force became important to the construction of the police radio by police reformers as a technology that effectively extended both the reach and presence of policing. This allowed for an extension of the police practice of the dragnet, the rounding up of potential suspects by foot patrol officers. The use of police radio allowed the reformers to articulate their more provisional use of radio (there was no national police radio network) with the mode of electronic omnipresence encouraged by both its mode of reception and its organization into national networks. In linking radio content with radio's form, radio dramas constructed the idea of inevitable apprehension: the dragnet effect. Police radio thus emerged not only as a tool of policing but also as a potent symbol of police presence.

This chapter discusses the way that shifting relationships of time and space impacted both police practices and narratives about policing. Drawing on the work of Bakhtin and considering the use of sound, it examines the creation of the dragnet chronotope within the narratives of the crime docudrama. It then focuses on the ways that radio crime dramas blended the narrative content of the docudrama with the technological forms of radio. By examining the relationship between the geographical uses of police radio and the geographical scope of different crime dramas, this chapter considers how the idea of police omnipresence was constructed as a piece of popular American discourse. A key to this relationship was the ability of radio to effectively simulate its own experience, especially the experience of simultaneous communication over vast geographical spaces. Finally, this chapter examines the fate of the criminal in the world of constant police presence as enabled through radio.

AUTOMOBILITY AND THE PROBLEM
OF CRIMINAL APPREHENSION

As criminal apprehension emerged as the dominant goal of policing during the second wave of the police reform movement, the problem of criminal mobility loomed large. According to reformers, criminals not only had become more organized, but through the use of automobiles and modern communication, were taxing poorly equipped and uncoordinated law forces. Criminal mobility was a characteristic of both urban gangs and rural bandits. In a comment on the Wickersham Commission report, August Vollmer (1932) noted that "criminals may reside inoffensively in one section where the police are efficient and operate against society in a nearby community where the police system is less effective" (723). This created problems because while "professional criminals know no political boundaries," "officers of the law are hampered by these same boundaries" (723). A speaker at the second annual meeting of the Interstate Commission on Crime, a meeting of state governors, judges, and police chiefs held in Boston in August 1936, addressed the attendees with his concerns about a "little Caesar," who from his headquarters in San Francisco:

> can order a henchman in New York by a secret telegraph or telephone message to rob a bank, to intimidate and collect money from storekeepers, to kill an enemy in cold blood, or to do about anything which he himself does not have the courage to do. His orders are carried out without his stirring from

his underworld headquarters on the West Coast. Murders by the score, rackets by the hundred, robberies, and other crimes by the thousand continue as an ever growing plague in our nation because artificial state lines aid the commuting gangster, the sit-at-home little Caesar and his accomplices in all parts of the country who remain in their branch headquarters awaiting orders from whatever chief of whatever gang has the stolen money with which to pay for further crimes. . . . I think this shows the present situation. (13)

Whether it was urban gangsters using communication and transportation technologies to organize their activities like modern corporations or rural bandits using automobiles as a form of quick escape, police reformers from around the nation were clear that changes would be necessary to fight these modern criminals.

What police departments and reformers found particularly vexing about criminal mobility was the ways that it strained the existing organization of policing to its breaking point. Few things more clearly pointed to the fractured and disorganized organization of policing in the United States than wanton criminality. Freely crossing city, county, and state lines, criminal mobility was both enabled by and a burden to decentralized and highly localized police forces. The rise in criminal mobility was part of the general rise in mobility made possible by the post–World War I Federal Highways Act (Potter 1998).[1] The combined power of the automobile and the rapid development of communications technology added a new dimension to criminal mobility. Taking advantage of highways and telephones, criminals flaunted their mobility as a mode of escape from police apprehension.[2] Possessing neither a coherent organizational structure nor an adequate communication apparatus, separate police forces were left to do what they could on their own despite the uneven spread of their resources and manpower. The highly localized development of policing in the United States rendered cooperation between various municipal, county, and state police departments almost nonexistent.[3]

To conquer this problem, modernizing police departments combined automobiles with a slew of emergent communication technologies. Police turned radios, telephones, and teletype machines into vital weapons for fighting local crime. Each of these allowed for the coordination between station houses and police cars, and perhaps more important, they created unique opportunities for intrastate and interstate communication. Radio came to play the most important role in this respect. Its unique ability to work as a medium of both point-to-point and broadcast communication combined with advances in its portability rendered radio particularly suited to the needs of law enforcement. It was the radio, more than the telephone or the teletype, that also dominated popular imagination in the 1930s.[4] Radio served a dual purpose as a key aid in controlling criminal mobility and as a key tool for improving the public image of the police.

This is evident in the earliest uses of police radio. Urban police forces were the first to explore the possibility of adapting radio to police work. While claims to the first working system were made by both Berkeley, California, and Detroit, Michigan, by the early 1930s, larger municipalities across the United States were installing two-way police radio systems. By combating criminal mobility, police radio was celebrated for enhancing police efforts at criminal apprehension. In a breezy, enthusiastic tone, numerous reports represented the technology as an active partner in policing. Among police reformers, city managers, and citizens, radio was frequently celebrated not simply for its ability to conquer space but, in some ways even more spectacularly, its ability to conquer time. The speed of radio as a method of conveying information regarding crimes guaranteed that criminals could sometimes be caught in the act. William Rutledge, another key reformer of the era, provided this exciting account of the merits of police radio according to the Detroit Police Department:

> Snaring criminals in a radio network, woven by broadcasting to radio-equipped pursuit cars, has become a matter of seconds. Seconds are precious to the law-breaker. They spell the difference between escape and capture. The wider the margin of time, the better his chances to escape apprehension.
>
> By the use of radio we are catching the criminal red-handed. We are eliminating the introduction of circumstantial evidence in trials by indisputable proof of guilt.
>
> Murderers have been caught at the scene of the crime before they had a chance to dispose of their weapons. Burglars have been captured while still piling up their loot in homes.
>
> Bewildered auto thieves have gasped as a police car roared alongside of them a few moments after they had stolen a car.[5] Speeding hit-run drivers

have been captured and returned to the spot where they had run down and left their helpless victim a few seconds before.

Thugs have been captured while in the act of robbing their victims. Racketeers and bad-check passers have been caught. Bank stick-up men have been in handcuffs within sixty seconds of the time they fled the bank. ("Catching Crooks Red-Handed by Police Radio Broadcast" 1930, 46)

Throughout the 1930s, different municipalities proudly reported decreases in their crime levels. St. Louis, Missouri, reported "highly gratifying" results, as the city police department noted that it had been able to make a number of arrests that would have been impossible before the use of radio ("Proofs That Police Radio Reduces Crime" 1935). In New York State, Nassau County declared that in the year after installing police radio, arrests had risen 20 percent, while crime had dropped 20 percent ("Radio Drops Crime Twenty Per Cent in Nassau Country" 1936). In 1937, New York State reported that, due to widespread use of police radio, twenty cities had witnessed a drop in crime ("Police Radio Facts and Result in New York Municipalities" 1937). Stories also circulated about the ability of police radio to act as a deterrent to crime. Noted Jo Ranson (1937), "Does police radio scare off potential criminals? You bet it does and there is excellent proof in the records filed away at the New York Police Headquarters. 'I got so scared when I saw how radio worked. So I quit.' These words were uttered in a confession of an alleged kidnapper at Police Headquarters" (6). Radio was one of the most efficient and successful aids in criminal apprehension and a key source of publicity for suffering police forces. The wondrous success of police radio could be mobilized to build public faith in the police.[6]

THE RADIO CRIME DOCUDRAMA AND THE PROMISE OF INEVITABLE APPREHENSION

As argued in chapter 1, the radio crime docudramas, centered on the activities of the police and working within the discourse of police reformers, broke in important ways from existing genres of crime fiction, including classic and hard-boiled detective fiction. This was especially true in their emphasis on apprehension rather than identification of criminals. This focus on apprehension was further evident in the way radio crime dramas dealt with the relationship between space and time. As police used communication and transportation technologies to collapse the relationship between space and time in their practices, so did the relationship between space and time change in the narrative structure of programs like *Gang Busters* and *Calling All Cars*. Police use of communication technologies to coordinate their activities, hasten apprehension, and extend their reach was a dominant theme of the radio crime docudrama.

The rearrangement of the relationship between time and space was a key component of the ideological effect of radio crime docudramas. Bakhtin (1981) argues that one way to consider the ideological effects of literature is to consider its chronotopes, the relationship between space and time in the narrative that determines the kinds of relationships and actions that can take place. For example, classic detection was marked by the parlor chronotope. The parlor was the space of private encounters that marked the action of the classic detective, which was based on the revelation of secrets. He writes that because they center around "private lives," classic detective stories are about "snooping about, or overhearing 'how others live'" (123). The key to the story is the exposure of a private life, as "made public in a criminal trial, . . . by inserting criminal activities into private life, or circumstantially and conditionally, in a half-hidden way, by utilizing eyewitness accounts, confessions of the accused, court documents, evidence, investigative hunches and so forth" (123). Classic detective fiction was organized into a closed world of secrecy and privacy marked by individual encounters. The goal of the narrative was the revelation of such secrets in order to correctly identify the criminal.

The radio crime docudramas worked with a different organization of time and space that is closer to what Bakhtin calls the chronotope of the road, which is marked by the possibility of chance encounter. It is these chance encounters that organize the relationships between the characters and the action in the narrative. However, one significant difference marks the organization of time and space in the radio crime docudrama. The effective collapse of time and space created by the radio made encounters no longer a matter of chance but of inevitability: the dragnet chronotope. The dragnet chronotope was a key narrative component of the dragnet effect. It was the linking of the narrative of inevitable apprehension to the technological and cultural form of radio that created the condition for the dragnet effect. Drawing on the technological capability of radio as a medium capable of collapsing the relationship between space and time, radio as an aural medium proved especially apt at enacting this refigured relationship to create stories based not on the revelations of secrets but on inevitable apprehension.

The emphasis on space and time further distanced the radio crime dramas from the visual emphasis on detective fiction and even earlier efforts at police reform, best illustrated through the switch in emphasis from photography to radio and cars. Tom Gunning (1995) argues that photography was important to both policing and detective fiction at the turn of the century because both dealt with questions of criminal identification in the spaces of circulation in the modern city. Both photography and classic detective fiction revolved around questions of identification as criminals played on and escaped into the hidden corners of urban space. However, in its emphasis on the constant presence of police, the radio crime docudrama was less about finding what was hidden than about making the entire system of circulation visible and controllable. It was not the intelligence of the hero that guaranteed apprehension but the power of the radio and other communications technology that conquered mobility through their simultaneous, instantaneous address across space.

Rendering these tales of mobility through an aural medium was an important achievement. Whether dramatizing movement within a particular municipality or across city, county, or state lines, radio professionals could not ignore the growing centrality of the radio and the automobile. Because they were the key symbols marshaled to improve the public perception of policing, they must certainly play a central role in these apprehension narratives. As discussed in chapter 2, in compensating for what many in the industry determined were the particular challenges of writing for radio, producers like Phillips H. Lord developed devices that created a kind of intimate authority held by the police. However much radio professionals labored to produce meaning through sound alone, writers of the time did recognize a distinct advantage of radio vis-à-vis film or theater. The most widely recognized advantage was that of mobility. Simply put, radio easily allowed for significant jumps through time and space.[7] Whereas theater action was tied to the proscenium and cinema relied on some sort of accuracy in its visual representations, representing movement across space in either was expensive; the faster or farther the movement, the higher the cost. Through the use of sound effects and dialogue, radio easily could move its characters without losing any plausibility in its representation or incurring any additional expense. Furthermore, as many writers noted, whereas cinema created two-dimensional space and theater created three-dimensional space, radio, because it was unhindered by the need for visual representation, could create four-dimensional space in the minds of its listeners by effectively obliterating the point of view necessitated by vision (Cantril and Allport 1935, 233). This advantage made radio an especially useful medium for portraying the problem of criminal mobility while also showing the advantages of the police use of radio as a tool for dealing with that mobility.

It was out of consideration of the strengths and weaknesses of radio, as an aural and commercial medium, that radio crime dramas developed a number of recurring narrative and sound effects. As police forces turned to communications technologies as a method to ensure criminal apprehension, radio crime dramas, through plots, dialogue, and narrative devices, were able to create a sense of law as an ever-present, invisible force that was always monitoring criminal behavior and from which no criminal ever could hope to escape. The communications technologies most regularly celebrated were those that seemed to offer the police the greatest leverage against criminal mobility: the police radio, the teletype, and the telephone together allowed police to coordinate their work and allowed for contact between police and citizens. These technologies were most often simulated through the use of a filter, "a device used to distort voice quality by eliminating upper or lower frequencies, or both" (Barnouw 1939, 103). Originally developed as a method of simulating phone conversations, the "naturalistic" use of the effect to simulate "telephones, radio, Victrolas, police broadcasts" (103) had become ubiquitous and instantly recognizable to the radio listener. Used as a way to convey information regarding the narrative, the simulation of police broadcasts and teletype messages was also a key component of the creation of a multidimensional dragnet effect, moving beyond the creation of a new chronotope by linking radio form and content.

SIMULATING SIMULTANEITY

In these tales of apprehension of mobile criminals, developing ways to represent the relationship between communication in the form of technology and mobility over geographic space was essential to constructing the ideology of inevitable apprehension. The dragnet effect was produced by playing on key aspects of radio and by, over time, expanding the scope of geographic reference in the programs. First, communication technologies played a key part in the narrative structure of the radio crime docudramas *Police Headquarters, Calling All Cars,* and *Gang Busters.* Second, the industrial organization of commercial radio was articulated with police use of radio. This was done by symbolically connecting police radio to local commercial radio and, especially, by articulating police radio with the structure of regional and national networks. Third, through the use of sound effects and dialogue, radio professionals simulated the experience of police radio. In doing so, the radio crime dramas drew on key aspects of the experience of radio, including its simultaneity, dailiness, and penetrative power, thus articulating the experience of police radio with the experience of commercial broadcast radio. Taken together, these representational and discursive strategies constructed an idea of constant communicative presence. These techniques were used to represent two key aspects of police radio. The first was the use of police radio by urban police forces to centralize and coordinate urban police activities and wrest power from urban machine politicians. These representations were key to constructing the call-and-response model. The second was the use of police radio to coordinate activities at the state level and among different police agencies through a relentless focus on criminal mobility. These representations were key to constructing an imagination of police omnipresence.

Call-and-Response: Representing Urban Police Radio

As mentioned previously, urban police forces were the first to see the potential power of radio as a remedy to the increasing mobility of Americans made possible by both the growing use of automobiles and the increasing construction of new roads and paving of existing roads. Radio could be used to report crimes instantly to squad cars on patrol in a way that greatly improved previous forms of urban police communication, especially the call box. In purveying the merits of radio, many officers began to argue that call boxes made it difficult to coordinate police efforts. A police officer on the beat was required to stop at one of the call boxes located at specific locations throughout a municipality in order to call in to his station; if no officer called in or was near the call box, there was no way to communicate. Commenting on the advantages of radio over the call boxes, Thomas Rochester, chief engineer of the Police Department of the City of New York, noted that

> with the old signal box system it took a patrolman 20 minutes or more to reach the scene. . . . Now radio gets there in 45 seconds and these 45 seconds are significant since it has been estimated that the small holdup job takes just about this length of time to carry out. Thus the criminal is very likely to be caught in the act or at least apprehended before he has time to make a getaway. Should he escape from the scene his dash for freedom is short lived as a general alarm is broadcast and every radio car along the line of escape is on the lookout. (Ranson 1937, 4)

Another disadvantage of call boxes was that criminals might cut the wires leading to the box, rendering them entirely useless. Two-way radio was the remedy.[8] Unthreatened by cut wires, radio messages could be instantly transmitted to officers patrolling in their squad cars, who could likewise radio their replies to the dispatcher, thus coordinating efforts of apprehension. Radio communication guaranteed speed in response that makers of the call boxes could barely imagine, making instant response to calls a key measure of police effectiveness and success.

Urban uses of police radio were frequently represented in the radio crime docudramas and were the exclusive focus of *Police Headquarters,* a program whose stories were set in a single urban police department. In many ways, the narrative structure of the program simulated the ideal relationship posited between citizens and police in the call-and-response model. Each episode was initiated by a simulated telephone call to the unspecified police headquarters. Someone would call to report the crime in question, be it a kidnapping, missing person, murder, or robbery. The phone was answered by an unnamed operator who, upon the ring of the phone, would simply say "police headquarters." The caller spoke through a filter device, further indicating to radio listeners that they were hearing a phone call. Upon hearing the purpose of the call, the unnamed operator forwarded the call to the appropriate division, such as the chief of detectives or chief of homicide—a reference to the hierarchal organization of police departments. At this point, in many episodes, the officer in charge would request a call go out over the police radio to available beat cops. The call itself was sometimes dramatized, but often it was simply discussed. After the call was issued, the listener was instantly transported to the scene of the crime, with the speed of the narrative standing in for the speed of police response.

While offering a specific narrative economy to a program that was only fifteen minutes long, this standardized structure quickly oriented and informed listeners and dramatized the power of radio to coordinate police activities, suggesting that calls to the police would be met with swift action. The compactness of the program further indicated the speed at which police radio could guarantee apprehension, suggesting early on an inescapable dragnet. For example, in the "Laundry Truck Kidnapping" (1932) episode, when a man calls in to say his son has been kidnapped, the officer tells him that a radio patrol will be at his house in "two minutes." In the "Silver Collection" (1932), a woman calls while being attacked. When the detective receives the call, he races to a squad car and tells the officer to "step on it." The phone call told the listener what kind of crime would be investigated and suggested the kinds of relationships that should develop between police and citizens, and the radio calls, sent out to different cars, suggested an organized, coordinated, quick-to-respond police force. Therefore, rather than simply detailing the successes of radio in fighting crime, these short dramatizations were organized around the use of communication and transportation technologies that were key elements of urban police reform.

The simulation of urban police operations spoke most directly to audiences as citizens served by local police departments. After all, when people call the police, they do not call a national police force, but a local force, for immediate response. To this day, modern 911 systems are linked to local police departments. This understanding was encouraged not merely by setting the show in a single municipality but by the lack of any specific references to a particular location. This meant that the program, airing in different cities, might be read as a dramatization of the police in whatever city a listener heard the program. As a syndicated program made available to individual radio stations on electrical transcription disks, the program could be scheduled in accordance with local needs rather than dictated by a national network. In addition, the program left plenty of "time" available at the beginning and end of each fifteen-minute episode for the placement of local spot advertisements. Russo (2004) explored the development of spot advertising during the 1930s. He argues that although scholars commonly associate the practice with television rather than radio, spot advertisements were often used on radio during this period. The presence of a local sponsor's message in the program would further heighten the program's connection to the listener's municipality. In this form, people were constructed to see themselves as citizens of a specific city and to support their local police forces in order to protect their communities from crime.

Based on cases from the Los Angeles Police Department, urban uses of communication technologies were also frequently highlighted by *Calling All Cars*. Each episode began with a simulated "calling all cars," as recited by real-life Los Angeles Police dispatcher Sergeant Rosenquist. In some episodes, police radio itself was featured as the star of the episode. For example, the "July 4th in a Radio Car" (1934) episode begins with Los Angeles Chief of Police James E. Davis, explaining police radio to the radio audience:

When you citizens chance to hear the police broadcast, you no doubt feel after you've been tuned in for a few minutes that they are rather dull. All you hear is "see a man," "ambulance follow-up," or "a disturbance." But behind each of these calls is a story, a slice of factual life, much more dramatic than the wildest dreams of fiction. Every time a radio car receives a call while cruising its district, the officers cannot be sure that death does not await them at their destination, as they streak down the street, sirens screaming. There is rich drama in the daily prowling of the radio cars, and there is highly amusing comedy. . . . The incidents you will hear dramatized on tonight's broadcast are all true, and all occurred on the fourth of July. Incidents of this same nature have occurred to day, are occurring just at this very minute. A regiment of officers and a fleet of police cars are cruising the streets of this city, keeping the peace, keeping a vigil which never ends, 24 hours a day, seven days a week, 365 days a year, year in and year out.

Davis addresses the possible disappointment that such excited rhetoric of police radio might have produced when matched against reality by emphasizing the dedication, sacrifice, and constant presence of police officers. The episode presents a number of short vignettes of various radio calls, connected, as are most episodes in the series, by short segments of orchestra music. Each snippet is introduced by the familiar simulation of a "calling all cars" broadcast, which sends a car to the scene of some kind of disturbance. Woven together are scenes involving domestic violence, a man knocked out by a gang, a mistaken complaint regarding possible gunfire, and an ambulance follow-up on a hit-and-run accident. In this way, police are represented as roving public servants responding to citizen calls. More than that, the reference to their around-the-clock and calendar availability constructs the police as a constant presence.

The program ends with Chief Davis giving a second speech: "Such is a typical cross section of a day's log from the Communications Division of the Police Department. Every day in the year your police officers are answering similar calls and by their quickness and alertness furnishing the often needed oil to make the machinery of metropolitan life run smoothly." Here the "machinery of metropolitan life" is not the corrupt practices of local politicians working in concert with organized crime but the smooth running of a technologically enhanced modern professional organization dedicated to serving the public by responding to their calls and needs. The crimes responded to are ones against private persons and property and do not involve public forms of disorder.

The specific powers of police radio were also discussed by the characters in *Police Headquarters*. In one instance, two officers are called to investigate suspicious activity at a local delicatessen. As they approach, they see a man trying to enter but wait to make sure he enters illegally before they arrest him. While they wait, the officers discuss the futility of the suspect's actions: "Some day these 'yegs' are gonna get smart and figure out you can't beat the police radio" ("Man Stealing Food" 1932). In an episode involving a missing woman, the officer in charge of the investigation instructs his men to broadcast the description of the woman on police and broadcast radio as well as to print it in the newspaper because they will "need some quick action on this thing" ("Dr. Thornton's Wife Disappears" 1932). In most episodes, the officers on the case drive around in a police car; therefore, the program makes early use of mobility as a central theme, demonstrating the ease with which officers are able to travel and their powerful organization as enabled by the police radio.

Command and Control in Police Headquarters

Municipalities found in two-way police radio a method not only to conquer criminal mobility but to centralize and depoliticize police operations. After all, second-wave urban police reformers worked diligently to remove policing from the influence of ward politicians. The installation of radio systems with centralized dispatch centers effectively allowed urban reformers to break the authority of ward politicians by rendering district police stations less autonomous. The ability to use a single dispatch center to organize the dispersal of officers in patrol cars offered a centralized command structure to control the actions of police officers. The installation of centralized dispatch also meant that citizens were asked to call the police rather than visit their local precinct or turn to local politicians for help. As Samuel Walker (1998) suggests, the centralized dispatch system also allowed for surveillance of officers on duty. When reporting on the city's new police radio system, the *Mason City Gazette* (May 8, 1939) noted that in addition to stationing full-time operators to receive and relay messages, the receiving equipment would also be placed in the offices of the police chief and captain, in the fire department, and even in the city manager's office; in this way, police work itself could be monitored at all times, as could the comings and goings of the Mason City residents who called the police department.[9] The newspaper also reported that officers leaving their cars were required to report the approximate length of and reason for their absence. In these urban uses, police radio was linked with reform efforts to control social mobility. The dispatch center was often featured in publications aimed at police and general readers. With their array of telephones, wires, lighted maps, and uniformed officers, the image of the dispatch center powerfully symbolized urban police centralization and organization.

This centralized control, or "headquarters," was a frequent feature of the radio crime docudramas. Of course, one of the earliest programs to consistently focus on the idea of a centralized headquarters was *Police Headquarters*. The name of the series is not an accident, as it is the police force in general that serves as the program's protagonist, and its most consistent face is that of headquarters, as embodied in the voice of the nameless operator who answers the telephone call that initiates each episode. The officers on patrol are constantly in contact with headquarters, and all actions are coordinated through that location.

Gang Busters used the site of headquarters as the place from which investigations were coordinated and through which information flowed. Because most cases dealt with criminal mobility, Lord wanted to make sure the cases presented were as clear as possible to the listening audience. Fearful that audiences might be disoriented by too many voices, each episode centered on a single headquarters represented by one chief. From this site, most episodes deployed one pair of officers who followed the case through to the end. This was done despite the reality that most of the *Gang Busters* cases involved more than one force and any number of individual police officers. Authors used this method in their attempt to make their plots seem less confusing to the radio listeners. Lord and the people who wrote for him were well aware of the narrative devices necessary to ensure dramatic consistency in the program in order to keep the action easily recognizable to listeners. The use of headquarters dovetailed with the reform discourse by constructing police forces as organized, coherent, modern forces capable of managing criminal mobility and citizen calls.

The Network as Dragnet

If radio was vital to the coordination needed between municipal police stations and their squad cars, it was equally important, if not more so, as an aid in intrastate and interstate coordination of police efforts. As criminals moved quickly across municipal, county, and state lines, coordination between these levels of law enforcement became a necessity if criminals were to be caught. A key problem for local law enforcement officials was how to deal with the new highways. City, town, and county police forces could not be responsible for policing the highways: there were simply too many miles of road to cover and not enough manpower. Moreover, laws regarding the use of the highways were often state laws, and local police forces could not always be counted on to follow their instructions. At the state level, the answer was the formation of either state police or state highway patrols (Kaloupek 1938; Mayo 1917; Smith 1940; Vollmer and Parker 1935).[10]

State police patrols created new problems for communication not only between their own units but also between state and other police forces. Initially, state forces relied on a network of telephones for contacts, usually located at gas stations or other businesses close to the highway. When a call came through, the storeowner would put out a colored disk, which the officer would see when he passed. The officer would stop, call in to a central command unit, and receive his instructions. This cumbersome problem was greatly alleviated by the use of the two-way radio (Smith 1940, 162–63). The shortwave radio used by police forces was especially suited to covering long distances, so police cars in a large radius could pick up the same warning and be prepared. In addition, stations in nearby towns could be notified by telephone, and these stations could radio their own officers. Thus, police radio became important not only to municipal police forces but also to county and state forces as well.[11]

The teletype and radiotelegraph machines were as important as the radio in coordinating crime fighting. Like radio, some police departments used teletype in the late 1920s, but as the technology improved and the need for coordination grew, teletype systems became more widespread. The teletype often required state-level coordination between various municipalities in order to create a network system that guaranteed farther coverage. Among the special features of teletype were

> the simultaneous transmission of detailed descriptions, data and instructions to a number of locations, as opposed to the necessity for individual communication with each location and the subsequent loss of valuable time; the reliable transmission of messages in printed form; eliminated misunderstanding or garbling due to messages passing through intermediaries; the introduction of coordinated police activities as the result of the operating flexibility of the service; the definite fixing of responsibility through the printed record; reporting back to headquarters the solution of crimes or recovery of property; and the advantage of secrecy, so that the criminal cannot avail himself of information pertaining to police operation. (Harrel 1931, 84)

Teletype would be used to develop "Crime Thwarting Networks" that could prove in some ways even more useful than radio. While criminals themselves might use radio for their own activities or to overhear broadcasts regarding their own potential apprehensions, teletype, by virtue of the special equipment needed and the security of its transmissions, was virtually secret. By the early 1930s, reports on the success of the teletype machine in crime fighting became commonplace. Westchester County in New York proudly stated that in six months of operation, the teletype system had helped them recover 45 percent of stolen vehicles. The instant transmission available via teletype made it possible for police officers to block all county exits once they received report of a stolen vehicle. The police also made increased use of radiotelegraph systems, particularly in interstate communication. Requiring less power than voice—hence different frequency allocations—and transmitting in code that prevented citizens from listening in on messages, and simply being more efficient in terms of time, radiotelegraph increasingly was used for routine communication between different police forces, while voice transmission was used primarily for communication between radio stations and patrol units (Ranson 1937). In state police discourse, web imagery was frequently used to celebrate the power of communications technology over vast tracts of space. Graphic depictions in articles and advertisements aimed at police professionals frequently represented radio and teletype as webs covering entire states.

As a regional program, *Calling All Cars* often dramatized cases that emphasized, in addition to communication and coordination between police headquarters and patrol cars, the communication and coordination among different police departments. The program was able to construct the idea that through radio and teletype, the police had created an inescapable dragnet conquering both time and space, as illustrated in the "Unwritten Law" (1934) episode. The episode deals with the shooting of a police officer and the efforts of the San Jose police department to capture the shooter. After San Jose Police Chief M. Black introduces the episode, the scene shifts. The listener finds Chief Black addressing the city council on "one of the single greatest inventions" in police work, the police radio. The chief demonstrates the power of police radio to the city council and, by extension, to the radio audience. Explaining that he has set up both a telephone and a radio set tuned in to the police radio band, the chief calls headquarters and asks for a police car to come right away. The city council listens in amazement as the captain's message is transferred immediately into a radio call for

Police radio and teletype were frequently pictured as webs covering large swaths of geographic territory. Advertisement in *American City* 54 (March 1939).

Car 5 to proceed to the auditorium. The chief marvels that during the "90s," it would take the police half a day or more to receive news of a murder that had occurred a mere five or six miles away, giving the criminals a substantial lead in escaping the police. Now, he continues, the radio allows the police to create an "invisible dragnet" before the criminal even leaves the scene of a crime. As he speaks, officer John Buck walks in and asks if anything special is needed.[12] In the short time of the chief's presentation, Buck had come a distance of ten blocks in response to the radio call. When Buck returns to his partner in their radio car, he tells him that the captain is "showing off radio efficiency to the citizens." It is shortly after this that Buck is shot, an event that pulls Chief Black away from the city council meeting, leaving those in attendance horrified to know that the officer they met just moments before has been mortally wounded.

In addressing the city council, the chief in this episode also addresses his radio listeners, who, like the invisible council, are treated to an education on the merits of police radio. The power of police radio is heightened by the poignancy of having a familiar officer shot while on duty. This also allows for a further demonstration of the power of radio in bringing such vicious criminals into police custody. Once the chief returns to police headquarters, he begins to put into action the invisible dragnet. After receiving a description of the shooter's vehicle from Buck's partner, the chief has this description sent by radio and teletype to other police stations in California. This is dramatized for the listener through a filtered series of "calling all cars" announcements for the police of San Jose, Oakland, and San Francisco. While the chief puts out more radio calls, the radio audience listens as the shooter, Joe, argues with his girlfriend, Bonnie, about his malicious act. Having been injured by Buck before killing him, Joe commands Bonnie to bandage his wounds because they need to "highball it outta here," realizing the police will be searching for him.

It is at this point that the radio audience can begin to imagine the full force of the invisible dragnet, as the announcer narrates with musical accompaniment:

> While Bonnie bandages her wounded sweetheart, the law's invisible dragnet has stretched across the peninsula and the Bay Area. The police radio

spins an escapeless web as it deploys officers to all strategic points leading out of San Jose and into San Francisco and Oakland, [musical pause] and up and down the coast from Eureka to El Centro, from the Sierra's to the sea [voice hurries now], the police teletype ticks out the warning to all officers to pick up the wanted black coupe. [musical pause] The Bayshore Highway is barricaded and every passing car is stopped and its occupants are scanned and questioned. The Bay bridges and ferries are watched to prevent escape to the north. [musical pause] Route one hundred and one is blocked between Gilroy and San Jose. Officers are stationed outside Livermore on Route 99; escape to the south is cut off. [musical pause] On a pitch black lane along the main road from San Jose to Oakland is a parked police car, its lights out. Quietly its two occupants watch the infrequent cars that pass the spot.

In this case, the local use of radio as a device to coordinate activities between police and headquarters is transformed into a regional device with the power to spread across time and space.

While the program used simulated radio calls in its theme and earlier in the episode as the chief demonstrated the power of police radio, when it came to more fully exploring radio's ability to conquer space, the program turned to narration. Music, rather than any sound or voice effects that would signify "radio" as a way to dramatize its power to conquer space and time, accompanies this expository scene. That said, this narration achieves a great deal of power because it does not merely describe the idea of a dragnet but uses specific geographic references, which would certainly help some of the program's regional listeners fully imagine the power of the radio in its ability to coordinate officers across a large geographic expanse and across multiple departments. This use of specific geographic reference most likely resonated powerfully with Depression-era audiences. After all, one of the earliest uses of radio by the public was precisely the search for distant signals, a practice that continued on shortwave radio. In his famous study exploring why the infamous *War of the Worlds* broadcast caused panic in some listeners, Hadley Cantril (1940) found that many listeners were persuaded of the broadcast's veracity because of its specific reference to locations in New Jersey and New York. The use of references in *Calling All Cars* is highly suggestive of the power of radio in aiding the police in capturing mobile criminals. As a source of communication that promises instant response and the ability to conquer space and time, police radio is here imagined as extraordinarily potent.

The use of police communications technology to spread this dragnet and to coordinate different police forces is repeated throughout a number of episodes. In an episode detailing the capture of a man who murdered a railroad security officer, information about the suspect is broadcast around the country until he is traced to an Ohio railroad yard. The Stockton, California, police travel there and, with the cooperation of local police, bring the suspect back to California ("Cinder Dick" 1937). In another case, in which an officer is shot while on duty, the police follow a woman from Los Angeles to San Francisco, suspecting her of harboring the fugitive. Through cooperation with the San Francisco police, she is brought into police head-quarters for questioning ("Lt. Crowley Murder" 1934). "Tobaccoville Road" (1937) details the efforts of a national dragnet to capture a bank robber, who San Diego police learn is traveling with a woman to Tobaccoville, Virginia. After the pair successfully eludes the police between San Diego and Norfolk, Virginia, they finally are snared by a Norfolk dragnet, set into motion by the San Diego police upon learning that the fugitive has relatives in that city. As the name of the series, *Calling All Cars*, suggests, the cases selected for dramatization pay significant attention to criminal mobility. The series began to demonstrate how police radio and teletype allowed for the creation of an inescapable, invisible dragnet.

While occasionally dramatizing cross-country police chases, *Calling All Cars* primarily dramatized solved police cases set in the Southwest. This strong geographic orientation was doubtless intensified by its appearance on the regional Don Lee/CBS West Coast Network with regional sponsor Rio Grande Oil Company. Rio Grande's sponsorship was based precisely on its status as the sole provider of gasoline for the automobiles of the Los Angeles Police Department, a fact emphasized by its weekly promise that its cracked gasoline offered "police car performance for your vehicle." The program reveled in references to the Southwest, situating Los Angeles as belonging to the entire region. Russo (2004) notes that regional networks, such as the Yankee Network in New England, prided themselves on selecting and developing programming that spoke specifically to regional audiences and interests. The ability of the Don Lee/CBS West Coast Network to coordinate local radio stations into a network capable of authorizing a professional production like *Calling All Cars,* with production values not far removed from those of the national networks, bolstered the police departments' claims that through modern communication technologies, they were able to coordinate their efforts in order to ensnare even the wiliest criminal in their mediated dragnet.

While this regional program suggested an articulation between the power of the regional network and the police radio communications, *Gang Busters* makes a stronger claim to be the only national program dramatizing actual police cases. In dramatizing solved police cases from across the nation, the program often featured criminals who traveled over large geographic regions, especially the Midwest, and who were often described as blazing a trail of crime. This emphasis on interstate crime in part stems from its start as *G-Men.* After all, a key justification for the creation of a federal police force was the need to combat interstate crime and compensate for the localism that characterized policing in the United States. For example, in the dramatization of Bonnie and Clyde, the writers present an effective aural montage that creatively, quickly, and dramatically represents the pair as not only brutally violent but also as extremely mobile:

LORD: Sheriff Jordan, the number of crimes committed by this Barrow Gang is unbelievable—

CHIEF: It was the cruelest gang of killers ever to organize, Mr. Lord. They killed without warning—needlessly—They actually had target practice twice a week—If you had had a short wave radio and had tuned in on the south during this period, you would have heard such police calls as—

FILTER MIKE

April 27, Hill County Police—Barrow Gang just murdered Samuel Mellow— escaping in Ford V-8, heavily armed—shoot on sight.

August 5, Aloka, Oklahoma: Barrow Gang just killed Undersheriff Moore— escaping in stolen car toward Clayton, Oklahoma.

April 13, Missouri State Police: Barrow Gang have just killed and wounded officers at Oak Ridge Drive—escaping in Packard car. Close all roads.

July 18, Missouri Police: Barrow Gang escaping from gun battle at Red Crown Point along Highway 71—Bandits badly wounded. Buick car riddled with bullets—heavily armed—shoot on sight.

July 23, Iowa Police: Barrow Gang escaping after gun battle in Dexter Park—
2 of gang shot—Clyde and Bonnie Parker escaping in sedan toward Dale,
Iowa. Watch for airplanes overhead which are trying to spot them. If
airplane spirals, gang has been sighted and close in—they are killers.
January 15, Texas State Police: Clyde and Bonnie Parker just drove into the
State Prison Farm, opened fire with machine guns—mowed down convicts
and guards—five lifers escaped—car racing toward state border. Shoot on
sight. (5–6)

This clever sound montage succinctly conveys to listeners information
about the range of geographic territory covered by the pair in a relatively
short period of time. Providing the highlights through this particular technique drew attention not only to the violence of the couple but also to their
mobility. These criminals would seemingly turn up anywhere as they wantonly challenged a system of law enforcement based on localism. Using
automobiles to cross state, city, and county borders, criminals seemed to
flaunt their mobility as a mode of escape from apprehension. If the legacy
of local policing in the United States left the country with a patchwork of
various policing agencies, often with little sense of how to communicate
with each other and certainly no coherent plan to coordinate police efforts
in apprehending these mobile criminals, the simulated radio in this montage offered the solution by offering some instrument through which to
track and ultimately contain such mobility.

Gang Busters most fully articulated the dragnet effect both through the
kinds of cases it dramatized and through its development of a series of narrative devices and sound effects. Like *Calling All Cars, Gang Busters* focuses
on criminal mobility and frequently refers to communications technology, only going one step further. Whereas *Calling All Cars* frequently relied
on narration to explain the setting up of dragnets, *Gang Busters,* through
the use of sound effects and narrative transition devices, enacted the dragnet, placing the home radio listener, hearing only disembodied voices, in
the middle of its invisible web. For example, the script résumé for "The
Sacramento Post Office Robbery" (1936) reads as follows:

The script opens with an interview between Mr. Lord and Chief of Police
at Sacramento. The Chief begins to show how an entire smooth working

scientific machine goes into operation the minute anything unusual in the way of crime is reported at Police Headquarters.

The scene is dramatized as the information about the mail robbery comes into headquarters. Radio cars are contacted, all roads out of Sacramento are watched and clues are sent out immediately as the necessity appears. The Federal Bureau of Investigation and neighboring police forces are contacted. The minute description is obtained . . . the clues are sent out over the various channels.

This summary reads like something that might have been heard as narration on *Calling All Cars.* The reference to the "smooth working scientific machinery" echoes James E. Davis's statement to radio listeners that police communication technologies allowed for the "machinery of metropolitan life [to] run smoothly" ("July 4th in a Radio Car" 1934). The description of sending "clues . . . out over the various channels" recalls the use of police radio dramatized in the "Unwritten Law" (1934) episode of *Calling All Cars.* This summary also indicates the self-consciousness of the writers in such programs while constructing police presence as pervasive and constant. However, while this summary closely resembles the narrative content of *Calling All Cars,* the makers of *Gang Busters* used these ideas as starting points for dramatization.

The turn to dramatization made *Gang Busters* unique among police-centered radio crime dramas. This was achieved through the use of sound effects that simulated radio, telephone, and teletype messages not merely to suggest but to place the listener at the center of a well-oiled machine—one from which escape was impossible. With a sound "(CLICK OF PHONE)" the listener is brought to Sacramento Police Headquarters, where there is a telephone report of robbery. An Inspector Markson hears this and requests that a radio "flash" be sent to "block off all roads."

> VOICE: Calling all cars—cars four and six—cars four and six cover U.S. Mail
> Robbery Post Office—all other cars cover all roads leading from city—
> more instructions following.
> (OCCASIONAL TELEGRAPH)
> (DOOR)
> BOBS: (FADE IN) All plain clothes men standing by, Inspector.

INSPECTOR: Notify Postal Inspectors—Flash the FBI Office San Francisco. (CLICK OF PHONE) Hello—Sacramento Police calling—State Police—Post Office Robbery—escape in car—cover all roads—full description follows. (CLICK OF PHONE)

BIZ: (VAN DYKE CALL HEADQUARTERS—FILTER MIKE)

FLANDERS: Hello—Hello, Postal authorities—United States Mail Robbery at Sacramento Post Office—(CLICK OF PHONE)

BOBS: (OFF MIKE) Federal Bureau of Investigation—Sacramento Police Calling—Mail Robbery—escaping in car—we're blocking all roads—we'll keep you posted. That's all.

FLANDERS: Your radio flash, sir.

INSPECTOR: Turn it on.

(FILTER MIKE)

VOICE: Reporting to headquarters—have only poor description of criminals— One wore striped overalls—Robbery was perfectly timed and executed— robbers cool and deliberate—escaped in black Pontiac Sedan—that's all. (7–8)

Gang Busters was unique among the crime docudramas in the ways it frequently used sound effects to create simulated broadcasts that demonstrated to listeners the organization and power of the police in responding to crime.

One cannot underestimate the decision to use the filter and typewriter as a way to communicate information. Without visual cues, the use of sound effects had to be finessed carefully so they did not confuse listeners. When they were used well, they were capable of conveying a great deal of information and adding infinite layers of meaning to the events transpiring in the narrative. During the program's early years, many in the radio industry praised *Gang Busters* as an example of a program that made innovative use of sound effects. Using simulated police communications as a narrative device not only conveyed information that was important to the narrative but also took advantage of radio as an aural medium and placed radio listeners inside an invisible, multidimensional dragnet, which conveyed an idea of an omnipresent police force. While the adoption of such communications technologies did change policing, it was the dramatic reenactment of such technologies that created an impression of police omnipresence.

The instant transmission of messages via telephone, teletype, and, most important, radio allowed for the seeming simultaneous coordination of police efforts. The program worked to put its listeners in the middle of the invisible dragnet, which the police created through the use of communications technologies. The important thing here is the double effect created not merely by telling the listener about the dragnet but by enacting the effect of such a dragnet in a way that puts the listener in the center of the representation. The listener hears simulated radio calls on the radio, thus plausibly bridging the gap between real and representation and between radio form and content. The radio listener is positioned to experience the power of radio and communications technologies to conquer the vexing problem of criminal mobility on the very same medium that brings listeners into a simultaneous connection across, as the program promises in its opening, the entire nation. Here is radio, the medium that covers the entire country, at the same time enacting precisely this power of constant presence.

Such simulations were a powerful force at a time when the representational rules of the medium were still under negotiation. The most significant example of this power must be the aforementioned panic caused by the infamous *War of the Worlds* broadcast in 1938. Similar to *Gang Busters,* the program simulated not only the content of radio but, as Williams (1974) describes it, the very experience of broadcast flow. Structured as a series of "news bulletin" interruptions to the "regular" program line-up of dance music, representing the voices of scientific experts, and invoking the authority of the state, the program offered a condensed simulation of radio itself. Miller notes that shortly after the broadcast, the Federal Communications Commission "restricted the simulation of news programs within radio dramatizations" (107).

From the simulated telephone calls, radio calls, and automobile sounds to represent the workings of a metropolitan police department in *Police Headquarters* to the thrill of the chase in the regionally produced and broadcast *Calling All Cars* to the imaginative use of sound effects and dialogue to simulate the experience of radio in *Gang Busters,* the radio crime docudramas effectively constructed the idea of police omnipresence: the dragnet effect. The dragnet effect was not merely the result of narrative representation. The effect was created by the articulation of police radio with the organization of commercial radio, whether as regionally or nationally linked networks. The power of commercial broadcast radio to link citizens together as denizens of the same city, of a specific geographic region, or of the nation itself and to bring these linked listeners the stories of action and adventure could easily spill over into understandings of police radio.

This leakage could extend to other key aspects of commercial broadcast radio. Beyond the articulation between police radio and the networked structure of commercial broadcast radio that promised simultaneous communication across the space of the entire nation, police radio was further articulated with one other key aspect of commercial broadcast experience: its constant availability.[13] Commercial network radio in the United States, and entertainment radio in general, was organized around what Williams (1974) called flow—the guarantee of a continuous stream of available programming.[14] As audience attention was one of the main goals of radio professionals, pauses in the schedule would be considered a great liability, leading to a loss of audience. In exploring the phenomenology of broadcasting, Paddy Scannell (1996) argues that one of its central organizing principles is dailiness. Broadcasting is presented as an always-available, always-at-hand, regularized service. It is consistent, dependable, and oriented to quotidian life. While early commercial radio had not yet achieved the level of flow, or perhaps even dailiness, as would be achieved after World War II, during the Depression, commercial broadcasters were moving in this direction. Police departments had long engaged in a range of activities across the space of the day. But in the use of radio, the idea of police presence was constructed not only as simultaneously covering vast expanses of space but also as conquering expanses of time through its constant communicative presence. Policing itself becomes quotidian.

In this there is the final linkage between the commercial broadcast radio and police radio: the joining of the network and the dragnet. While there were state police radio systems, police radio remained highly localized. There was no national police radio system. However, the impression given by these programs was that police radio was a constantly available service. This is key to the development of the call-and-response model. For the model to work, quick response must be promised. This promise is achieved through the construction of radio as a constant communicative presence, a pan-acoustic presence that works in a way similar to Foucault's (1979) description of the form of constant visual presence in Bentham's panopticon. While the dragnet effect is in some sense also tied to vision, it is the penetrative, unseen power of radio to cover and reach all spaces that is key to understanding the police as a constant presence. After all, radio's unseen waves penetrated the divide between public and private spaces. While this construction was meant to discipline criminals and control mobility, it can also be seen as producing the conditions for mobility by suggesting that the roads are not isolated, dangerous spaces.[15] It also worked to assure the idea of inevitable apprehension. There simply would be no escape from the increasingly extended arms and eyes of the law. If criminal actions are futile in a world where apprehension is inevitable, citizen interaction with the call-and-response model is celebrated by the promise of fast response no matter location or time.

CRIMINAL CLAUSTROPHOBIA: THE FATE OF THE CRIMINAL UNDER THE DRAGNET

Radio docudramas portrayed a technology-enabled, omnipresent police force focused on the goal of apprehension. They also worked to show how this force bore down upon the criminal, rendering efforts at escaping the law futile. The most common motif was the portrayal of a criminal cracking under the claustrophobic pressure of the dragnet. The results of these mental breaks varied but most often led to the criminal's capture when he became careless because of his paranoia or, in the most severe cases, when he committed suicide. In either case, the audience clearly was not meant to side with the criminal but to view his (or, occasionally, her) suffering as a positive outcome of police omnipresence.

A good example of criminal claustrophobia can be found in the *Gang Busters* episode of July 1, 1936, detailing the criminal exploits of "Tony the Stinger" Cugino. As the program developed, *Gang Busters* came more and more to focus on the activities of the criminals as framed through the actions of the police narrators. This shift in narrative content had to do with a stated desire on the part of the show's producers to convey a sense of omnipresence regarding the police to the listening audience. A letter from Lord's associate, John Ives, to Ken Stowan of station WCAW, dated June 27, 1936, explains the producers' intentions:

If you have an opportunity to talk to Captain Malone with regard to the script, would you be kind enough to point out to him some of the difficulties in doing a case of this magnitude in six or seven scenes which cannot run more than twenty-two minutes on the air, due to time limitations. We have developed the case from a rather unusual angle, and instead of showing the painstaking clever detective work in detail which tracked Tony the Stinger, we have attempted to show the effect of such work on Tony the Stinger, and the agony of mind it caused him as time went on. We have used Detective Jimmie Ryan as the symbol of the law's relentless pursuit, and it would be somewhat difficult to say that Stinger hated two men, namely Ryan and Sullivan, as the embodiment of the law. However, we will do anything possible, or anything that Captain Malone suggests to give equal credit to Detective Sullivan.

Lord sets up the important distinction here between a focus on criminals as a voyeuristic peek into the glamorous aspects of the underworld and a focus on the desperation, isolation, and fear of living in a world with such technologically enhanced, modern police forces. *Gang Busters* would spend time dramatizing the exploits of Tony the Stinger but only in reference to his relationship with the police, which seems will cause him to exist in a constant state of anxiety.

The episode begins with Lord introducing as guest host, an "outstanding criminologist of the Philadelphia Police Department," Captain Shooey Malone. The two share the following exchange that demonstrates to the listener the cause of Tony's persistent anxious state:

LORD: Captain Malone, what did you mean when you said the case of Tony the Stinger illustrated the Ghost of the Law.

CAPT. Well, Mr. Lord, the law is an intangible force but, its represented by hundreds of Federal men,___police officers,___soldiers,___sailors, and 125,000,000 people. When a man becomes a criminal this tremendous force haunts him night and day—he sleeps with this fear—he eats with it until it suffocates him. [Blank spaces in the original.] (1)

The episode proceeds in a series of scenes that demonstrate how "the ghost of the law" works: Cugino becomes increasingly agitated regarding its seeming omnipresence, as embodied in the figure of Officer Jimmy Ryan. The episode begins with a flashback scene during which Ryan, "with the lather drying on his face, . . . dashed into the street, gun in hand," and apprehended Tony for the Armitage Diamond Robbery in Baltimore. Sentenced to fifteen years in prison, Stinger kills one man during his time but is still paroled after twelve years. Once out of prison, the audience finds him "standing and talking to three underworld characters on the corner of Sixth and Fitzwater streets in Philadelphia," when he meets Jimmy Ryan (4). After a brief exchange in which Ryan expresses his dismay that Cugino was released, the Stinger tells his friends to convey a message to Ryan: Stinger plans to kill him! Ryan, not intimidated, has a message delivered to Stinger: that he will be watching him.

As the episode progresses, Cugino grows increasingly agitated. As he perceives himself under constant police pressure, he commits several murders out of fear. He murders two of his associates for standing up for Ryan; he murders police officers because he is afraid they might be after him; and he ends up murdering more of his accomplices and their girlfriends. When he is killing one of the women, she "screams in stark terror," leading Cugino to respond, "Shut up, you, do ya want the coppers down on us? Yollin for the law, yollin for the law. Everybody I know yollin for the law" (19). Malone explained to the radio audience that "Stinger felt this intangible force bearing down on him—he was terrified, and thought if he could kill a few more—he'd be safer, but he was really just getting in deeper and deeper" (15).

After running from New York to Washington, to Chicago, and back to New York, Tony the Stinger finally comes face to face with the "Law," as embodied by Jimmy Ryan, in a New York City subway station, while trying to board a train with his girlfriend. As the train pulls away, Officer Ryan comes up and tells Cugino to "Put 'em up. . . ." Stinger "(SCREAMS) The law" (26). Stinger attempts to get Ryan to protect him from the New York City police officers, but Ryan refuses, telling him, "A streak of yellow a mile wide. Stand up, rat, and take a breath of fresh air, because you're going to a place where they don't breathe the air" (27). Malone comes on to tell the listeners, "That night, Mr. Lord, Tony the Stinger was behind prison bars—but that Ghost of the Law was at him—he was in a frenzy—pacing his cell" (27). No longer able to stand up under the pressure of constant police presence, Stinger finally kills himself out of desperation, leading Malone to assure the radio audience, "Once a criminal knows the law is after him—that dread fear will hound him to his grave" (30).

A criminal cracking under the pressure of the seeming omnipresence of the law is an enduring device used throughout the *Gang Busters* series. Tony the Stinger was not the only criminal featured in the series who committed suicide because of the unending pressure of police presence. By the end of the episode "Midget Ferenkes" (1936), Ferenkes, having been driven to desperation by the police, kills himself. The guest chief tells Lord and the listeners, "Midget Ferenkes could have been a great leader, Mr. Lord— a great scientist—he could have made the world a better place to live in— could have gone down through the years loved and remembered—instead of that, he was dumped into a pauper's grave without ONE person caring. When he killed himself, all he had in the world was $20 and an old second hand car" (25).

The prediction that cowardly criminals would commit suicide when threatened by the police was used purposely to create such an outcome in the *Gang Busters* episode "Edward Metelski" (1936). Metelski and his partner, Whitey Morton, kill two state troopers when they are pulled over during a routine traffic stop. The two escape into the New Jersey marshes, leading to a massive coordinated manhunt, which includes citizens and police. Finally, Metelski is caught by a pair of officers, and despite lying about who he is, he is identified by his fingerprints and photographs. On finding a movie stub from a Philadelphia theater in Metelski's pocket, a detective, Weaver, travels to Philadelphia to ask the local paper for help.

WEAVER: Well, we've got Metelski—had to take him alive but what happens is this. When a crime is committed, there's a lot of publicity—then time passes and when the criminal is caught, there's very little. The impression is left with the public that there are many times as many crimes committed as solved.

EDITOR: That's very true, Detective.

WEAVER: It'll be a fairly long time before we can catch Morton. He'll hole up. Now we want to clear this case while its hot—and we're going to force Morton's back to the wall.

EDITOR: What do you mean?

WEAVER: Scare him to death. He already knows we're after him and he thinks that Metelski has cracked and told everything. I'm spreading the news through the underworld we'll shoot Morton on sight and we want you to print a gallery picture of Morton and ask all good citizens to be on the lookout for him and report to police when and where they see him. Morton will see the picture—he'll be scared to death.

EDITOR: We'll do it, Detective Weaver—and I hope you get this killer. (24)

As the newspaper editor exhibits the kind of cooperation between the press and the police that these dramas advocated, Weaver continues his plan to scare Morton. This desire to pressure Morton, perhaps to his own death, is clearly motivated in part by citizen criticism of the police. Weaver suggests that police tactics are not to blame for either too short or too long a delay in capture; instead, an impatient and inattentive public is at fault. Armed with this desire to manipulate his capture, Weaver goes to Morton's "haunts" and begins to spread the word that the police are after him. They arrest Morton's girlfriend so that he has no one to turn to for help.

Three days after the arrest, the audience hears Weaver at the Philadelphia police headquarters chatting with the local detectives about Morton's possible whereabouts. While the Philadelphia police suggest that he might have left town, Weaver confidently affirms that "he's in town somewhere, holing up. The underworld is getting messages to him that we're out to kill him—he's probably seen his picture in the paper. He'll blow his brains out—or take the gas pipe—or jump out the window" (26). At that moment, a message comes through the police radio, as indicated by the use of the filter device, that a man has been found dead. Upon hearing that this man committed suicide by sticking his head inside a gas stove, Weaver is positive it is Morton, telling the local detective, "That's the news I've been waiting for—it's Whitey Morton, all right," and continuing that he "won't object to seeing Morton on a slab, either" (27). The scene shifts to Lord and guest host Norman Schwarzkopf, as Lord approvingly explains that this is the first time he's heard of "getting a criminal that way" (27). Here, then, criminal claustrophobia is not only a result of the dragnet effect but it is a specific outcome of the deliberate action of the characters in the narrative.

While suicide was an occasional and often pointed outcome, in general, *Gang Busters, Calling All Cars,* and even *Police Headquarters* relied on the strategy of portraying criminals cracking under the pressure of constant police presence. In "The Blonde Tigress" (1939), as discussed in chapter 3, Eleanor Jarman is portrayed as a particularly vicious and gutsy criminal. When the police begin to close in on her, she becomes quite anxious, leading to her eventual apprehension. Early in the episode, one of her partners in crime, Minicci, telephones the police out of desperation to surrender himself. He tells Officer Brady, "I'm on the spot—between 10,000 cops and the Tigress, it's a bullet any way I turn. I'm out to save my own skin." Brady pressures him, trying to get information on where Jarman is, but Minicci replies, "It's myself I'm looking out for now—I'm going nuts, cooped up here in one room not knowing what second you guys or the Tigress'll burst in here with guns an' kill me—I can't stand it no more—I got to save myself—so come get me—I'll give up" (8). Once Minicci has saved himself and revealed Jarman's whereabouts, it is Jarman's and her other accomplice, Kennedy's, turn to crack under the pressure of hiding from the police. Kennedy edgily asks Jarman to stop playing with guns, leaving her to respond "(FLARING BACK) What about me! You think I like it being cooped up in these four walls—like a—like an animal!" Fearing that Minicci has "squealed," she expresses her growing anxiety of staying hidden, menacingly telling Kennedy, "But we can't stay here forever. I feel like taking pot shots at the people in the street, just for the fun of it" (25–26). As a knock on the door interrupts their conversation, Jarman assures her accomplice that "(LOW) If its cops—I'm killin' the first one that comes through that door" (26). When the person at the other side of the door turns out to be a grocery deliveryman, the increasingly jittery Jarman tells Kennedy that she will not only shoot but also beat any stranger who approaches their door. Originally confident in her schemes and power to manipulate those around her, Jarman is reduced to desperate violence in a futile attempt to avoid apprehension.

It is important to point out that this criminal claustrophobia was not exactly the same thing as a guilty conscience. A guilty conscience would imply some redeeming quality to the criminal in question. This difference is clearly seen in an episode of *Police Headquarters,* the program that had begun only to *suggest* rather than fully *enact* the dragnet chronotope. An episode that features the guilty party committing suicide highlights the difference. In "Dr. Thornton's Wife Disappears" (1932), Dr. Thornton calls police headquarters claiming that his wife has been missing for two days, and he believes robbery accounts for her disappearance, as she had been carrying $160,000 with her. Upon hearing this, the police captain asks Dr. Thornton why he didn't come to them sooner. The doctor claims he and his wife had an argument the last time he saw her, and he assumed she was punishing him by not coming home, which is something she had done in the past. Saying we "need quick action on this," the captain begins to put a dragnet into effect, broadcasting Mrs. Thornton's description on the police and commercial radio and publishing it in the newspapers.

As the detective assigned to the case begins to investigate the doctor's story, he finds an increasing number of inconsistencies. When Mrs. Thornton fails to turn up, the detective correctly assumes that she is dead. This leads to another deployment of the dragnet, this time in search of information about Dr. Thornton. As the information accumulates, it becomes clear to the police that he murdered his wife. When the police finally confront the doctor with all the evidence they have accumulated, he begins to unravel. After spending some time questioning him, the captain tells him he will leave him alone with his conscience for a while. Once alone, the doctor is plagued by his guilt. His interior guilt is exteriorized by the use of two female voices, who, through a filter device, repeat, "What are you going to tell them doctor?" To this is added the sound of a ticking clock, and the clock and voices speed up and finally stop, telling the doctor to write his confession. Seeing the gun the captain left behind, the doctor shoots himself. Upon hearing the gunshot, the captain tells the detective that the doctor's conscience must have been too much for him. While certain elements of the dragnet are enacted in this episode, they are not enacted in the same way as in *Gang Busters*. Although the criminal commits suicide here, he does not do so out of fear of the police; he is not suffering from claustrophobia but from his own guilty conscience.

The narrative device of criminal claustrophobia was an enduring one. The March 27, 1942, episode of *Gang Busters* is devoted to the story of "Bruno Salek," who suffers from "bull fever," an underworld term for fear of the law. The episode begins with a conversation between host Norman Schwarzkopf and guest Commissioner Millhauser, which echoes the opening of "Tony the Stinger":

COMMISSIONER: Colonel Schwarzkopf there have been some who thought they could get away with a crime like that, but they forget one important angle of the law. I want to state a few facts,—because the solution of this case tonight depends entirely upon them.

(STACCATO—MARCH-OF-TIME TEMPO)

MILLHAUSER: (FILTER) There are one hundred and ten thousand uniformed police officers in this country.

COP: (FILTER) Thousands of plainclothes detectives.

MILLHAUSER: 50,000 short-wave police radio sending sets!

COMMISSIONER: (NO FILTER) There are 10,000 scout cars criss-crossing the nation's streets and highways. 2,500 G-Men working across State lines, 12,000 State Troopers—the Secret Service—The Postal Inspectors—the Customs Service—

MILLHAUSER: (FILTER) And don't forget there are 104,000,000 miles of telephone wires to trip the criminal.

COP: (FILTER) One hundred and fifty crime detective laboratories!

COMMISSIONER: In other words, Colonel Schwarzkopf, when a man commits a crime, all these forces of the law form a tremendous dragnet which automatically closes in on him. What's more, the criminal, himself, knows it.

COLONEL: And that knowledge makes the net of the law all the more inescapable. (2)

The "facts" about the communication network that ensnares Salek were specifically requested.[16] A week later, the information that appears in the beginning of the Salek episode is sent back to New York. While the FBI would not give out all the information the program requested, it gave enough to present the idea of an inescapable presence.

That Salek, a small-time robber hunted across eight states, eventually should crack comes as no surprise to the radio listener. In fact, Salek's breakdown is initiated by his listening to a radio broadcast warning citizens and police to be on the lookout for him. The episode begins with Salek committing a nightclub robbery. Before the police even have identified him, Salek begins to suffer from "bull fever" and acts increasingly paranoid. While in their hideout, Salek's girlfriend and the other accomplice tell Salek to calm down and suggest he turn on the radio for some music. Instead, they hear an announcement about Salek on the radio, causing Salek to panic. The three take off in their car and drive forty-eight hours straight to try to escape an eight-state dragnet set up for their capture. When they stop at a campsite for a night of rest, they hear an announcement about themselves coming from the camp owner's shortwave radio. As they continue to drive, Salek grows increasingly mad, killing an officer who routinely pulls them over. His girlfriend eventually confesses to Salek that she would rather be dead than live the life of a fugitive from the law. Salek's other accomplice swears he will give up his life of crime once they are safely outside the police dragnet. However, growing increasingly paranoid, Salek is convinced that police cars are chasing them, when, in fact, there is nothing behind them. In his panic, he crashes into the side of a house, injuring the three. When they are taken to the hospital, the two are identified by authorities. As a result, Salek and his accomplice are eventually sent to the electric chair.

Criminal claustrophobia was a clear result of the dragnet effect and its logic of inevitable encounter enabled by radio's ability to extend simultaneity across vast reaches of space. The technology used by the police allowed for the creation of the dragnet, an extension of their power into the private lives of criminals and citizens. As a device used in the docudrama, and by police forces themselves, to justify their increased presence, the dragnet, which was organized around the idea that apprehension was inevitable, offered no hope for escape. Each program demonstrated that criminals could not succeed, but *Gang Busters* offered an additional element—the criminal could not escape. In classic detective fiction, all that mattered was the identification of the guilty party. In hard-boiled fiction, identification also mattered. Because radio crime docudramas dealt with solved cases, the identity of the criminal was secure—apprehension was the goal. The dragnet ensured that this would always happen.

CONCLUSION: CONSTANT COMMUNICATIVE PRESENCE

The dragnet effect was part imagination and part fact, part discursive hope and part technical reality. It was about reveling in the thrill of the chase while safely guaranteeing that the outcome was always the same. A heady combination of cross-country motion, adventure, prowess, and control, the radio crime docudrama played on the contradictions of a society becoming at once more mobile and more privatized. Radio's ability to both link and collapse the distance between the public and the private, the mobile and the fixed, time and space, communication and transportation, state and citizen, and industry and listener was distilled in the imagination of police omnipresence as positive and productive.

For police reformers, modern communication and transportation technologies promised the smooth and efficient pursuit of criminal apprehension in an increasingly mobile and complex society. In keeping with the American fascination with fetishizing technology as offering technical solutions to political and moral questions (Carey and Quirk 1992), reformers imagined radio as a technical solution both to the problem of criminal mobility and to the political problems of policing. In the quest of municipal police forces to wrest power, including power over the police, away from ward politicians, radio offered a way to consolidate police operations through a centralized dispatch system. Police commanders, and not ward politicians, would coordinate and determine the activities of police. The use of two-way radio further guaranteed that the technology would be used not only in the surveillance and control of mobility but also in the control of police officers. Radio proved a key technology for redefining the relationship between police and citizens. The symbolic power and excitement generated by the radio, already an object of consumer adoration, was mobilized to garner support for police modernization efforts. At the same time, the promise of police omnipresence offered a compelling reason to call the police. The promise of instant aid in the case of a crime against person or property indicated the police would serve citizens even as professionalization rendered citizen input in matters regarding crime, policing, and public disorder unwelcome. That is, citizens could make demands on the police, but the relationship was predetermined.

The unique qualities of radio, as developed by commercial broadcasters, made it an ideal site through which to imagine police omniscience. The dragnet effect was secured by linking communication and transportation and their dizzying ability to collapse space and time. Radio's ability to conquer space and time without wires offered the ability to oversee the roaming nature of mobility produced by the automobile. Linking the imagination of the industrial organization of radio and the organization of police radio furthered the dragnet effect in the minds of radio listeners. On the one hand, radio's localism allowed for an articulation between the identity formed by local stations and the relationship between citizens and their local police departments. On the other hand, the technological organization of radio into regional and national networks contributed greatly to the imagination of its covering huge expanses of geography. This was consistently reinforced both through the production of imagery, such as maps, and through constant reference by the networks to their national audience. *Gang Busters* began each episode assuring listeners that it offered the only national program dramatizing the work of the police. While police radio remained localized in its organization, its representation in the radio crime docudrama effectively articulated it to the imagination of national radio, promoting an imagination of police radio as coherently covering the nation, offering no space of escape. Finally, the dragnet effect was produced by linking the experience of radio as shaped by the commercial broadcast industry with the simulation of that experience in the dramas themselves. What better space to represent the liveness and dailiness of the commercial broadcasting than on a commercial broadcast, where the simulation and original experience were close enough to potentially register as indistinguishable.

Trade publications, professional literature, popular literature, and radio crime docudramas presented police radio as capable of effectively and efficiently conquering space and time. Using language and imagery consistent with the national networks, radio was figured as the ideal medium for casting its net over ever-increasing geographic spaces. Radio's ability to provide simultaneous communication over space, to collapse space and time, was offered as further proof that radio was the ideal foil to criminal mobility and proof of the ability of modern police to conquer time as well as space. This spatial-temporal relationship was completed by the articulation of police radio with network radio—by drawing the representational power of radio to simulate its own experience—and, more specifically, to simulate the experience of network radio itself, to draw on the experience of radio and radio's specific relationship to temporality—its flow, its dailiness, its everydayness—to create a sense of constant communicative presence. This was constructed through the narrative organization of these crime docudramas, whose narrative was centered less on domestic space, encounter, and the revelation of secrets than on a chronotope that suggested that apprehension was always inevitable. Constant communicative presence constructed through the dragnet effect guaranteed apprehension.

The Shadow of Doubt and the Menace of Surveillance

LORD: Then Manovitz was really the murderer of the old Russian couple, Chief Coglin?

COGLIN: Beyond the shadow of a doubt.

—"The Chicago Kid" episode of *Gang Busters*

As argued up to this point, the radio crime docudrama was developed as an entertainment formula that was largely complicit in naturalizing a progressive definition of policing as a profession producing, and thus possessing, its own body of expert knowledge about criminality, policing, and the proper role of citizens. This was achieved both through the narrative content of the programs, which continually worked to construct the police as professional laborers, and in the formal elements that were particular to the production of meaning in the radio medium. The narrative content constructed the police as self-assured authorities in matters of policing and criminality who never erred in their efforts at criminal apprehension. As the quote from "The Chicago Kid" suggests, these programs deployed self-confident, boastful claims to authority in order to improve the public image of the police; their methods of identification were infallible, their methods of apprehension inescapable. The use of sound effects and articulation of police radio with the industrial organization of commercial broadcasting fostered the imaginative possibility of an inescapable dragnet under which criminal apprehension was inevitable. While the meanings of the crime dramas were not always so read, especially in regard to the representation of criminality, the representation of police authority was largely conservative in its aim to bolster the social standing of the police during a time of social upheaval. The growth of police power was tied to the overall adoption of post-Progressive reform measures by both the government and professional organizations in a move that rendered citizen involvement in the definition of social problems, and hence the kinds of solutions required, increasingly unwelcome. While policing was defined as a public service through the development of practices such as call-and-response, the struggle over defining what constituted the activities of the police and definitions of criminality would now be a matter for professional police forces to decide rather than be the object of public debate.

Yet, the pro-police discourse that celebrated proceduralism and apprehension was both contradictory and incomplete in nature. This chapter focuses on the ways in which the strongly pro-police ideology of the radio crime docudrama was challenged. First, the docudramas sometimes produced counterdiscourses that called into question the very model they were constructing. Such moments were rare but no less significant. Counterdiscourses most often took the form of reversing one of the consistent elements of the program either by creating sympathy for the criminal or by calling police proceduralism into question. Other times, the claims made by the producers of the programs to define situations in a particular way were challenged by the police or by the criminals themselves. What constituted the correct narrative was often less clear than the strongly didactic tone these series suggested. Second, another kind of crime drama, rooted in pulp and hard-boiled detective fiction, found loyal radio audiences. Programs such as *The Green Hornet* and *The Shadow,* like their docudrama cousins, drove home the strong moral message that crime never pays, but they did so in a way that replaced Progressive reform claims to professional expertise and attempts to use reform as a way to control social mobility with a more ambivalent take on the growth of police and state power. This ambivalence was expressed through character, plot, sound effects, and other elements specific to the radio medium. In all these instances, a shadow of doubt was cast over the police and their claims to being the professional keepers and makers of knowledge about crime and policing.

CRACKS IN THE ARMOR

As has been argued, there was a remarkable consistency to the radio crime docudramas' representations of policing, criminality, and citizenship. As their definitions became reified in the formula of the programs, the constant reproduction of these categories became a matter of course. The writers, producers, and audiences knew what to expect, if not in terms of the actual action that would ensue, at least in terms of the characterization of the police and criminals. Yet, occasionally, these programs disrupted their own flow in a way that called into question the very model of policing they attempted to construct. Because these moments so clearly stand apart, their significance extends beyond their rarity. *Police Headquarters, Calling All Cars,* and the more confessional *True Detective Mysteries* were the programs most likely to depart from their usual characterizations, primarily by evoking sympathy for the criminal and even occasionally calling proceduralism into question. *Gang Busters* was more consistent in its representational strategy; however, correspondence from listeners, police officers, and judges indicates that there were those willing to challenge the program's self-confident narration of the events that transpired. That people wrote to challenge the program's claims to factualness is not entirely surprising, but correspondents more significantly called into question the authority of the program to define events and the character of individuals.

Sympathy and Moral Ambiguity

As chapter 3 argued, radio crime docudramas worked to strip all glamour from criminals and to render them as unsympathetically as possible in order to leave no space for audience identification with the plight of lawbreakers. The goal was for Depression-era audiences to stop idolizing gangsters and desperados and to instead support the police. The radio docudrama criminal was therefore constructed as needlessly brutal and beyond redemption.[1] Occasionally, however, these programs broke from that pattern to present listeners with more morally ambiguous representations of criminality. In rare instances, they called into question their own boastful self-confidence in the correctness and effectiveness of police procedures.

As a nascent series focusing on the police, *Police Headquarters* largely represented the police as intelligent, competent, and well organized into a clear hierarchal chain of command. Yet the program could occasionally call some of these elements into question, such as in the episode, "Man Stealing Food" (1932). Two beat cops in their car answer a radio call about a possible break-in at a delicatessen. When the officers arrive, they see the man attempting to enter the deli but wait until he gets in before arresting him, so that he cannot "beat the rap." When they finally approach him, they do so with the typical tough attitude of the documentary-style radio crime drama, pulling their guns and addressing him as a "yellow rat." The man, Tim, quickly responds that he is unarmed and is trying to get food to feed his sick baby. Worse yet, he himself has not eaten meat for a month. Rather than arresting him, the police grab some food and drive him back to his home. Against Tim's protestations that his wife is too sick for visitors, the officers climb up a long flight of stairs and arrive in a dark apartment with only candles for light. Tim's wife and baby are clearly ill, so one of the officers calls a doctor to attend to them. The officers also try to reason with the delicatessen owner, paying him for what they took and asking him not to press any charges. When the officers report their activities to the lieutenant, to their surprise they find him uncooperative: he wants an arrest regardless of the circumstances. It is at this point that the "crazy Irishman" Mike puts his unorthodox plan into action. Calling on his underworld contacts, he spreads the word that the delicatessen has a great deal of money and that it is easy to get into the store. Sure enough, a smalltime crook named Wheezy attempts to rob the store. Having laid their trap, the officers are there to arrest him, thus fulfilling the lieutenant's desire for "some action" on the call.

This episode works against the dominant narrative thrust of the series in two ways. First, the episode elicits sympathy for the "criminal," Tim. Forced to commit robbery under desperate circumstances, especially poignant to a Depression-era audience, Tim does not deserve punishment for his act—a point stressed in the scene that takes place in the apartment. Although hungry himself, Tim's first concern is for his wife and child. Worried that his wife will be afraid when she sees the officers, they volunteer to lie, saying they are there to help Tim get a job with the railroad. When his wife hears this, she is relieved. A victim of circumstances beyond his control, Tim is someone who deserves the understanding of both the police and the home listeners. The program does not go so far as to suggest all criminals deserve our sympathy, however; it demonstrates through the somewhat pathetic character of Wheezy that most criminals deserve what happens to them. Second, the program calls into question police reform. The officers disagree with their lieutenant, and while not exactly resisting his orders, they do not follow them either. The officers thus call into question a system of authority that has no space for understanding the circumstances surrounding actions in its single-minded emphasis on criminal apprehension. In addition, while *Gang Busters* especially worked to deethnicize the police in accord with the reform desire to close policing down as an avenue of social advancement for the ethnic working classes, here *Police Headquarters* marks "Mike" as Irish, and his sympathies clearly lie with class interests rather than with the professional norms advocated by reformers. Like many beat cops of the reform era, Mike bristled under the attempts to control his actions, a key element of the police reform movement. At the same time, the officers in this episode are further frustrated by the definitions of what constituted crime during a time when resources were so unevenly distributed throughout the population.

In another *Police Headquarters* episode, "John Fleming Confesses" (1932), a frail, sickly man comes to police headquarters and tells them he knows who committed a recent murder in front of a subway terminal: John Fleming. The elderly man tells a story about a farmer who was well liked by everyone in his community except his neighbor Andrew Adams. One day, Adams's house burned down, leaving behind a body burned beyond recognition. The body had two gunshot wounds, and the bullets were traced to John Fleming's gun. Despite maintaining his innocence, Fleming was convicted Adams's murder and served over eighteen years as a model prisoner. Released with nothing but twelve dollars and a "cheap suit," he returned to his hometown and found work with a trucking company.

One night, Fleming returned to his rented room to find Andrew Adams—the man he had been convicted of killing! As revenge against Fleming for marrying his sweetheart, Adams had faked his own death by stealing Fleming's gun, shooting a drifter, and burning down his house. Adams was cruel. He said he had hoped Fleming would die in prison, and would kill him now were it not obvious Fleming was terminally ill. Fleming's suffering makes Adams happy. A few days later, a dumbstruck Fleming purchased a revolver and arranged to meet Adams at a downtown building. Adams was incensed, believing Fleming wanted his help. Instead, Fleming complimented him on his diabolical scheme but pointed out one important fact that Adams forgot: a man cannot be convicted of the same crime twice. While Adams pleaded for his life, Fleming shot him. When the old man finishes his story, the police ask if he knows where Fleming is, as they still might be able to arrest him. The man reveals that he himself is Fleming.

This episode offers another example of sympathy for the criminal. While Adams, whose murder is the central crime of the episode, evokes no sympathy, the man who murdered him does. Fleming tells his own story without an excess of maudlin emotion, indicating he still possesses some dignity. At the same time, the various trials he suffered are in themselves emotionally poignant. This is a case where the law has failed, sentencing an innocent man on the basis of seemingly infallible scientific evidence—a ballistics report matching the bullets in the burned body to Fleming's pistol. This episode therefore calls into question the self-confident police discourse of inevitable apprehension as the police so clearly failed to identify the correct criminal in the first instance. It also allows the audience to feel sympathy for someone who in the end is a murderer himself.

Sometimes, moral ambiguity was featured more strongly than actual sympathy. This moral ambiguity dealt with more personal matters, people who made bad choices in their lives. In the "William Spencer Killed" episode of *Police Headquarters* (1932), for example, the investigating officer, Captain Frasier, knew the victim while growing up. Frasier knows that Spencer has had trouble in the past due to his penchant for gambling. In fact, Spencer is killed as a result of his gambling debts. Frasier had once told him that he would bring him in dead one day, either by Frasier's own hand or by someone to whom he owed money. Despite having chosen a life of crime, Frasier expresses a great deal of sympathy for Spencer, making it his personal mission to apprehend his killers.

The more confessional tone of *True Detective Mysteries* lent itself readily to expressions of sympathy for the situations of the criminals, especially when a woman committed the crime.[2] Crime dramas offered sympathy to men doing the best they could to provide for their families, like Tim, thus demonstrating their attempts to fulfill the norms of masculinity. Women, however, were afforded sympathy based on those ideas of femininity circulated by confessionals, which portrayed women as overemotional and irrational. For example, in one episode, a woman murders her philandering and abusive husband. "The Buddha Man Mystery" (1937) begins with a phone call from a Mrs. Anderson to the operator. Desperate to find a doctor, she explains with panic in her voice that her husband won't wake up. The doctor and police arrive to find Mr. Anderson dead, apparently from an accidental overdose of chloroform, which he regularly inhaled to help him sleep. As the police investigate the case, they find a number of possible suspects, but finally it is clear to them that Mrs. Anderson killed her own husband. When confronted, she tearfully explains her history with Frank Anderson, including how he stole a passionate moment with her bridesmaid right before their wedding ceremony. The night she murdered him, Frank had threatened her with a beating when she suggested to him that his Hindu philosophy was hurting his work as a meteorologist. Explaining to her that under Hindu philosophy, the woman is the slave, he proceeded to beat her while telling her he never cared for her. Unable to bear it any longer, Mrs. Anderson waited for her husband to inhale chloroform, which he called the "nectar of the gods," and once he was sufficiently sleepy, she forced him to inhale more chloroform, thus administering the lethal dose. Despite committing murder, Mrs. Anderson was sentenced to one to ten years in the Connecticut State Prison on manslaughter charges, indicating that her sentence was influenced by her mitigating circumstances.

Another woman in desperate circumstances is Helen from the "Murder at Sunset" episode of *Calling All Cars* (1939), which tells the story of a woman in love, who "strived to transform life to the color of her dreams." Helen is married to Harry, who insists on hiding their marriage from his mother. Although initially happy to have love in her life, the burden of keeping their relationship a secret begins to try Helen's patience and happiness. Helen finally complains about the time Harry spends with his mother and threatens to tell her about their marriage. Harry responds with threats of physical harm. In a strange sequence, the program intimates that Helen is pregnant when Harry sends her away to take care of her "problem," threatening to kill her if she does not. When she comes back a year later, she spends two happy days with Harry, who then states his intention to spend New Year's Eve with his mother rather than with Helen. Helen protests and threatens to tell his mother, provoking a violent outburst from Harry, who burns their marriage certificate and then threatens to kill her if she shows up at the New Year's Eve party. Unable to bear the silence or loneliness, Helen arrives at the party. Intercepted by Harry, the two go out to the car where they struggle with the gun. Helen claims the gun went off by accident, but no one will believe her. Distraught over the loss of her husband and over her incarceration, Helen literally wills herself into a prolonged state of unconsciousness.

As she lays unconscious, the radio listener is allowed to listen in on the thoughts racing through her mind, which center mostly around Harry. When she finally awakes, she asks only to be allowed to return to sleep. Of course, at the end, the host assures the listeners that "no matter how much we sympathize, taking a human life is a crime, and crime must never pay." Helen, as represented in this episode, is unlike Bonnie Parker or Eleanor Jarman in their *Gang Busters* treatments. Whereas Bonnie and Jarman are afforded little sympathy, instead represented as wantonly and ruthlessly violent, *Calling All Cars* represents Helen as a sympathetic victim of violence, forced to make horrible choices to gain the love of an undeserving man, again stressing her basic feminine emotional weaknesses. While not condoning her actions, this dramatization nonetheless allows the audience to feel for her. Like the warnings on the gangster films that tried to remind audiences that they were stories of criminal suffering, episodes such as these called into question the self-confident faith in apprehension more frequently constructed by these programs.

Police reformers reasoned that once citizens sympathized with the plight of a criminal, identification and possibly emulation could not be far behind. While films were understood as glamorizing criminals, chapter 3 argued that radio crime docudramas worked to completely deglamorize urban gangsters and rural bandits, representing them as needlessly and wantonly violent. While the programs, drawing from progressive theories of juvenile delinquency, suggested that social causes might account for a young person's entrance into a life of crime, once such a path was embarked on, there was no turning back. Stripped of any humanity, these were ruthless men and women who warranted a powerful and total police presence to guarantee their apprehension and protect the innocent. On rare occasions, however, the docudramas represented criminals as men and women who were victims of circumstances beyond their control or understanding. These were people who deserved the sympathy of the listener and even of the police. In breaking with the typical representation of criminality, the docudramas infrequently but significantly called into question their own justification for expanded police power and the apprehension-based model of policing.

Refusing Compliance

While the programs occasionally confounded their own formula, more significant was the noncooperation of citizens with the model of policing advocated by the docudramas. No matter how much effort reformers expended on improving their public image and developing new relationships with citizens, there were those who questioned the growth of police power. For example, fingerprinting, the crown jewel of scientific policing, met with disapproval from the American Civil Liberties Union, which argued that fingerprinting had little actual relation to crime, as more knowledgeable criminals would most likely use gloves. But, more than this, the ACLU feared that mandatory fingerprinting might lead to future kinds of compulsory activities and strengthen the power of the state at the great expense of civil liberties ("G-Men Collect Six Million Clues" 1936). In addition, as Potter (1998) notes, the young men employed by the Civilian Conservation Corps, expressing their concern for the growth of federal power, refused to have their fingerprints taken (128). Labor groups were critical and suspicious of growing police powers. Cartoons from the 1930s often represent the criminal as a small figure being loomed over darkly by some larger figure, such as a group of federal agents or, in one case, a menacing eagle claw. Popular resistance could also be found in the persistent tendencies of Americans to glamorize and identify with the criminal lifestyle. Gangsters were often as much heroes as criminals to many Americans. Even state police forces were seen as troublesome extensions of police power. Such was the case in Iowa, when in 1935 the state legislature voted to establish a state highway patrol rather than a state police force (Kaloupek 1938).

Even police radio, the most potent symbol of a modernized, professional police force, became a site of struggle. Toward the mid-1930s, as police radio gained in popularity, there were reports that citizens were actually hampering law enforcement efforts. Curiosity seekers began to turn up in greater numbers at the scene of a reported crime. This fact was dealt with in the "July Fourth in a Radio Car" (1934) episode of *Calling All Cars,* which begins with James E. Davis asking his listeners for "assistance on behalf of the radio police." Explaining that as listeners' "radios are capable of tuning in on the police radio broadcasts," he is afraid that too often they are "tempted when a call is broadcast . . . [to] rush to the scene of the disturbance." Unfortunately, he continues, though this "is a natural thing to do . . . it often hampers the work of the policeman." Davis warns his audience against such a behavior, telling them, "You can be of the greatest assistance if you refrain from doing this. The radio police can much more successfully complete their duties if they are not hampered by crowds of curious citizens. . . ." Knowing that they seek to "cooperate" with police to the "fullest" extent, he tells them that this can be best achieved "by staying away from any call you might hear over the police radio." Rather than the citizen compliance and cooperation that reformers hoped police radio would encourage, it encouraged meddlesome behavior. Curious onlookers were not the only problem: ambulance chasers, commercial auto-wrecking companies, and others who stood to profit from the victims of a particular crime also interfered with crime scenes.

Worse yet, criminals could monitor the police efforts at monitoring them. Police were unable to stop criminals from listening to their radio broadcasts, but by forbidding shortwave radios in automobiles and using a code system, police tried to limit what criminals could learn from their radio transmissions. In some cases, criminals complained about the intense level of surveillance they were put under, as in the case of Bonnie and Clyde. Police also feared that criminals could use radio to coordinate their own activities. When *Gang Busters* was turned into a fictional serial film in 1942, it began with a broadcast made by the criminal to the police over a hijacked police radio. Citizens interfering at crime scenes, criminals monitoring the police radio, and criminal broadcasting all suggested that the control over mobility and publicity offered by radio could be turned against them.

Talking Back

The files for *Gang Busters* contain a number of examples of people who challenged the authority of the program to construct criminal and police activity. Elena Razlogova (2006) details these interactions in "True Crime Radio and Listener Disenchantment with Network Broadcasting, 1935–1946." Examining the dramatization of conflicts among the interests of police, broadcasters, listeners, and criminals, she argues that "because the program reenacted actual confrontations between poor people and state authorities, it inspired its working-class and non-white listeners and informants to articulate popular dissatisfaction with the emerging impersonal corporate power in the broadcasting industry" (139). She asserts that for many listeners, populist interpretations of the activities of bandits "constituted the dominant meaning of *Gang Busters*" (145). Interested in the development of broadcasting as an institution, she considers the ways that audiences' interaction with the program spoke to the growing sense of disappointment working-class audiences felt toward the powerful corporations in control of radio. When read against the rise of the police reform movement, we can see that these instances of talking back were also aimed at the growing professional power of the police. Correspondents who talked back refused to adopt the progressive police point of view and questioned the complicity of broadcasters in accepting their claim to professional authority and expertise. Many of these complaints centered on the program's claim to factualness. In some instances, state officials wrote to the program either challenging Lord's right to broadcast certain information or suggesting that Lord had information that he kept from the authorities. Some of those who wrote to Lord specifically questioned the characterization of police and criminals. The files also contain many clippings from magazines and newspapers that challenged the program's dramatization of events. Even when simply questioning the program's claims of veracity, these letters and articles indicate that as much as the program tried to present itself as an important space for police efforts to improve their public image, this self-proclaimed role did not go unchallenged. Citizens, police, and criminals themselves called into question the program's self-confident discourse of factualness.

Julius Haycraft, a judge in the Seventeenth Judicial District, Chambers District Court of Fairmont, Minnesota, expressed his concern over the broadcast dramatizing the career of Bonnie and Clyde. His concern centered on the claim made by the program that the Barrow "gang" had robbed a bank in Minnesota, a crime for which Mildred and Floyd Strain had already been tried and sentenced. That the right persons were in jail was not the problem. That the Strains might use the episode to gain early parole was. After detailing the successful capture of the couple, now serving time in state prison for robbing a bank, Haycraft continues:

> The Barrows gang did not rob the Okabena bank. Pictures of members of the Barrows gang were shown to the identifying witnesses, in the trial of Floyd Strain, and each testified that the pictures were not of the bandits who robbed the Okabena bank. The identification of the Strains was positive and emphatic. I wanted this information, first, to learn just what was said in the broadcast, and I would like to know from what source your information was

obtained stating that the Barrows robbed this bank. I want the information for this purpose: These bandits will apply, or are applying for a parole or pardon, and they will insist that it was the Barrows gang and not they that perpetrated the robbery. I want the information to the contrary that can furnish the Parole and Pardon Boards. I feel sure the claim will be made that it was broadcast over the radio February 19, 1936, that the Barrows gang were the robbers. (1936)

What is especially ironic about this, in addition to the program possibly being used to set convicted criminals free, is that the central "lesson" of the two-part dramatization of the criminal careers of Bonnie Parker and Clyde Barrow was to urge legislators and citizens to "stop wholesale paroles" ("Bonnie and Clyde, Part 1" 1936). Not only does Haycraft call into question the program's claims to have truthfully documented the careers of Bonnie and Clyde, but he also suggests that their very mistakes constitute a harmful interference in the legal process itself. He also validates the power of the program to persuade listeners that the stories it presented were indeed factual.

A more pointed letter comes from retired inspector of police, John Mitchell, in response to the "The Scarnini" (1936) episode. He claims that either the information presented by the program was untrue or the program introduced new evidence pertinent to the case, which should be handed over. This writer's critique cuts to the heart of the premise of the program, explicitly challenging the right of its makers to turn real-life crime stories into dramatized entertainment. He accuses the sponsor, Colgate-Palmolive, of "commercializing crime for self gain and deceiving the public with a lot of rot, purporting to be facts." He notes that the program's "SLOGAN: CRIME DOES NOT PAY, SEEMS TO BE A JOKE, because I can disprove it very easily and prove to you and the ONE HUNDRED AND TWENTY-FIVE MILLION PEOPLE THAT CRIME DOES PAY: THAT I AM BASING MY STATEMENT ON FORTY YEARS EXPERIENCE AS A POLICE OFFICER [emphasis original]." The writer of this letter clearly exposes the ultimate commercial intent of the program. No matter how sincere Lord was in his production of the program, in the end it was a program designed to make money for Lord, the program's sponsor, and the network.

Resistance to the program's claims to factualness and its condensation of events was often expressed by the refusal of participants in the dramatized cases to have an actor impersonate them. In a telegram dated April 27, 1936, R. F. Cunningham, chief of police of Steubenville, Ohio, refused to give his consent, arguing that the "DRAMATIZATION BY RADIO OF THE CAPTURE OF THE D'AUTREMONT BROTHERS IN STEUBENVILLE STUDY OF YOUR SCRIPT FOR RADIO USE SHOWS IT TO BE POORLY CONCIEVED UNNECESSARILY EXAGGER-ATED AND ALMOST WHOLLY INACCURATE." Not only was this a problem in terms of representing the police, but Cunningham also states that "IF FOR NO OTHER REASON I WOULD OBJECT TO ITS TRANSMISSION OUT OF RESPECT FOR RADIO LISTENERS WHO CAN ONLY BE MISLED AND CONFUSED BY THE ALMOST PURE FICTION YOUR WRITERS HAVE CONCOTED." He tells Lord that he may be referred to as "A MEMBER OF THE STEUBENVILLE POLICE DEPART-MENT." Despite the insistence of the program that it was made with the full cooperation of law enforcement officers, many people objected to the writ-ers' habits of exaggerating and condensing certain "facts" in order to turn sometimes complicated police investigations into half-hour radio dramas.

Sometimes criminals themselves objected to their dramatizations. For example, as discussed in chapter 3, criminals were given standardized ways of speaking that marked them as unintelligent and nonspecifically ethnic. A Toledo newspaper reported on one such objection to the "Livacoli Gang" (1936) episode of *Gang Busters:* "Smooth talking Yonnie probably will be very much peeved to learn that his 'voice' talked like a 'mug' during the drama." In fact, Thomas "Yonnie" Livacoli had used his gang activities to gain access to upper-class life, living in fancy hotels and then purchas-ing a mansion in a respectable area of town. Upon moving his family into his new house, the dramatized Livacoli notes in his "mug" accent that "our neighbors is very classy people."

Livacoli bristled against this voice characterization, which was consis-tent with the imagination of radio professionals but had only a tangential relationship to the actual person.[3] Declaring his plans to sue the network, Livacoli further objected to the representation of himself and criminals in general, stating, "We all have some bad in us. But these commercial radio programs try to paint all of us as the blackest criminals in the world. There is some good in all of us." Livacoli accuses Lord of having made a career of distorting facts for publicity, noting that "this is the man who sent out two S.O.S. messages from his schooner, the *Seth Parker,* and caused a war ship to race halfway across the Pacific Ocean to find out that aid was not needed. A lot of people suggested at the time that Mr. Lord just had queer ideas about how to get publicity." Livacoli further questions the definitions of his activities as constituting a "gang." Emphasizing the populist appeal of the Prohibition-era gangsters, Livacoli told reporters that the prosecutor "pictures me as a big gang leader ordering death for this man and that . . . I'm no cannibal. The only law violation I was ever guilty of was selling good liquor to good people. I was mixed up in no gang. I directed no gang." Livacoli links his own career to the public dislike of and often open opposition to Prohibition, maintaining his innocence and challenging the "facts" presented.

On other occasions, the family and friends of the criminal protested representations of their loved one. In the "Machine Gun Kelly" (1935) episode of *G-Men,* the controversy surrounds the program's characterization of J. C. Tichenor as "a well-known character of the Memphis underworld" who had taken in Kelly and Kelly's wife as boarders. The program suggests that Tichenor knew who the Kellys were and was guilty of harboring known fugitives from the law. In fact, Tichenor was successfully tried on this count, although he served only several months in jail. Lord received correspondence from Tichenor's friends challenging the claim that he was an "underworld" member. Mrs. A. H. McNeely wrote on September 12, 1935, giving a detailed description of Tichenor's upbringing and unique circumstances. Tichenor was born into a wealthy family and was college educated, but the death of his father and mismanagement of the family business by his brothers left him penniless. Trying to find work to support his wife and child, Tichenor, "a victim of infantile paralysis" who "weighed less than one hundred pounds," had a difficult time finding work. When his wife and child were away, he rented out rooms in his house. As to Tichenor's conviction, McNeely was adamant in placing the blame on the tactics of the police, clearly referencing those third-degree tactics that brought so much public criticism of policing. She explains that Tichenor "was yanked from his bed, taken to headquarters and grilled all day without food or even a drink of water, not allowed to communicate with even his wife, and when he was thoroughly exhausted, and in so much pain he was crazy, a paper was thrust before him and we was told to sign his name." Of course, in the wake of such treatment, Tichenor did not read what he was signing, rendering his false confession a direct result of police brutality.

McNeely notes that even with this confession, Tichenor had the support of "his next door neighbors, his employer, and a lawyer who was donating his services, members of his family and many others in that court room at his trial." But that was to no avail. Because "they did not have a chance to say a word," Tichenor was "convicted . . . on the signed statement, and that was that." After serving only six months of his four-year sentence, because "the court knew he was innocent, and the people of Memphis knew it," he was able to get his job back, but left Memphis, trying to forget the experience for the sake of his son. The writer admonishes Lord that "it is just not fair that you should have to send this false story out over the air. . . . These are the kind of people you hurt, you and the G-men, you, who have put on the programme of Seth Parker, and sung so often, 'Throw Out the Life-Line.'" Lord was advised by NBC and Rex Collier, who helped provide the material for the program, to simply ignore a lawsuit brought against him. While the files do not indicate what happened to the lawsuit, McNeely's letter reveals that some people understood what was at stake in the power of both the FBI and the program to define the situation as they saw it. McNeely also hinted at another issue of contention among those who chose to talk back: the tension between national and local interests. She states that Tichenor was a respected member of his community and, in her characterization of his sentencing, that it was mitigated by this local understanding.

Other complaints about the program centered on its status as a national broadcast. Of particular concern was that the program, in the name of whatever "chief" whose permission for impersonation the program secured, did not give proper credit to the work of various local authorities. For example, a clipped article from an unidentified newspaper in response to the "Arthur Boccadero" (1936) episode of *Gang Busters* questions the program on two counts.[4] First, the program is called to task for its cavalier dramatization of police procedures. On the basis of a bullet matching a gun he had stolen a year earlier, Boccadero, "the cat burglar," was convicted of murdering a man during a house robbery. The original gun owner had fired his weapon on New Year's Eve, and the police were able to locate the bullet by searching the owner's garden. The writer of this article complained that the program made solving a crime seem like a result of "one of those inspired visions on the part of master detectives" when in fact crimes were solved through routine, painstaking detective work. Second, the writer criticized the program for failing to properly acknowledge one of the key law enforcement agencies, in this case the Glen Ridge, New Jersey, Police Department, involved in bringing Boccadero to justice. The writer suggested, probably correctly, that this was because the chief of the Glen Ridge Police Department had died between the solving of the crime and its dramatization by *Gang Busters*. Without the proper host chief available to fill its narrative slot, *Gang Busters* simply ignored the efforts of this department.

The tensions between national broadcasting and local situations came to a head following the broadcast of *Gang Busters'* dramatization of the capture of "Homer Van Meter" (1936), a member of Dillinger's gang, in St. Paul, Minnesota. The Federation of Women Teachers in Minnesota objected to the broadcast because they believed it too directly interfered with an upcoming local election. Federation secretary Helen Conway wrote on April 30, 1936:

> Public opinion, generally, considers that the material of a coast-to-coast broadcast should be of national and not local import. The aforesaid broadcast, with its partisan attitude toward local issues, coming as it did near the end of a heated political campaign in St. Paul, seemed to the members of this organization, as well as to others associated with them, to be contrary to a sense of fair play. This broadcast unquestionably left the feeling that it was beneath the dignity of such a firm as the Palm Olive and unworthy of the attention of a great organization such as Columbia Broadcasting Company.

The Federation of Women Teachers express a fear of the loss of local control over their local political situation to a national agenda and a set of national concerns. They question the authority of *Gang Busters* to define what constitutes an important political matter for St. Paul, Minnesota, residents. While chain broadcasting might have meant participation in national consumption trends, these women expressed the desire that some matters be left to local control.

The attitude of the advertising agency and Lord's production company was condescending. In the advertiser's quest to reach a national audience and the desire of Lord's production company to live up to its claim of producing the only national program dramatizing real-life police cases, the concerns of these writers simply did not register. A letter dated May 8, 1936, from Theodore Bates at the Benton and Bowles advertising agency to John Ives reads, "Dear Johnny: I am attaching a letter from the Federation of Women Teachers in St. Paul, which expresses the opinion of the Federation about our *Gang Busters* program in which we tried to make the fair city of St. Paul free from criminals, and a lovely place in which to live." The cavalier sarcasm here is translated into a letter to the Federation, sent under Lord's signature, in which the agency wishes to express "that we do not have any feeling locally or otherwise, one way or another; that it is our sincere aim to conduct a true crusade against crime which will be effective nationally; and that in order to do this, we use local examples of excellent police work" (Lord 1936). While for this organization the local was an arena for the negotiation over what constituted proper policing and justice, for the makers of *Gang Busters,* the local was simply one of many examples of a national fight against crime, and it was at the national level that such negotiations should take place.

DARK SHADOWS: THE MENACE OF AUTHORITY

Listeners were not always satisfied with the way crime and policing was represented on the radio crime docudramas or with the circumscribed role suggested for citizens by the police. In working to construct the police as authoritative experts on crime and policing, these shows largely erased the concerns of ethnic and working classes. The same cannot be said for a group of programs that, drawing from the pulp fiction of the 1920s, focused on the activities of vigilante crime fighters and their attempts to secure law and order. These programs were centered around the actions of a single character who dominated the program, a figure MacDonald (1979) calls the "glamorous detective." MacDonald argues that the "glamorous" detective programs did not take themselves as seriously as the "realistic" detective shows. The primary characteristics of the glamorous detective were his vigilantism and his mobility. Glamorous detectives worked outside of the law, usually on their own, to bring criminals to justice. He writes that glamorous detectives "symbolized the direct action not affordable to most citizens" (177). As a vigilante, the detective could fall back on simplistic notions of good and evil and act unfettered by laws. MacDonald notes that "when the pressures of existence in the twentieth century produced alienation and boredom, the romantic dynamism of the Shadow provided listeners a model that was exhilarating and desirable" (177). A key part of this exhilaration was the mobility of the vigilante characters. "Free of restraint, save their inbred codes of justice and honor, these heroes alluringly embodied the desire of many to wander uninhibitedly" (177).

In considering the relationship between the glamorous detective and the official forces of law and order, MacDonald writes that they usually get along. He notes that sometimes more hostility is expressed toward the police but believes this is simply a literary residual from the pulp fiction of the 1920s from which the programs drew inspiration. MacDonald is correct in seeing these programs as a significant departure from the realistic detective story, but he does not consider the ways in which these programs expressed more ambivalence toward the official forces of law and order more confidently portrayed on the radio docudramas. In fact, it is precisely in the "literary residual" of 1920s pulp fiction that these programs created a space to articulate a more populist position toward crime and policing. These residual elements are based on the recollection of a populist sensibility founded on a distrust of the state to ensure justice and a desire for more direct citizen action.

This particular sensibility was a key element of hard-boiled detective fiction, which arose on the pages of pulp magazines such as *Black Mask* in the 1920s and, though the genre evolved, remained popular in its pulp form until the overall collapse of the pulp industry in the 1950s. But hard-boiled fiction had long ago found new homes with more literary publishing houses, in movies, and on radio and television programs. While more fully recognizable, hard-boiled characters did not begin to populate the radio airwaves until the 1940s, and especially in the postwar period, 1930s radio crime dramas drew some elements from the literature. One of the most important elements of hard-boiled detective fiction was its purposeful break with the tradition of classic detective fiction. While the significance of this break has been interpreted in different ways, the break itself is what is essential. The solitary genius of the classic detective bent on solving domestic parlor crimes was replaced by the solitary private detective, a lone voice of honor in a world awash in corruption. Cawelti (1976) suggests some important differences between the hard-boiled and classic detectives.

First, the dramatic action of the plot in hard-boiled detective stories was not motivated by the revelation of the solution but by bringing the criminal to justice. Second, rather than the gentle finger-waving of the classical detective story, the hard-boiled detective story is one of intimidation and violence, often directed at the protagonist himself. Third, unlike his moneyed classic detective predecessor, the hard-boiled detective usually comes from and lives among the lower classes on the margins of society. The class background of the hard-boiled detective has been noted by a number of scholars. May (2000) argues that the film detectives of the 1930s, such as Hammett's Nick Charles, frequently came from the working classes. Slotkin (1992) argues that the hard-boiled detective occupies a position between the propertied or managerial classes and the more radical labor organizations. Finally, Cawelti (1976) argues that city functions as an important backdrop in the broken down, hard-boiled world.

It is in these breaks with the conventions of classic detective fiction that the hard-boiled detective represented a voice of dissent against certain developments in 1920s U.S. culture. Hard-boiled fiction resists the authority of the state, a culture based on expertise, and the growth of corporate monopolies. Thus, for example, McCann (2000) argues that whereas the classic detective story focused on the individual, the hard-boiled fiction focused on the state. Hard-boiled authors witnessed the failure of classical liberalism and understood the appeal of a new form of liberalism that stressed expertise, efficiency, and modernity but also understood that this new liberalism was antidemocratic. These were the same principles embraced by second-wave police reformers. However, if reformers embraced these principles, hard-boiled detective writers expressed anxiety about this new culture of expertise and the power of the state. McCann writes that in Hammett's hand, "the detective story would no longer be about the way that social consensus was threatened and recreated, but about the way in which people could be shaped, molded and manipulated by the very institutions and beliefs that once seemed transcendent" (111). Slotkin argues that an important element of these stories is the focus on a private eye rather than on someone who works as part of an organization, such as the Pinkertons. This private eye harkens back to the days of the pre-Industrial artisan or entrepreneur. Ronald Thomas (1999) argues that the hard-boiled detective doubts those "mechanisms of truth" that the classic detective and police forces had put so much faith in: the fingerprint, lie detector, and photograph. In comparing the writings of Edgar Allan Poe and Dashiell Hammett, he argues that "if Poe's story sought to reconcile the conflicting voices of a nation made up of many nations and voices, Hammett's tale repudiates the privileges of an economic system in America in which certain voices are privileged over others" (106). Denning (1996) argues that these pulp fiction detective heroes formed the basis of the persistence of the cultural front in the Hollywood film noir films of the 1940s and 1950s.

That these glamorous detective programs were potentially subversive of the model of law and authority constructed in the docudramas was recognized by certain groups during the 1930s and 1940s. Of particular concern was the way such programs distorted understandings of the real functioning of law and order. Writing about radio crime dramas and their potential effects on children for a study conducted by Ohio State University, Howard Rowland (1942) states, "Insofar as radio crime drama deals with the theme of justice, there is gross distortion" (8). Rowland was especially critical of the focus on apprehension: "The dramas invariably end when the crooks are captured or exterminated and in the serials this results in long-drawn-out plots in which super-heroes or super-sleuths are in pursuit of elusive villains in order to maintain a perpetual state of suspense among young listeners" (8). In addition to overstimulating young listeners, the programs contributed to "misconceptions about the nature of the police and the courts in the minds of young listeners" (8). Yet it is precisely in this distortion that these programs expressed more anxiety about than support for changing definitions of policing. In their single-minded focus on pursuit of the criminal with little concern for how he or she is brought to justice, these programs both mirrored and critiqued the radio crime docudramas. First, in these pursuits, it was not the official forces of law and order that were in control but the vigilante, whose action was usually precipitated by some failure on the part of the police. In this way, programs like *The Shadow* and *The Green Hornet* revised the relationship between citizens and forms of institutional authority as represented in the radio crime docudramas where criminals and citizens, rather than the failure of institutions, were the sources of disorder. The vigilante dramas often questioned state authority. Second, in the use of sound effects and their emphasis on communication and transportation, they mirrored some elements of the radio crime docudrama. But this was a funhouse mirror, where the self-confident guarantee of apprehension was represented as menacing rather than comforting.

The Problem with Authority in The Shadow

The most famous of radio's glamorous detectives, the Shadow, began his career in the pages of *Black Mask,* the same magazine that featured many of the most successful hard-boiled writers. The Shadow was the alter identity of Lamont Cranston, a wealthy playboy who made it his mission in life to fight crime. To do this, Cranston made use of secrets he learned in "the Orient" to read criminals' minds and to render himself unseen. In many ways, the dominant anticrime message and strong morality of the programs can be seen as naturalizing new methods of crime fighting. A number of programs began with the following introduction to the premise of the show:

> The Shadow, Lamont Cranston, a man of wealth, a student of science, and a master of other people's minds devotes his life to righting wrongs, protecting the innocent and punishing the guilty. Using advanced methods that may ultimately become available to all law enforcement agencies, Cranston is known to the underworld as the Shadow, never seen, only heard, as haunting to superstitious minds as a ghost, as inevitable as a guilty conscious.

The Shadow's methods, though learned in the Orient, were not that far removed from the growing register of existing police surveillance techniques expressed through the narrative elements and sound effects increasingly familiar to radio listeners from the crime docudramas. However, *The Shadow* was far more ambivalent about the growth of police power and their claims to authority and expertise. This ambivalence was expressed in the Shadow's relationship with the police and in the program's use of many of the same sound effects and narrative techniques of the docudramas, but in this case for the creation of unease rather than assurance.

The Shadow and the Police

One of the most consistent themes in *The Shadow* is the relationship between the Shadow and the police, as represented by police Commissioner Weston. Although the Shadow supports the efforts of the police—

he believes in law and order—he often finds them incompetent. They are simply not up to the task of guaranteeing justice. Their failings are exemplified in three key ways. First, the Shadow knows things that the police do not. Despite police professionalization, the police were still limited in their thinking. The program continually cast into doubt the certainty of the police's instruments for securing identification and truth. Second, the Shadow often expressed concern that the police would cause more harm than good and, especially, that they would create more violence and death than he himself would. Finally, the Shadow's relationship with Commissioner Weston demonstrated the Shadow's greater competence and, more important, made fun of Weston's antipopulist attitude toward citizen knowledge of and involvement in crime fighting.

Most episodes feature the Shadow/Cranston stating a clear lack of faith in the official forces of law and order. Sometimes this lack of faith is in the observational and investigative powers of the police. For example, in "The Blind Beggar Dies" (1938), Cranston and Margot recognize that the blind beggar is the victim of a vicious beating rather than, as the police suspect, a hit-and-run accident. In a number of episodes, including "Death Speaks Twice" (1942), "The Precipice Called Death" (1940), and "The Return of Anatol Chevanic" (1942), the police suspect the wrong man of committing the crime, and it is the Shadow who makes sure the real criminal is brought to justice. In "The Cat That Killed" (1939), Margot is confused when Cranston will not tell the police that a suspected killer they are dealing with is a large cat or, more likely, a man who disguises himself as a cat. Cranston explains that he has an edge over the police because they have no idea what to suspect or look for and he does. Implicit is the fear that even if they did know what to look for, they would still not be able to stop the murders. In "The Ghost on the Stair" (1940), Cranston and Margot investigate a series of strange deaths at a hotel in the South. After the first death, late at night, the two poke fun at a southern sheriff who, after collecting the body, leaves the scene, stating that he will begin his investigation in the morning. Cranston notes that the criminal will have plenty of time to get out of town. It is the lack of a specific smell that proves to the Shadow that a leopard accused of a series of murders in a zoo cannot be the real culprit in "The Leopard Strikes" (1941). From his experience on an African safari, Cranston knows that leopards have a unique scent that is not present at any of the crime scenes, leading Cranston to the conclusion that a man dressed as a leopard is the actual murderer. He and Margot agree not to pass this information on to the commissioner because he would only laugh.

An episode from the program's first year expressed the tension between the Shadow and the police most clearly. In "The Death House Rescue" (1937), the Shadow tries to save a wrongly accused man from state execution. Early in the episode, Margot, concerned for his safety, tries to convince Cranston to give up his double life after gangsters threaten the Shadow. When Margot suggests that he could be more effective if he worked openly with the police, Cranston replies with a sneer, "Don't you realize Margot that my entire usefulness to the organized forces of Law and police lies in my remaining outside those forces, in remaining always, The Shadow. Would they approve my methods? Would they believe in my science?" While Margot continues to implore him to share his secrets with the police, Cranston remains firm that they are not be trusted. First, they might allow such knowledge to "fall into the hands of organized crime." But more compellingly, they simply lack the imagination to understand what the Shadow does. He tells Margot, "Why do you think I've invested countless hours to investigating electrical and chemical phenomenon? Why do you think I went to India, to Egypt, to China? What do you think I studied in London, Paris, and Vienna, except to learn the old mysteries that modern science has not yet rediscovered." These are secrets that modern professions such as "psychology" are only "beginning to understand." Cranston thus casts doubt on the ability of the police to see beyond their training. In this case, the Shadow is not simply more intelligent than the police but has devoted his life to learning scientific methods that help in solving crime. Although the police possess science, their methods are still tied to conventional ways of thinking, which hinder their ability to understand the evidence before them. In this particular episode, the doubt cast on the police is extended to the legal system.

The innocent man awaiting death in prison is Paul Gordon, who got mixed up in a crime because he was desperate for work in order to support his family and to take care of his sick child. When going to a local bar to ask the bartender if there is any work available, explaining that he has a car, his desperate pleas are overheard by a pair of bank robbers. When the bartender tells Paul he has no work available, the scheming bank robbers call him over and arrange to pay him for use of his car and driving services. They instruct him to meet them in front of a bank the next morning. Not suspecting any foul play, Paul goes to meet them, but the robbery goes wrong and the robbers end up murdering a police officer. Jumping into the car, they tell Paul to speed away, which he does, but he insists that he wants no part of their criminal activity. The two sneeringly relent and take off, leaving the murder weapon behind. The police soon catch up with Paul and, finding the gun, assume he is the murderer. In this case, even the judge is convinced: "Paul Gordon, the jury have found you guilty of robbery under arms, and statutory murder. You have been shown to have both motive and opportunity. The prosecution is part of a mass of incontrovertible evidence, and I myself have no doubt of your guilt. Therefore, in accordance with the law, I direct that you be taken from here, to the place from whence you came, and that there you be put to death in the manner stated by the law, and may god have mercy on your soul." Even the judge is willing to give greater credence to the physical fact of the evidence than to Paul's account of the happenings. Not only is Paul wrongly imprisoned, he is wrongly sentenced to death. As Thomas (1999) argues, hard-boiled detective fiction often threw doubt on the traditional reliance on physical evidence as a way to secure the truth.

Although he believes Paul's account, the Shadow knows that it will take physical evidence to exonerate him. Thus, while still questioning the police's faith in physical evidence, he nonetheless mirrors the discourse of police science by telling Paul that every criminal leaves a clue behind: there are no perfect crimes. To find out what has been overlooked, the Shadow reads Paul mind, confident that he has merely overlooked some piece of evidence, which will help set him free:

SHADOW: Now Gordon, listen to me. No crime is perfect. There's always
    somewhere a loose end. The only reason that all crimes aren't solved is
    because there is some one fact that someone knows and doesn't tell. And
    sometimes they don't tell because they don't know that they know.
PAUL: I told everything I know in court. They wouldn't believe me then.
SHADOW: Because you couldn't prove what you said. We're going after the
    proof now. You and I. . . .

PAUL: How? (somewhat startled)

SHADOW: I'm going to think with your mind.

After describing how he will read his mind "like television," the Shadow is able to see that Paul remembers one of the gang members adjusting the rearview mirror, leading the Shadow to observe, "Now we've got it. That's the loose end. That's where his thumbprint will be. Gordon, now I can save you. You've told the truth you didn't know you knew." Based on this information, the Shadow is able to force the bank robbers to find the car to remove their fingerprint evidence. Still, this tortured route to discovering the physical evidence indicates that the police cannot guarantee that their observation of any crime scene is enough to prove who really committed any crime. More than that, the program demonstrates a clear awareness of the discourse created by the radio crime docudramas, and the Shadow acknowledges the ubiquity of reform in his attempt to prove Paul's innocence in a way the police will understand. Yet, while the crime docudramas were boastful about the power of their scientific methods, the Shadow points to their fallibility.

While the Shadow peers into Paul's mind to find the evidence that might free him, Margot is left with perhaps the more difficult task of securing Commissioner Weston's cooperation in helping Paul. Like the officers on the scene and the judge, the commissioner is all too willing to put his faith in the power of the physical evidence rather than trust people:

MARGOT: But Commissioner. . . . .

COMMISSIONER: I'm sorry Ms. Lane, but I don't see what we can do.

MARGOT: But I tell you Paul Gordon is innocent. The men who committed the crime are free.

COMMISSIONER: Where did you get this information, anyway?

MARGOT: That I can't tell you.

COMMISSIONER: Ms. Lane, Paul Gordon was convicted of murder by due processes of law. Tonight he pays for his crime in the electric chair. If the police listened to every crank who came in here claiming new evidence. . . .

MARGOT: But they can't send an innocent man to the chair, they can't do it. . . .

COMMISSIONER: No, but they can send a guilty man, and according to the evidence Paul Gordon is guilty.

MARGOT: Commissioner, suppose that afterwards, when it's too late, they discover that Paul Gordon wasn't guilty after all. And suppose I testify that the police refused to listen.

COMMISSIONER: Well, what do you want me to do, if it's within reason I'll do that.

MARGOT: I want you to send some men to that garage. I want you to catch the guilty men and see that justice is done. . .

In addition to expressing his faith in evidence, Margot's threat to testify against the police points to the concerns that police had with controlling their own image and demonstrates the awareness that many had about police attempts to do so. Finally relenting, Weston sends his men to "that" garage, where Paul Gordon's car is stored. Having learned about the existence of one of the bank robber's fingerprints in the car, the Shadow visits them and manipulates them into going to the garage, knowing that Margot was working on making sure the police would also be there. Thus, as Paul is exonerated right before he is to be put to death, the guard states that he should be thankful to the governor. Paul knows better, and states that all the credit in this case belongs to the Shadow.

The entire legal system comes under attack in "The League of Terror" (1938) when a group of racketeers terrorize locale merchants and then prevent them from testifying by threatening members of their families. A frustrated Cranston tells Margot that the legal system is being compromised by violence and terror and that, as the Shadow, it is up to him to defend the poor people who cannot defend themselves. Scarier still are the events of "The Three Frightened Policemen" (1941). When Margot and Cranston return from a trip to Chicago, they ask Commissioner Weston to meet them at the airport. At the airport, a Detroit policeman, Officer Sloan, approaches them with another man in tow. Showing the commissioner a police circular, Sloan claims that he has just arrested Tony Vitor for the murder of a Chicago gangster. While Vitor denies that he is the man in the picture, Commissioner Weston uses fingerprints to successfully identify Vitor, and thinking the case is closed, puts Vitor in jail. However, Cranston is suspicious of the situation and, more specifically, of a local printer's mark on what Sloan claimed was a Chicago Police circular. Thus, as Thomas (1999) might point out, the circular and its photographic guarantee of identity are called into question. When Vitor dies in prison, the police assume it is suicide, but the Shadow knows he was murdered. When Vitor's ex-wife is murdered, her roommate Elaine is falsely arrested. Again, only the Shadow knows that she is innocent. After a series of missteps by the police, the Shadow finally ensnares the real killer of all of the victims, Officer Sloan. Sloan had lied on his application in order to be hired by the Detroit Police Department. This episode shows that the local police failed to recognize the deceit, and it actually presents an evil policeman, suggesting that the police cannot always be trusted.

In "The Phantom Voice" (1938), surveillance became the subject. In this episode, an upstanding senator is accused of taking bribes from a local gangster. During the trial, the crooked prosecuting attorney plays a film secretly made during a real meeting between the senator and the gangster. The film shows the back of the senator's head as he seemingly verbally agrees to take the bribe. Those present in the courtroom are shocked, and even the Shadow's faithful assistant, Margot Lane, is forced to confess her doubt in the senator. Cranston convinces her that, as suggested by the ancient Greeks, she believe only half of what she sees and nothing that she hears. The Shadow discovers that the lawyer had found someone to imitate the voice of the senator and had dubbed the film. In the end, the truth prevails, but surveillance is rendered problematic and even untrustworthy. Again, criminals might use the same methods being developed by the police. Scarier still, information obtained by surveillance might not even be accurate; thus, rather than punishing the criminals, it might serve as an instrument to persecute the innocent.

Another consistent concern the Shadow expresses regarding the police is his fear that the police might somehow ruin a case or create more violence than is necessary. In the "Circle of Death" (1937), a madman with a hatred of crowds starts setting off bombs in different parts of the city. When the Shadow learns about the next attack, Margot suggests they phone the police, but Cranston refuses, worried that the police might bungle the case and lead to the death of hundreds of people. In "The Ghost Building" (1941), Cranston willfully ignores the instructions of Weston and rushes into a boardroom, which has been flooded with poison gas, just in time to save the men inside. Weston's smug confidence in his ability to protect the men by posting police officers around the entrance to the room ignores the possibility that death might be delivered in other ways. When a rash of explosions cripples a navy base, Margot worries as the Shadow finally goes to face the mastermind behind the sabotage plot ("Sabotage" 1938), and she wants to call the police. The Shadow emphatically warns her to hold off on her call. He knows that the culprit possesses delicate explosives and fears that the police will bungle the job, causing unnecessary damage and death. When an "Oracle of Death" (1938) predicts that a power plant at one end of town is going to explode, Weston foolishly sends all his men there, leaving the rest of the city unprotected. Thankfully, Shrevey, a cab driver and Cranston's sometimes driver, tells him about all the activity over the radio. Recognizing a trick, Cranston has Shrevey tell the commissioner to move his men to a facility on the other side of the city, where, as the Shadow, he is able to thwart a dastardly plan to shut down the city. Even more significant about this episode is that it uses a series of "calling all cars," delivered through a filter, to enact Weston's initial orders to deploy his men. In this case, a familiar motif used by the radio docudrama as a sign of police omnipresence leads to the absolute opposite, at least until the Shadow intervenes.

The thorny relationship between Commissioner Weston and the Shadow calls into question police claims to authority. Weston is somewhat like the police of the radio crime docudramas in his extreme confidence and his distrust of those who try to meddle in police affairs. As head of a modern urban police force, Weston has every reason to feel confident in his abilities. What is striking, however, is how little Weston actually accomplishes. More often than not, it is the Shadow who must come to Weston's rescue, much to Weston's consternation. For example, a continued problem that Weston faces is criticism of his job performance. Someone is always threatening to fire him. In "Firebug" (1937), the fire chief publicly chastises Weston and his department for not finding an arsonist. Of course, it is the Shadow who finds the arsonist, but knowing that Weston's reputation is on the line, Cranston lets him take the credit.

When a narcotics ring infiltrates the city in "The Temple Bells of Neban" (1937), a prominent city official threatens Weston for allowing his son to come home with the "DT's." Cranston knows that one of the group members responsible for the narcotics smuggling is Saddi Bel Adda, who knows Cranston from his days in the Orient and thus also knows that he is the Shadow. Of course, the Shadow outwits Saddi in the end. When Weston arrives to find her dead and the rest of the ring fearful and ready to turn themselves in to the police, the Shadow sarcastically comments, "Thanks for coming Commissioner, you were very helpful." In "The Poison Death" (1938), the mayor threatens to fire Weston if he doesn't find the person responsible for a rash of poisonings throughout the city. Seeing no rhyme or reason to the pattern of poisonings, the police have been unable to identify any clues or find the source of the poisoning. Cranston figures out that the poison is being delivered through the water system, and after a specific threat leads to the death of the commissioner of the water works, Cranston tells Margot that the logic of the case is so simple and straightforward, it is little wonder the police had been unable to figure it out.

If Weston often feels aggravated at the involvement of the Shadow, his attitude toward Lamont Cranston is sometimes one of gentle condescension. Weston's feelings toward the interferences of Cranston or the Shadow are varied. Despite all the help he receives, Weston foolishly keeps insisting on his professional expertise, denigrating Cranston and the Shadow's efforts in bringing the criminal to justice. In earlier episodes, Weston is often dismissive of Cranston's efforts to help. When trying to infiltrate a prison, Cranston asks Weston for permission, claiming he is writing a book on crime and its causes. Weston expresses doubt that such an "amateur Sherlock Holmes" could possibly know anything about crime, but he relents. When Cranston, Margot, and the commissioner work together on a case, Cranston takes the lead and exhibits the most bravery ("Ring of Light" 1941). When they smell fire in a building, Cranston insists they find what someone is trying to burn before escaping. Frightened, Weston simply wants to leave. When they hear screaming, Cranston tells a nervous Weston to stay with Margot while he checks the situation, a suggestion Weston willingly follows. Thus, it is Cranston, not Weston, who leads the investigation.

In "Traffic in Death" (1938), Weston again accuses Cranston of being an amateur criminologist who would have avoided a lot of trouble if he had come to the police from the start of a case of murder in a sanitarium. In this case, the beginning is heralded by a call to Cranston from his old friend, Doctor Lee, head surgeon at the sanitarium. Lee is suspicious of a number of deaths at the hospital, which the medical examiners have attributed to hemorrhages but which he knows resulted from exsanguinations. However, when Cranston and Margot arrive, they find that Lee has been murdered. When Hardwick, a foreign laboratory worker, happens upon Cranston and Margot with the body, he calls the police and accuses them of the murder. When Weston arrives, a few quick questions assure him that the pair is innocent, but by this time, Cranston realizes that Hardwick himself is the killer and begins to follow him around as the Shadow, leaving Margot alone. When Hardwick happens upon Margot, he confesses that he has been killing the patients in order to sell their blood back to the sanitarium. Then he tells Margot he will do the same to her, and even though the Shadow is there with them, he cannot prevent Hardwick from taking her. In an exciting sequence, Hardwick prepares Margot for the draining of her blood while the Shadow searches madly for her. When he finds them, he tells Hardwick that the police are after him, leading Hardwick to commit suicide. When Weston comes upon them after hearing the shots, he is very stern in his chastisement. Then he suggests that he knew all along that Hardwick was the killer, though he offers no reasons for why he might think so. When searching for something to offer in their defense, Margot and Cranston reassure Weston by saying that at least the Shadow wasn't needed to solve this case. Weston defiantly exclaims that the Shadow would not be able to solve the case "in a month of Sundays"—he's just another amateur criminologist.

The Shadow and the Radio Medium

In his dealings with the police, the Shadow clearly countered the self-confident, boastful discourse of the radio crime docudramas. But the program worked at a different level to express a more diffuse anxiety about the growth of police power, enabled in part by police use of communications technologies. This anxiety was specifically expressed through the Shadow's ability to "cloud men's minds" and render himself invisible, functioning as the dystopic possibilities inherent in intimate authority and the dragnet effect. In its many print forms, the Shadow was a person who headed a gang, which, like the FBI, used ultrasophisticated technological instruments to catch criminals. On radio, the Shadow was likewise embodied, until Orson Welles took over the role in 1938. Welles made the Shadow invisible, exploiting the eerie, disembodied nature of radio (Maxwell 1979). As a disembodied voice, the Shadow served as a clear metaphor for radio itself, but not a comforting one. Drawing on the work of Chion, Miller (2002) argues that the Shadow functions as an acousmetre, "a kind of voice-character specific to cinema that in most instances . . . derives mysterious powers from being heard and not seen" (221). As Chion (1999) elaborates, radio itself may be defined as acousmatic, that is, as composed of sounds that have no visual reference. Chion argues that the acousmetre has four important powers: "the ability to be everywhere, to see all, to know all, and to have complete power. In other words: ubiquity, panopticism, omniscience, and omnipotence." Miller (2002) argues that these qualities allow us to understand

> that when Lamont Cranston becomes the Shadow, he also becomes an acousmetre. The Shadow sees all, he is omniscient, and can enlist this omniscience in action (solving the crime). As a show broadcast on radio, *The Shadow* is from the outset operating in an acousmatic medium. The Shadow becomes acousmetre when his voice is responded to by all characters with a panic derived from their inability to see the source of the voice but their knowing that it is near, that it has impact. The Shadow wears a sonic mask that grants him secret power—one that is only effective if the correlation between The Shadow and Lamont Cranston remains a secret. (51)

These characteristics echo the representation of police radio in the radio crime docudramas in the creation of the dragnet effect and in the power of address achieved through making authority intimate.[5] But as the technological symbol of a generalized force rather than of an individual voice, the police radio, though acousmatic, is not quite an acousmetre. Even if the specific voice speaking through the police radio is unidentified, both home audiences and characters in the dramas know that it comes from the body of a police officer.

In the figure of the Shadow, the power of the police radio is condensed onto an individual who already elides the categories of good and evil by operating in both worlds. In this way, the invisibility of the Shadow as acousmetre was associated with a general "creepiness," and it was through this register that *The Shadow* called into question the growth of police power in two important ways. First, the program drew on the sense of radio's electronic presence as a blanketing omnipresence (Sconce 2000) and suggested that this might serve as a source of subjugation rather than connection and community. The Shadow's omnipresence invoked fear and horror as much as reassurance in the radio network, including its use by police. Second, the program expressed a longing for the prenetwork days of radio in its celebration of a decentralized person-to-person mode of communication across distances.

As an omnipresent force from which no criminal could escape, the Shadow's powers of invisibility and mind reading, accompanied by his free-roaming mobility, directly mirrored the dragnet effect discussed in chapter 4. This similarity extended into the mode of its aural representation. As police communications were simulated through the use of a filter device, so was the voice of the Shadow. While Cranston's voice was conveyed in a normal register, as soon he shifted into the character of his alter ego, the Shadow, his voice was altered through a filter, giving it a tinny, distant quality. Eric Barnouw (1939), in his book on radio writing, praised the program for its innovative use of the filter device. He noted that whereas the filter was frequently used "naturalistically" to simulate communications technologies, including the police radio, it could by used "supernaturalistically" to represent "ghosts, goblins, invisible people, inner voices, God" (103). These supernaturalistic representations were thus associated with explicitly creepy forms of presence, precisely those presences that were associated with radio in its early years (Douglas 1999; Peters 1999; Sconce 2000). In the case of the Shadow, his invisible presence was much like the representation of police omnipresence created by the dragnet effect. However, unlike the self-confident representation of the dragnet in the radio crime docudramas, the Shadow's omnipresence was often eerie and frightening, even for the innocent.

In this way, *The Shadow* stood for the development of the specific form of procedural, technological police power of the Depression. The invisibility of the Shadow, like the invisibility of radio, suggested a panacoustic power. However, the effect was often unsettling rather than reassuring. For example, as chapter 4 discussed, a key component of the dragnet effect was criminal claustrophobia. In *The Shadow*, this device is used to eerie effect as the Shadow becomes the acousmetre, a disembodied voice that suddenly speaks to criminals, some of whom are driven to the point of madness by the Shadow's constant berating. In "Murder on Approval" (1938), the Shadow menaces not the masterminds behind the plan to kill the U.S. Army with a deadly disease but their helpless coconspirator, Dr. Harris, who has discovered that his own nephew has been infected. As the Shadow speaks to him, Dr. Harris begins to rant madly, believing he is going insane. When the Shadow later approaches Dr. Harris in a laboratory, the doctor drops a medical flask and begins to cry out in mad desperation when the Shadow finally speaks. In "Aboard the Steamship Amazonia" (1938), the Shadow drives a servant to madness. In "Death under the Chapel" (1938), the Shadow speaks to a young Mr. Bragg, who has been forced into a murderous plan by a former professor of Lamont Cranston. Bragg quickly crumbles under the power of the Shadow. What is significant in these cases is that it is not the criminal mastermind the Shadow terrorizes, but the poor helpless sap of a middleman, sometimes in desperate circumstances— someone with whom the audience might identify.

In these instances, the Shadow's ability to be everywhere, unseen, is made even more invasive by his ability to read minds. Sconce (2000) argues that by the 1930s, the dominant mode of the electronic presence of radio became the network, a blanketing presence that spread everywhere, even into the private spaces of the home. While the network offered a solution to what some thought was the etheric chaos of the 1920s, it also threatened to force listeners to become part of a larger community of which they wanted no part. Particularly threatening was radio's ability to instantly bring frightening and traumatic events into the home. In this way, Sconce argues, the network as a mode of presence became associated with subjugation. He interprets the *War of the Worlds* broadcast as a sign of this fear, asserting that the broadcast successfully mimicked the conventions developed by the network for delivering traumatic events. The dramatization of the invasion of the world was an event that, like so much of what was conveyed through the radio set, was simply beyond the control of listeners— there was no meaningful way to intervene. Even the resolution to the invasion was beyond human control: the alien creatures were conquered not by humans but by germs. While radio crime docudramas attempted to ease such possible threats to the disruption of the public–private divide by rendering authority intimate, *The Shadow* exploited such threats as a key source of its central character's unique power. It is probably not a coincidence that

Orson Welles was the voice in that broadcast as well as the first voice of the invisible Shadow. Welles was known for his innovative work in radio, which Denning (1996) links to his antifascist politics. In fact, Denning argues that when Welles arrived in Hollywood in 1939, "he was immediately drawn to the anti-fascist thriller; after all, he was a veteran of pulp radio, having played Lamont Cranston . . . the Shadow" (378). Thus, in the Shadow's ability to read minds, this blanketing web extends into the most private thoughts, a power that, when used to drive people insane, could seem entirely unsettling. While the representational strategies of *The Shadow* might not have expressed any direct political intent by those involved in its production, it is clear that the uneasiness promoted by this disembodied presence was inflected with a more strongly leftist orientation than the radio crime docudramas ever aspired to.

In suggesting that such a blanketing network was as much of a threat as a comfort, it is not a surprise that the program also spoke to a longing to decentralize the transmission of communication by breaking away from the omniscient presence of the network. There was no more potent symbol of this intent than the Shadow's frequent use of his shortwave radio to call Margot Lane. Harkening back to the days of the amateur, when radio was still thought of as a medium of point-to-point communication, the Shadow, except in rare instances, uses his radio only to call Margot. The radio is also no longer a feminized domestic device, fixed inside a decorated cabinet in the living room, but a mobile device, returned to it roots in masculinity, that allows the two to communicate in various circumstances. Like police radio, it is mobile, and the Shadow mimics the call of the radio crime docudramas, "calling all cars," when he intones, "Calling Margot Lane, come in Margot." But whereas the police radio system is firmly anchored in the dispatch room of headquarters, the Shadow's use of the radio is entirely mobile.

The Shadow completely decentered the radio. Predicting the use of the cell phone, the Shadow uses the radio in a way completely unchained from any sort of network, usually to advise Margot to call the police. In "Death under the Chapel" (1938), he has her call the police to avert a mad bomber. In "Sabotage" (1938), the Shadow calls Margot on the radio and asks her to stand by as he pursues a man who is bombing ships at a navy base. While the communication in these cases tends to be one way, from the Shadow to Margot, in comparison to the existing uses of radio, the Shadow's use was startlingly decentralized and personal. While the radio announcers felt themselves addressing a mass of faceless listeners, the Shadow knew whom he was addressing, and Margot knew precisely who was addressing her. If Lamont Cranston "appeared" as a voice without a body to all whom he encountered as the Shadow, Margot Lane always knew the body behind the voice. For these characters, use of the radio guaranteed connection despite the fact that both were mobile.

In adapting the radio for police use, reformers drew on the understanding of radio as a blanketing presence in order to suggest that through the use of radio they could control the chaotic mobility of the criminal population. The radio docudramas used this sense of presence in the creation of the dragnet effect, a positive presence meant only to search out the guilty while leaving the innocent untouched. *The Shadow,* however, played on existing anxieties about this blanketing presence as one that seemed to offer no hope for privacy or escape from the larger, often traumatic, world of the public. This anxiety was expressed in two contradictory yet equally important ways. First, as Loviglio (1999) argues, the Shadow, through his expert mastery over and use of modern means of communication, functioned like an expert capable of singlehandedly controlling disorder. In this sense, his use of communication technologies mirrored that of the police. The Shadow's omnipresence and power to penetrate even the boundaries of personal thought might be considered a positive development in the same way police radio was constructed. However, the Shadow's disembodied omnipresence is always rendered sinister by the use of sound effects that suggest unease more than comfort. The second way the program suggested unease with the growing power of the police was through the Shadow's own use of communications technologies in a way that was removed from any centralizing power, such as commercial broadcast networks, the police, or the federal government. Thus, in a contradictory manner, the Shadow sometimes invoked the omnipresent power of the radio network and at other times countered the centralized power of network by using communication unchained from any such network. However, even when invoking the power of the network, the sinister register of the Shadow's presence suggested unease more often than comfort with his and, by extension, the radio network's omnipresence.

While the radio crime docudramas waxed boastful and reassuring about their power and expertise, *The Shadow* continually called these claims into question. As a private citizen, Cranston refused to defer to police claims to authority and instead acted on his own to bring criminals to justice. In this way, Cranston adopts a potentially populist attitude toward crime and policing. Loviglio (1999, 2005) argues that the Shadow's expert knowledge and distrust of the public mark him as a technocrat, someone who embraces what McCann (2000) calls liberal realist thinking. Reflecting Walter Lippmann's loss of faith in the ability of the public to make sense of a complicated world in an era of mass communication, Loviglio argues that *The Shadow* often dramatized publics too easily manipulated. In many ways, this attitude toward the public is similar to the one expressed in the radio crime docudrama. However, *The Shadow* plays with the logic of the police-centered dramas. While programs like *Gang Busters* blamed the press and culture industries for manipulating the public into valorizing criminality at the expense of the police, in calling into question and playing with the conventions of the docudrama, *The Shadow* questions the ways the state increasingly manipulates public opinion. Instead, in acting alone rather than as part of an organization, and by continually questioning the authority of the police, including their methods for securing the truth, and of the state, *The Shadow* created a counterdiscourse to that of the radio crime docudramas. The discourse of the program, in its lack of faith in democracy in the age of mass media, does not quite embrace the cultural front populism Welles would later be associated with. But in figuring a citizen at its center, the program can be read as potentially critiquing police claims to authority.

The Antistate Discourses of The Green Hornet

If the Shadow was not exactly a populist hero, the Green Hornet emerged as more of one, only this time more firmly to the right. Created by Fran Striker for WXYZ in Detroit, *The Green Hornet* resulted from the desire of station manager George Trendle to create a program that would educate young listeners on the necessity of vigilance against political corruption (Russo 2001; Osgood 1981). Like the Shadow, the Green Hornet was an alter ego, in this case of Britt Reid, a newspaper publisher. For Trendle, the decision to make Reid a publisher allowed the character to have knowledge of political corruption (Osgood 1981). Reid was usually led to cases he examined through leads discovered by himself or other reporters. When fighting crime, he donned the outfit of his alternate persona, the Green Hornet, and sped off in his special car, Black Beauty, all with the help of his loyal Japanese valet and master scientist, Kato.[6] While Cranston often worked to make sure that the Shadow was recognized as a crime fighter rather than criminal, Reid did not share the same concern about his alter ego and was willing, in the name of fighting corruption, to let the Green Hornet be a suspect in certain crimes.

Alexander Russo (2001) persuasively argues that throughout the 1930s, the program primarily revolved around incidences of political corruption. Even more than the police in *The Shadow*, the police in *The Green Hornet* were incapable of solving these political crimes:

> *The Green Hornet*'s focus on civic corruption and criminality is an example of the ways in which social debates around the state's authority were being enacted in popular culture. At the core of debates around New Deal programs were assumptions about the proper extent of federal regulatory authority and how a state should function. Questions about a state's ability to perform properly were connected to questions about its right to regulate. (261)

By repeatedly representing civic institutions as corrupt, the program questioned the authority of the state to regulate the economy and business. However, produced in Detroit and dramatizing urban political and police corruption, the program spoke as much to the centralization of urban governments as to the growth of the New Deal State. The program continually suggested that individual action based on individual responsibility, rather than government action and collective responsibility, were the key to solving social ills. Russo argues that the character of Britt Reid "provided an example of how the failure of public institutions made operating outside of legal boundaries necessary" (263).

Even a cursory listening to *The Green Hornet* supports this claim. The very titles of the programs, such as "The Political Racket" (1938) and "The Parking Lot Racket" (1939) indicate the program's overwhelming emphasis on corruption. For example, "The Political Racket" (1938) tells of the Green

Hornet's attempts to bring to justice crooked ward boss Joe Desmond, who uses his position to take advantage of arriving immigrants by promising them citizenship papers for money but delivering insurance policies instead. After a high-speed chase, in which the police are briefly hunted by Desmond rather than vice versa, a newly arrived immigrant in police custody winds up murdered by Desmond. Simulated radio and newspaper reports bemoan the lack of police competence in dealing with these organized criminals, and the Green Hornet goes to work to expose Desmond and bring him to justice for his corrupt practices. The Green Hornet rarely used violence as a means to secure justice, and in this case, he tricks Desmond's henchman into testifying against him so that Desmond is ultimately forced to surrender himself. In "The Smuggler Signs His Name" (1939), a diplomat smuggles linens into the country under the guise of diplomatic immunity and conspires with the daughter of a large department store owner to get the items onto the shelves for sale to unsuspecting customers. The case is brought to Reid's attention by a reporter who is tipped off by a customs agent fed up with the rampant corruption of the customs office. In "The Parking Lot Racket" (1939), the police are helpless in the face of a particularly vicious group of racketeers who use escalating violence to secure payments from parking lot attendants from across the city. It is up to the Green Hornet to bring this group to justice.

In each of these episodes, the state is engaged in corrupt practices or is incapable of dealing with the rampant corruption that threatens the security and well-being of the city's inhabitants. The relationship between the politicians and criminals was rarely discussed on radio crime docudramas but was a theme aggressively pursued in the making and marketing of *The Green Hornet.* Throughout its history, the program aired alternatively on the Mutual Network and NBC and was sold to individual radio stations. In publicity material for transcription sales from 1940, the King-Trendle company attempted to sell *The Green Hornet* as an "adult-oriented" program. An advertisement for the program describes it as a "half hour drama portraying the adventures of a newspaper-man's singlehanded fight against 'law breakers within the law.' Modern and militant in plot; and sequences that develop comedy, satire, and seriousness, played by WXYZ's professional radio artists" (1940).[7] Another description of the program notes that through his own aggressive reporters and his friendship with the local FBI agency-in-charge, Britt Reid becomes familiar with crime, political lobbying and racketeering, the industrial labor disputes, and the "under-Federal-observation" characters. Thus, his sources provide him with a voluminous store-house of all kinds of information, much of which is not admissible in the liberal American courts.[8]

These specific references to various forms of political corruption stand in pointed opposition to the kinds of crime usually represented by the radio crime docudramas. However, the critique of the "liberal" courts and invocation of militancy indicate the program's clear shift to a more conservative populist discourse based more fully on distrust of the state. The program consistently reminds listeners that it is only through the extralegal efforts of a figure such as the Green Hornet that such corruption can be stopped. The state and the police cannot be trusted to stop it.

While *The Green Hornet* was more explicit in its exploration of corruption, it shared with *The Shadow* a resistance to the claims of the radio crime docudramas. Their final challenge is found in the programs' representation of ethnicity. While the radio crime docudramas worked to effectively deethnicize the police, by associating their heroes with colors and darkness, *The Green Hornet* and *The Shadow* had the effect of marking their white, upper-middle-class protagonists as embracing nonwhite identities. Both kinds of programs readily associated criminality with ethnicity and outsiders, such as the strong orientalist discourse of *The Shadow* (Loviglio 2005); the vigilante dramas more readily acknowledged that ethnic immigrants and members of the working class were often victims of crime. Many criminals prey on immigrants unfamiliar with the norms of U.S. culture. *The Shadow* especially represented ethnic and working-class criminals as forced by desperation into a life of crime. While full of stereotypes, when compared to the radio crime docudramas, *The Shadow* at least acknowledged that the relationship between working-class, immigrant, and ethnic populations was tied to broader social circumstances. Moreover, in the references to color in the names of their alter egos, their interaction with people and ideas from the Orient, and close ties to the underworld, neither the Green Hornet nor the Shadow occupied the space of whiteness that the radio docudrama policeman did.

CONCLUSION

This chapter explored public resistance to the boastful, self-confident claims to authority produced by the radio crime docudramas and, by inference, the model of policing they constructed. Sometimes, the radio crime dramas themselves resisted their usual narrative formulas to offer morally ambiguous constructions of policing and criminality. More significant were the number of people who resisted specific elements of the programs. Police officers resisted the programs' claims to authority by refusing to participate in their dramatizations. Criminals resisted the narrow and formulaic characterizations of themselves. Citizens resisted the programs' turning their local concerns into narratives for national entertainment. As the growing power of the police force was met with resistance, so was the discourse of the radio crime docudrama, which supported and helped construct the police as professional experts.

Radio also produced a set of counterdiscourses that, if not exactly resisting, nonetheless called into question the model of policing developed by the radio crime docudrama. In these dramas, despite all their claims to expertise and authority, the police could not be trusted to maintain order in an increasingly complex world. In *The Shadow*, the devices used to assure police command and control over mobile criminality became devices that were sinister and overly invasive. As much as the Shadow was a law enforcer, his use of communications technology was practically criminal. He was freely mobile, and he used the radio as a method of point-to-point communication, effectively severing it from any centralized control. While the Shadow's expertise and intelligence seemed a sign of his technocratic mastery over modern means of communication, his rejection of the network designed to control etheric chaos indicated his understanding that chaos was the condition of modern life.

By throwing the self-confident discourse of the radio crime docudramas into doubt, vigilante dramas suggested a view of crime fighting that refused to accept the police claims of professional authority. While police reform sought to secure the right of police forces to define the meaning of policing and criminality outside of public interference through their much-vaunted efforts at depoliticization, the vigilante dramas insisted that politics would always play a role. Whether at the city, state, or federal level, authority could not fully be trusted. At the same time that they called the authority of the state into question, these vigilante dramas shared with the radio crime docudramas a mistrust of the public. This distrust muted their critique and rendered these vigilante tales less consistent in their representations. Their faith in the authority of the state allowed the creators of the radio crime docudramas to be remarkably consistent in their avocation of a progressive model of policing and in their boasts of police expertise and authority. They possessed and advocated a coherent political philosophy that, once turned into dramatic formulas, could be infinitely reproduced. Drawing on a less coherent political and cultural philosophy, the vigilante dramas were often more ambiguous, at once supporting and casting doubt on Progressive reforms, depending on how fully attached the creators were to a cultural front populist politics or to the more conservative populist discourse of the right. Thus, while *The Shadow* and *The Green Hornet* supported the idea of law and order, they consistently questioned the ability of the police to guarantee it.

Hearing the Echoes

Through the radio the comprehensive assistance of all law-abiding citizens
can be coordinated and directed in augmentation of the activities of the
enforcement agencies. Through the radio the public can be informed of the
effective, exhaustive and scientific approach which organized authority is
making to the solution of the crime problem. Through the radio a respect for
law and order, a respect for organized authority, a respect for the courts and
judicial procedure, and a respect for heroes of peace, who have sacrificed so
much in the service of security, can be developed, not only in our enfranchised
citizenry, but also in our very important youth, to whom we must pass the
burden of the future and of whom so many have unfortunately succumbed to
the lure of crime, vice and depredation.

—COLONEL NORMAN SCHWARZKOPF, 1937

In this remarkable statement, Colonel H. Norman Schwarzkopf, head of
New Jersey State Militia and host of *Gang Busters,* made clear the lofty ex-
pectation that radio might somehow revolutionize the relationship between
police and citizens.[1] His faith in the ability of radio to transform this relationship seems at once hopelessly naïve and eerily prescient. In his hope
that radio might foster "a respect for law and order" among the "enfranchised citizenry" and those "youth" who so many feared had easily "succumbed to the lure of crime," Schwarzkopf certainly seems naïve. Yet,
replace the word *radio* with *telecommunications* in additional statements,
such as his hope that "through the radio, intelligence can be brought to all
our people as to who the criminals are, their method of operation, their
description, whereabouts, probable field of other endeavor, and their ren-
dezvous and havens of security," and he might just as well be talking about
any of the other "wars" in the more than seventy years since this statement
was recorded. If radio was heralded as a way to achieve social control during the Depression, new technologies today are adapted to and heralded as

ways to achieve control in the war on drugs or the war on terror. This statement does not seem that far removed from a pronouncement by any state
police force or the Department of Homeland Security.

Schwarzkopf makes clear what police saw as the advantages of radio in
marshaling public support for crime fighting. Police reformers broadcast
this sentiment across the nation as they began to envision the possibility
of radio as a way to reach citizens directly. While radio as a technology
capable of two-way and broadcast communication offered a technical solution to the problem of criminal mobility, as a commercialized broadcast
medium it offered more. Commercial broadcasting was organized around
a model of centralized transmission and privatized reception that relied
on the diffusion of radio sets into American homes. In cooperating with
the makers of commercial entertainment programs, police found a way to
reach citizens in the private spaces of their homes. As populations became
more dispersed and transportation technologies facilitated greater mobility,
and as police forces replaced the more personal foot patrol with the impersonal automobile patrol, the reach of radio became increasingly important.
Through police radio broadcasts and commercial entertainment broadcasts
structured around the authority of the police, police worked to forge a
more direct link between themselves and the citizens they served. This was
especially important, as at the same time, the discourse of police professionalization demanded the removal of citizen input through the trope of
depoliticization.

Police professionalism was rooted in the fetishization of scientific methods
and organizational perfection that promised to arrest forms of social and
physical mobility. Commenting on police efforts some thirty years after the
beginning of the second wave of police reform, sociologists Bordua and
Reiss (1966) argue that "bureaucratization can be regarded as an organizational technique whereby civic pressures are neutralized from the stand-
point of the governing regime" (68). Using the developed terminology of
sociology of the time, they point to the realization of the professional reform
movement's goal of removing policing from the realm of politics: "In the
development of the modern police, bureaucratization has been a major
device to commit members to the occupational community, and to its
norms of subordination and service to a degree where these commitments
take precedence over extra-occupational ones to family and community"

(68). Like other professional groups in society, including those related to health and the law, police reformers strove to build a hierarchical, centralized bureaucracy with a structure in place to produce and guarantee professional knowledge. This was an important method to secure power and protection against interference from "politics," defined as interference from those outside of the profession. It is through the expressive and structural elements of the radio crime docudrama that this idealized fantasy of police bureaucratic efficiency began to take hold in the imagination of radio listeners. By the 1960s, this model of policing came under attack, pressured from both above and below as those in the legal system and those victimized by this rationalized system began to question and push against the power of the police.

Is it any wonder that when the archetypical docudrama *Gang Busters* was replayed in the 1960s, it no longer made sense? Razlogova (2006) notes that these re-airings ran into a great deal of resistance from listeners who found it overbearingly pro-police. At the historical moment that the assumptions of the second wave of the police reform movement came under increasing scrutiny, the idealized imaginary police seemed more regressive than Progressive. By this period, the populist meanings that Depression-era audiences could attach to the representations of criminality in the program simply did not register with audiences separated from this moment by thirty or more years. This is significant because, as has been argued, these programs dealt with historically specific conceptions of crime and policing and were products of the Depression era. Nevertheless, a brief look at any television schedule filled with police dramas tells us that their enduring legacy is found in the police-centered narratives that view all other events and characters in these stories from the police perspective.

Like all historical studies, this is an interested one. This project has insisted that a focus on a narrow set of programs created to meet the complex requirements of a single medium and linked to a specific set of material, historical practices would lead to a better understanding of radio's role in the social changes of the Depression era. Yet many aspects of the relationships forged during this period continue to echo today. First is the enduring relationship between broadcasting and policing that is based on the needs of both institutions. Second, aspects of the crime dramas that were shaped by the uniqueness of radio as a communication medium continue to shape the ways crime stories are told and our cultural discourses about technology and policing. Finally, the confluence of radio's entertainment function and social control function continue to inform our most mundane, quotidian interactions with communication technologies.

BROADCASTING AND POLICING

This project emphasizes the need to expand our knowledge of radio's past by examining one of the overlooked genres of radio's golden age. Rather than examine these programs in relation to other forms of radio programming or in relation to broader discourses surrounding mass culture, this project considers the relationship between those dramas based on real-life police cases and a significant historical moment in the development of policing. Its focus on micropolitics illuminates key aspects of the programs, particularly the way the programs worked to construct and enhance the authority of the police as modern professionals. In the process, an enduring relationship between policing and broadcasting was created. In examining how police reformers and radio broadcasters forged a relationship between their respective institutions, this project points to the ways this period established important precedents for the representation of police on television. This work is significant because these programs are too often overlooked. While many acknowledge *Dragnet* as an early exemplar of the police-centered drama, often called the police procedural, they still attribute its unique style to the forms of film realism established by police photographers and the makers of 1940s film noir.

For example, when Malvin Wald passed away in March 2008, news stories blithely repeated his assertion that his 1948 screenplay for *The Naked City* represented the first pro-police narrative to enter the popular lexicon. The film is often heralded as an important influence on *Dragnet*. Yet, what do we make of Pat Weaver, who was involved in producing the radio version of *Dragnet*, having begun his career on the regionally produced *Calling All Cars*? More significantly, what do we make of the claims that *Dragnet* was unique in seeking the cooperation of the Los Angeles Police Department, when *Calling All Cars* routinely featured infamous Chief James Davis as host and dramatized solved cases from that department? These questions are not meant to belittle the significance or uniqueness of *Dragnet*, noir

films like *The Naked City,* or the post–World War II literary police procedural but to assert that placing professional police authority at the center
of narratives about crime and policing has significant roots in Depression-
era radio.

While not an origin story of crime stories in general, or even of police
stories more specifically, this project nonetheless argues that broadcasting offered a new cultural space that consistently privileged the police
as authorities on matters of crime and policing. This relationship continued throughout what scholars now call the network era of television. The
most obvious example is the cooperation between the Los Angeles Police
Department and the producers of *Dragnet.* Police expertise provided broadcasters with a way to justify potentially questionable representations, as Todd
Gitlin (1983) notes in his examination of the breakthrough 1980s police
drama *Hill Street Blues.* Popular books and press coverage celebrate the science of *CSI.* It is significant that the programs that would finally decenter
the police point of view would be broadcast on cable rather than the over-
the-air broadcast networks. Not bound by the same public-interest regulatory apparatus as broadcasters, cable outlets like HBO could revel in the
exploits of a modern mob family, *The Sopranos.* Basic cable outlet F/X
could unfold the story of an increasingly unstable rogue cop in *The Shield.*
Broadcast outlets, however, have remained a key space for forwarding a
police-centered view of social disorder. From the *Law and Order* and *CSI*
franchises to the reality programs *COPS* and *America's Most Wanted,* television continues to serve as a central site for negotiating the ever-changing
meaning of policing.

As this project argues, such representations were not simply part of
entertainment culture but often became part of the self-image of police
forces. Police forces frequently confronted the public-interest requirements
of U.S. broadcasting both in terms of justifying their own access to the airwaves and negotiating the ways commercial broadcasters would tell their
stories. In the process, they began to sharpen their own self-definition as
public servants whose goal was to protect citizens from crime and disorder.
The emergence of the concept of public-image management impacted the
desire of second-wave police reformers to more carefully control and shape
messages about policing. These messages were frequently pitched in terms
of public service, a tactic that suited the needs of police officials around the

The public safety... FIRST!

GOOD STREET LIGHTING

RELIABLE FIRE ALARM SYSTEMS

POLICE RADIO

EFFICIENT TRAFFIC CONTROL

THE tremendous losses ;both in life and property suffered from traffic accidents, crime and fire are arousing the public. They are demanding effective, *modernized* protection...electrical protection. Good street lighting, for example. It combats crime...accidents. Boosts business... Reliable and adequate fire alarm equipment...Police radio to speed up the long arm of the law...Efficient traffic control to reduce costly and dangerous traffic congestion...The logical source for this equipment is Graybar. Graybar offers not only a complete line of equipment, but also expert and experienced advice on how to use it most effectively. Write for information.

GraybaR

OFFICES IN 79 PRINCIPAL CITIES
EXECUTIVE OFFICES: GRAYBAR BLDG., N.Y.

During December we hope you will remember to mention THE AMERICAN CITY

Police technologies such as radio were considered a key part of the police mission to provide public service to the citizens they served. Advertisement in *American City* 51 (December 1936).

nation attempting to defend themselves against criticism and of commercial broadcasters who could justify their most brazen representations of criminal exploits through the claim that they were serving the public interest. The focus on the professional authority of the police is not the only part of Depression-era programming that echoed in the following years. In these programs, we see the construction of a dominant white identity that many scholars see as being specific to 1950s American suburban culture. Police reform itself was centered on deethnicizing the police corps and breaking the relationship between police and ethnic-based ward politics. This meant that police had vested interest in replacing ethnic and local community loyalties with loyalties to a profession. Radio played a key role in articulating this identity. As much as radio reveled in ethnic characterizations, the radio crime dramas about policing worked to downplay ethnicity in favor of professional and technical authority as expressed in speech. This mode of speaking, in which many references to ethnic or working-class culture were erased, indicates that the articulation of a white middle-class identity is not solely a product of post–World War II suburbanization and consumerism but is rooted in the Depression era. Additionally, these representations of white, middle-class, professional masculinity were clear harbingers of Whyte's (1956) "organization man."

Finally, in considering the relationship between radio and the concrete set of historical discourses and practices of policing, this project draws attention to the complicated relationship between radio and national and local forms of identification. Most scholarship on golden age radio focuses on the relationship between broadcasting and the articulation of a national identity. While David Hendy (2008) insists that recent scholarship on radio reveals "heterogeneity" and "hybridity" (132) as the intrinsic features of the medium, a vast majority of the scholarship on 1930s and 1940s radio considers it primarily as a *national* medium. The focus on the highly localized practice of policing demonstrated that even national radio programming could play a role in how people saw themselves tied to a particular locality. Radio was involved not only in the negotiation and expression of mass culture and politics but also in the negotiation of local cultures and micropolitics. One of the most important aspects of the development of policing in the United States has been its highly fragmented and localized organization. While the FBI attempted to nationalize crime fighting, the most significant developments in policing occurred at the municipal, county, and state levels. During the Depression era, stories about these various forms of local authority predominated in syndication, regional networks, and national networks. Rather than thinking of local and national as oppositional categories in radio, this project demonstrated that even national shows could be a source for thinking about local relationships and local change. This is a crucial observation to make at a time of tremendous shifts in the organization of mass media in the United States, including the breakdown of the power of the national broadcast networks, the growing use of the Internet, and the increasing fragmentation of media audiences. While it is easy to see how current media forms contribute to micropolitics, we all too easily overlook the ways that mass broadcasting also did.

THE RADIO MEDIUM

This project offers a sustained consideration of radio as a unique communicative space where the conventions of radio "realisms" shaped by the technological and industrial organization of commercial radio intersected with police reform discourses to emphasize specific elements of that discourse. First, this project examines the unique technical and institutional features of radio that shaped the stories it told, including its aurality and commercial function. Radio was the only medium that conveyed information through sound alone. Second, the project argues for the importance of understanding radio's organizational structure and the metaphors of its presence. Both played important roles in other uses of radio technology and in the form and content of radio crime docudramas. This is a question, then, about the role radio played in mediating its own influence on the social changes of the Depression. More simply put, how does a medium represent itself, and what are the meanings of those representations?

That radio communicates through sound alone is central to understanding radio programming, but it has received little attention from radio scholars. The one area that has been addressed is the vocal performance of race and class. While a growing number of scholars have explored the way that the voices were used to incessantly mark ethnic and racial differences, little has been done to explore the way vocal performances sometimes functioned to erase ethnicity by an increasing reliance on standard vocal performance styles that symbolized specific character types rather than ethnicity. Greater attention must be paid not only to radio voices but also to sound effects. Despite their constant and important presence in radio programming, they have received virtually no critical consideration. Yet sound effects played a central role in creating a set of ideological effects that could both support and call into question developments in policing. Those working in the radio industry during the 1930s and 1940s recognized the important role of sound effects in creating meaning and worked hard to develop a set of standardized uses and methods for the creation of such effects. The ability of such effects to create meanings beyond the narrative content should not be underestimated.

Through the simulations of police communication technologies, especially the radio, radio crime docudramas created the dragnet effect. The dragnet effect involved placing the listener directly in the center of the representation of the police deployment of their forces for criminal apprehension. Unbound by the need for visual, radio could plausibly representing swift-moving action across great gaps in time and space and was thus able to construct the police as an omnipresent force blanketing the entire nation. Through the use of sound effects that simulated radio and other communications technology, the programs created an additional layer of meaning beyond the bounds of the strict narrative content that created this ideological effect. In turn, beyond the level of specific narrative critique, the same sound effects could be used in a different register to create more subtle critiques of the police paradigm of omnipresence, as was the case in *The Shadow.*

It is important to think about sound in an era when the visual occupies so much scholarly attention. A growing number of scholars (e.g., Sterne 2003; Thompson 2002) have begun to assert the significance of sound as central to our experience of modernity. For many, sound studies is emerging as an academic field of interest in its own right (Hilmes 2008). This new interest represents a significant intervention in the ways we think about media. For example, when we think of representation of the police today, it is impossible to do so without some sort of visual image: the gritty cinema verite technique used by programs such as *Law and Order, NYPD Blue,* and *COPS;* the heightened visual effects used in forensic-based programs such those in the *CSI* franchise. The world of the crime drama is clearly a visual one. In many ways, the visual style of these dramas, with their urban backdrops and moody lighting, owe a debt to the film noir of the 1940s and '50s. However, stories of crime have been equally marked by their styles of speech and strong sound design features. From the hard-boiled speech of film noir detectives to the specialized language of television police officers, ways of speaking have played an important role in constructing our image of police and criminals. Equally important to ways of speaking is the creation of strong sound design features that, as much as visual indicators, signify policing. For example how different would our experience of *CSI* be without the graphic sound effects that punctuate the animated interior shots of bodies? How do such effects contribute to the idea of science as penetrative of the most intimate spaces of the human body? How dull would lab scenes be without the pulsing music that heightens the dramatic tension and excitement of otherwise routine scientific work? Sound effects and music continue to be important elements to frame representations of authority.

An equally important part of radio communication is the link between radio's technological and industrial form and programming. In the case of police radio, the radio crime docudramas represented radio as a positive social force whose ability to cross the line between public and private could only lead to an increase in the ability of the police to successfully apprehend criminals. Yet, by extension, these representations of radio also worked to allay more diffuse anxieties about radio's ability to blur social boundaries. In this sense, the content of radio drew on its cultural form, the network. Although it began as a medium of point-to-point communication, over the course of the 1920s, radio solidified into a broadcast medium of centralized transmission and private reception. These centralized networks combined with radio's penetration into the private sphere of the home led to the understanding of radio as a blanketing presence, penetrating everywhere. Representations of police radio, which was provisional in its organization, drew on this understanding of radio as a national presence to suggest that, like the commercial radio systems, the police radio system was omnipresent. These metaphors were central to understanding the meaning of police power and cause us to think about the ways current police policies are shaped as much by metaphors as by technical realities.

COMMUNICATION AS SOCIAL CONTROL

Finally, in the dragnet effect, we see more clearly how radio's use as an entertainment medium dovetailed with its use as a medium of social control. Police found in radio a way to link the management of physical and social mobility to the management of public perceptions of policing. Electronic communication media have always been linked to forms of control, yet in the case of police and radio, we see an important interrelationship being built between the explicit use of technology for commercial entertainment and its use as a device that allows the state control over mobile populations. The significance of this linkage cannot be underestimated. It is not a stretch to say that representations of policing are ideological and that they naturalize a particular model of authority. Yet, in saying so, the assumption is that such representations are separate from policing. This project demonstrates that radio's commercial and social control functions were essentially collapsed into each other. In the relationship between policing and radio developed during the Depression, it is impossible to find a firm dividing line between radio as an entertainment medium and radio as a political technology. Police reformers and commercial entertainment providers together formed a particularly enduring horizon of expectations about communication technologies and policing. Central to this was the dream of seamless coordination between disparate parts and aspects of society, including among individual officers and centralized command structures, among various police agencies, between the self-image of the police and the public perception of policing, and between police and citizens. In this post–9/11 era, it is easy to see the ways that these desires continue to echo among government and police officials today.

In the most mundane of our everyday expectations about policing and in the most quotidian uses of our increasing number of communication technologies, the significance of the linking of electronic communication media's entertainment and social control functions continues to register. In every phone call to a local 911 system, in the use of OnStar systems, and in the frequent news stories about delayed responses to emergency calls, the construction of the police as a constantly available presence continues to echo. In public reports that criticize the lack of coordination among various government agencies in the wake of events like 9/11 and Hurricane Katrina, the dream of using communication technologies to perfectly coordinate fragmented law enforcement agencies continues to echo. In every program that claims to document some realistic aspect of policing or follow the steps through some form of procedure, the use of media as a space to construct an idealized version of policing continues to echo. In the text messaging alert systems used by various agencies to directly contact citizens about potential dangers, the dream of forging a direct and intimate connection between police and citizens in a mobile society continues to echo. In our daily social use of all those technologies that keep us in constant communicative connection despite barriers of space and time in an increasingly mobile society, the dragnet effect continues to echo. As we live through a process of social change, variously labeled neoliberalism, globalization, and post- or advanced capitalism, police and security reform at the national and local levels continues to involve the attempt to gain control over increasingly global mobility enabled by advances in communication and transportation. As new technologies are adapted to this quest, new relationships will emerge. But in every effort of various actors to link the scattered functions of these technologies, we still hear the echo of that symbol of modern adventure: "Calling all cars!"

ACKNOWLEDGMENTS

Why did I write a book about radio crime dramas? This is still something of a mystery. Perhaps the answer may be found in my childhood experiences. When I was young, my Nana, who took pleasure in occasionally finding ways to scare my brother and me, would recite the opening lines of *The Shadow* as she stuck her bottom dentures out past her lower lip and rolled her eyes back into her head. Of course, initial fright became amusement, and she knew this would entertain us. I was well into adulthood when I heard this line issued by one of several actors who played the Shadow on the radio and was instantly struck by how accurate Nana's rendering was. At some point during my childhood, my father purchased a police scanner, and he, my brother, and I would listen on the weekends for various emergency calls and spend our weekends chasing mill fires in Lawrence, Massachusetts. In her later years, my Nana also spent her homebound days listening in on a police scanner. Radio crime dramas and police radio were, in fact, a part of my growing-up experiences.

The move from childhood experiences to scholarly study requires much encouragement. This book began as a dissertation at the University of Iowa. The comments of my advisors, Joy Hayes and John Peters, whom I happily thank for many years of intellectual and emotional support, were key in shaping this project. I value the insight and advice of my committee, including Bruce Gronbeck, Rick Altman, and the late Joanna Ploeger. Important financial support was provided by the University of Iowa through the Robert Olney Scholarship for Sound Research Travel, Ramona Tomlin

Mattson Fellowship, and Ada Louise Ballard Dissertation Completion Fellowship. I received crucial research assistance from Bryan E. Cornell and the staff at the Motion Picture, Broadcasting, and Recorded Sound Division of the Library of Congress.

What started as a dissertation has grown into something much more, and since leaving Iowa I have benefited from continued advice and input from a growing circle of wonderful friends and colleagues. My heartfelt thanks go to Joy Hayes, whose friendship and guidance well past my days as a graduate student have been essential to the intellectual reshaping of *Calling All Cars* and the preservation of my sanity through the process. Similar thanks go to Wendy Hilton-Morrow, at times my most critical and insightful reader, at times my most persistent and nagging cajoler, but most often a loving and supportive presence in my life. A number of friends and colleagues, including Naomi Andre, Rachel Andrews, Tim Anderson, Kyle Edwards, Kellie Hay, Tom Discenna, Lisa King, and Lisbeth Lipari, generously gave their time and effort to talk through central issues and to read and comment on many drafts. I owe special thanks to Elena Razlogova for sharing archival materials and important conversations about *Gang Busters.* This project has benefited immensely from wonderful reviews by Kathy Newman, who proved to be that perfect reader who often seemed to grasp the scope of my work better than I did. This book would not be what it is today without the guidance, advice, and insight of all of these individuals. My thanks to Alex Russo and Shawn VanCour for their last-minute advice. That said, there were certainly times when I did not follow their suggestions, so while the success of *Calling All Cars* is owed to all of these contributors, its failures are ultimately my own.

I am grateful for the support of colleagues in the Department of Communication Studies at the University of Michigan, the Department of Communication at Denison University, and the Department of Communication and Journalism at Oakland University. I owe an additional debt of gratitude to my department chair, Shea Howell, for her gentle reminders to finish, and to both my department and the Office of the Provost at Oakland University for their financial support of this project.

Throughout too many years of working on *Calling All Cars,* I appreciated constant support from friends and family, especially Robin Allen, Naomi Andre, Mark Andrews, Steve Andrews, Thomas Andrews, Tim

Anderson, Christina Battles, Patricia Battles, Steven Battles, Larissa Faulkner, Mary Garrett, Annie Gilson, Kellie Hay, Lisa King, Andrea Knutson, Lisbeth Lipari, Susan Mayer, Leslie Oh, Valeria Palmer-Mehta, Kyra Pearson, Rose Ribeiro, Erin Sahlstein, and Tom Wilson. I owe my parents, Mary Smith and Tom Battles, a debt of gratitude for never letting me forget that I had not yet finished. This book would not even exist without the continued love and support of my partner, Rachel Andrews. I owe you a lifetime of clean dishes.

NOTES

INTRODUCTION

1. See, for example, Doherty (1999), May (2000), McCann (2000), Munby (1999), Potter (1998), Powers (1983), Ruth (1996), Smith (2000), and Thomas (1999).

2. See, for example, Nachman (1988) and Harman (1992).

3. See, for example, Hayes (2000b), Hilmes (1997), Hilmes and Loviglio (2002), Loviglio (2005), McCracken (1999), McFadden (1993), Razlogova (2006), and Russo (2002).

4. See, for example, Newman (2004) and Razlogova (2004, 2006).

5. This discussion is based on a review of a number of sources, including Fogelson (1977), Kaloupek (1938), Lawes (1938), Marshall (1932), Potter (1998), Smith (1933, 1940), Vollmer and Parker (1935), and Walker (1977).

6. The Wickersham Commission was not the first such crime committee. Policing was the focus of a number of independent studies throughout the 1920s. These independent commissions, usually composed of and funded by local businessmen and professionals, gathered detailed information on the state of crime and policing in their municipalities or regions (Walker 1998).

7. For discussion of the New Deal state-building efforts, see Brinkley (1989), Skocpol (1992), Skocpol and Finegold (1982).

8. The Depression-era gangster film has received a great deal of scholarly interest. See, for example, Clarens (1980), Doherty (1999), Munby (1999), and Slotkin (1992).

1. POLICING PERCEPTION

1. At this time, the Don Lee Network was part of CBS/West Coast. Dunning (1998) lists the program as airing on CBS/West Coast; however, program creator William Robson (1966) clearly indicates that the program was created by and for

the Don Lee Network. For the purposes of this project, references for *Calling All Cars* will remain consistent with Dunning and list programs as airing on CBS/West Coast.

2. It was fairly common for programs, especially long-running ones, to change sponsorship and even networks. Because programs were made by advertising agencies, they were the not the property of either a single sponsor or a particular network.

3. The public affairs program *America's Town Meeting of the Air* also featured an episode on America's "crime problem" (Bryson 1936).

4. See, for example, Breuer (1995), Cooper (1935a), Cummings (1934, 1935), Hoover (1935, 1936), Lawes (1938), Lysing (1938), and Vollmer and Parker (1935).

5. *Eno Crime Clues* was a continuation of *The Eno Crime Club.* The original series, which aired from 1931 to 1932 on CBS, moved to NBC Blue in 1933. The original series was based on a series of detective novels of the same name. *Crime Clues* was not (Dunning 1998, 232).

6. Other *Police Headquarters* episodes feature this focus on detection, including "Jake Miller Knifed" (1932), "Tommy Wood Killed" (1932), and "Silver Collection" (1932).

7. Information about this incident is taken from Dunning (1996, 227), Grams (2004, 14–16), and the WOR Collection, Box 58, Folder "Publicity Material."

8. For excellent discussions of the arrangements in the making of *G-Men,* see Grams (2004), Powers (1983), and Razlogova (2006).

9. All passages from scripts are reproduced in their exact form, including unusual spellings, errors, and punctuation. The only change involves the replacement of multiple dashes generated by typewriters with the computer-generated em dash.

10. The material about the clash between Hoover and Lord comes from the Papers of Helen J. Sioussat at the Library of American Broadcasting, University of Maryland. These papers were shared with me by Elena Razlogova.

11. Stott (1973) argues that the radio soap operas were simply confessionals sliced up into a continuing format.

12. In addition to "The Black Legion," many episodes of *True Detective Mysteries* often feature "potboiler" elements that make them more akin to soap operas than to the radio crime docudramas. For example, episodes often feature organ music that sounds like soap opera music but, more important, often focus on domestic conflicts. For example, in "Horror in a Hospital Ward" (1937), the drama revolves around a nurse secretly married to a man who murders a patient out of jealousy. In "The Buddha Man Mystery" (1937) and "The Girl in the Iron Mask" (1937) episodes, women kill their husbands out of jealousy and greed.

13. This letter is summarized as part of a report on publicity, and the name of the author is not included. The letter is located in the WOR Collection, Box 58, Folder "Publicity Material."

14. This clipping is located in the WOR Collection, Box 58, Folder "Publicity Material."

15. Chevrolet's advertising copy is located in the WOR Collection, Box 58, Folder "Sponsor Material."

16. The derogatory use of the word *hangout* should not be overlooked. While it is clear that Livacoli went to some trouble to have such a secret room constructed in his otherwise respectable mansion, and that he was able to operate an impressive crime racket, this site is still clearly differentiated from police "headquarters," as discussed in chapter 4.

17. The debates over gangster films and the efforts to ban them are discussed in chapter 3.

18. These handwritten notes are located in the WOR Collection, Box 1, Folder "Bonnie and Clyde, Part 1." The page numbers refer to places in the script where these "lessons" were emphasized.

19. The handwritten note is located in the WOR Collection, Box 1, Folder "Fats McCarthy."

20. Chevrolet's advertising copy is located in the WOR Collection, Box 58, Folder "Sponsor Material."

21. All of the correspondence in this discussion is part of a typewritten report prepared by Lord's staff to demonstrate to Hoover and the corporate sponsor Chevrolet the impact of the program on audiences. The report lists the letters as being received between September 18 and September 21. The only information provided with each letter is the name of the letter writer, his or her title if available, and the name of the organization the writer represents. This report is in the WOR Collection, Box 58, Folder "Correspondence, Juveniles."

22. Powers (1983) deals extensively with construction of the G-men as action heroes during the Depression.

2. THE SOUND OF INTIMATE AUTHORITY

1. This was true in the film industry as well. See, for example, Altman (1992), Chion (1999), and Lastra (2000).

2. See, for example, Bain (1939), Fogelson (1977), Hoover (1935), Johnson (2003), Smith (1929b, 1940), Vollmer (1929), Vollmer and Parker (1935), Walker (1977, 1998), "Wickersham Report" (1931), and Wilson (2000).

3. See, for example, Fogelson (1977), Johnson (2003), Kaloupek (1938), Lawes (1938), Marshall (1932), Monkkonen (1981), Potter (1998), Smith (1933, 1940), Vollmer and Parker (1935), Walker (1977), and Wilson (2000).

4. Fogelson (1977) notes that during this period, rank-and-file police officers were not supportive of reform efforts. Only a "small but growing, articulate, and as the years went by, more influential subset of the rank and file," "dedicated to the force instead of the machine," could be counted on (160).

5. See, for example, Lysing (1938), Monkkonen (1981), Smith (1940), Soderman and O'Connell (1935), Vollmer (1935), Vollmer (1937), and Walker (1977, 1998).

6. The meaning of such difference is contested. Hilmes (1997) argues that programs like *Amos 'n' Andy* and *The Goldbergs* speak to the centrality of assimilation as the dominant model for newly arriving immigrant groups and to radio's cultural work in maintaining American race and ethnic hierarchies. McFadden (1993) argues that ethnic and gender difference on *The Jack Benny* program worked to bolster the authority Benny claimed as a white male. Douglas (1999) argues that the humor of programs like *Amos 'n' Andy* and *Burns and Allen* worked to challenge dominant hierarchies of race, class, and gender. May (2000) makes a similar argument about the meaning of difference in Depression-era film and argues that during this period film's appeal was found in its populist appeal to ethnic, class, and gender instabilities.

7. For an excellent discussion of the relationship between ethnic working classes and whiteness in the first half of the twentieth century, see Roediger (2005).

8. The perfection of the police type of "character" would come after World War II in the form of Sergeant Joe Friday on the enormously popular *Dragnet* series.

9. This is from an initial draft of the script. The names are confusing and were likely changed. In the scene, Pyke and Jackson are looking through pictures with a detective whose partner has just died. Earlier, the script notes that Detective Kenney died, while his partner, McCarthy, lived. The script indicates, however, that Kenney is the detective looking through photographs, then lists McCarthy as the officer speaking. No doubt this confusion was clarified for the final draft. What is important here is the dedication of these officers to their job despite the danger they face.

10. Given the rift between Schwarzkopf and Hoover over the search for the Lindberg baby, this must surely have been another affront to Hoover on the part of Lord.

11. Johnson (2003) offers an excellent discussion of Valentine's role in the New York City police reform movement during the 1930s, especially his attempts to improve public opinion of the police by publicly decrying the use of the third degree.

12. Altman (1994), in considering the relationship between radio sound and the sound of *Citizen Kane,* argues that even nonsponsored programming had a double discursivity. In the case of *Mercury Theater of the Air,* the program was authored by the network *and* Welles.

13. Cantril and Allport (1935), in trying to determine *The Psychology of Radio,* began with a famous experiment in which they studied the responses of different groups of listeners gathered to hear a well-known evangelist, one group inside the hall and an overflow audience listening through a loudspeaker in a separate hall. Using this case, the authors argue that the lack of copresence between speaker and

listener required very different forms of address that necessitated much more inti-mate, encompassing, and direct communication.

14. The piece was completed in the late 1930s but never published until discov-ered in Paul F. Lazarsfeld's papers at Columbia University.

3. GANG BUSTING

1. See, for example, Powers (1983), Potter (1998), Munby (1999), Ruth (1996), and Smith (2000).

2. Less sensational summaries of the results were published in the previous year. See Blumer (1933), Blumer and Hauser (1933), and Charters (1933).

3. Even Roosevelt weighed in, announcing upon the signing of a federal crime bill in 1934, "Law enforcement and gangster extermination cannot be made com-pletely effective so long as a substantial part of the public looks with tolerance upon known criminals, permits public officers to be corrupted or intimidated by them or applauds efforts to romanticize crime" (quoted in Potter 1998, 150).

4. In fact, the gangster endured in film. See Clarens (1980), Munby (1999), and Doherty (1999) for discussions of the post–Hays code gangster films. Particularly odd reincarnations of the gangster film were the G-men films of 1935. Although ostensibly presenting a positive picture of the FBI, these films were as violent as their gangster movie cousins, leading to a quick stop to their production.

5. Paroles were early releases from prison granted by judges on the basis of good behavior. Developed as part of Progressive reform of the justice system in the first decades of the twentieth century, paroles were part of a series of reforms meant to facilitate criminal reform (Walker 1977).

6. Notes are located in the WOR Collection, Box 1, Folder "Bonnie and Clyde, Part 1."

7. All references are from the available scripts in the WOR Collection, Box 1, Folder "Bonnie and Clyde, Part 1," and Folder "Bonnie and Clyde, Part 2."

8. The Uniform Crime Reports are discussed by a number of historians of policing, including Fogelson (1977), Lovell (2003), Walker (1977), Wilson (2000). Samuel Walker (1977) argues that the most important failure of the UCR was its single-minded focus on crime fighting and that the data gathered failed to docu-ment what police did with most of their time. Thus, the UCR was based on and also reinforced the crime-fighting image of the police (155–56). Hall, Critcher, Jeffer-son, Clarke, and Robert (1978) similarly argue that crime statistics in general, though treated by government officials and journalists as factual, more accurately reflect the interests of those gathering the "facts" than the world that facts are supposed to reflect: "Statistics—whether crime rates or opinion polls—have an ideological function: they appear to *ground* free floating and controversial impressions in the hard, incontrovertible soil of numbers. Both the media and the public have enor-mous respect for 'facts'—*hard facts*. And there is no fact so 'hard' as a number—

unless it is the percentage difference between the two numbers. With regard to criminal statistics, these are not—as one might suppose—sure indicators of the volume of crime committed, or very meaningful ones. This has long been recognised even by those who make the most of them, the police themselves. The reasons are not difficult to understand: (1) crime statistics refer only to *reported* crime: they cannot quantify the 'dark figure'; (2) different areas collate their statistics differently: (3) police sensation to, and mobilization to deal with, selected, 'targetted' crimes increase both the number the police turn up, and the number the public report; (4) public anxiety about particular 'highlighted' offences also leads to 'overreporting'; (5) crime statistics are based on legal (not sociological) categories and are, thus, arbitrary . . . (6) changes in the law . . . make strict comparisons over time difficult" (9–10).

9. This note is located in the WOR Collection, Box 1, Folder "Michigan Enigma."

10. A similar version of this note is located in the WOR Collection, Box 1, Folder "Bonnie and Clyde, Part 1," and Folder "Scarnini Case, Part 1."

11. This note is located in the WOR Collection, Box 1, Folder "Scarnini Case, Part 1."

12. This note is located in the WOR Collection, Box 1, Folder "Bonnie and Clyde, Part 1."

13. Potter (1998) argues that the FBI actually worked to deny the existence of organized crime during the Depression. Although based on local police cases, the radio crime docudramas did not deviate from this. Criminals were constructed as belonging to gangs, but they were less commonly depicted as belonging to large syndicates linked to local politics through corruption and graft.

14. The script summary is located in the WOR Collection, Box 1, Folder "Gray Anthony Gang."

15. Potter (1998) offers an excellent overview of the ways that social reformers, the FBI, and other reform groups worked to define crime during the Depression. She especially focuses on the FBI's work to redefine the rural bandit as a "psychopathic public enemy," a theory "which fused older sociopathic and hereditary models with a postwar emphasis on moral decline among adolescents and young adults" (57–58).

16. A good overview of theories of criminality during the 1920s and 1930s is found in Ruth's *Inventing the Public Enemy* (1996, 11–38).

17. Of course, all *Gang Busters* episodes were professional studio productions. As discussed in chapter 2, the "chief," the official interviewed in each episode, was simply a device used to set up the stories and give their telling a sense of authority. All that mattered for Lord was that the chief who was "interviewed" be involved in some way with the case.

18. For example, Hoover often used FBI innovations in the collection of crime statistics to claim he had documented proof that crime rates were rising in order to

berate the middle classes into supporting federal crime legislation by suggesting that becoming a victim of a crime was an imminent possibility for all citizens (Powers 1983). Reporting to a Round Table Forum, J. Edgar Hoover (1936) presented such statistics regarding the invasion of crime into the American home: "Aggravated robbery, theft, arson, rape, felonious assault or murder annually is visited upon one of every 16 homes in America. Last year . . . there was a minimum of 12,000 murders and an estimated total of 1,445,581 major crimes. Thus, one of every of 84 persons in the United States was subjected to injury or death through the workings of this tremendous crime aggregate" (390). Hoover noted that crime cost each citizen a minimum of $120 per year (390). Attorney General Homer Cummings further emphasized these concerns in his public speeches. See Cummings (1934, 1935).

19. *True Detective Mysteries,* unlike *Gang Busters* or *Calling All Cars,* frequently followed its cases through to trial. Most episodes ended with some sort of dramatization of the presentation of the case in court.

20. This was somewhat more dramatic than the first-draft scripted version, which stated, "The underworld, racketeers and gangsters are an offensive insult to the name of our country. . . . You, the citizens, can help us. The Police are greatly hindered in their work by old obsolete laws protecting the criminal. We need criminal laws with teeth in them. The Police are forced to turn loose thousands of dangerous criminals every year because of old, useless, worn out legal technicalities."

21. The "Osage Murders" (1935) episode of *G-Men* explicitly takes on the cultural myth of the Old West manhunt as the FBI searches for the men responsible for a string of murders. Importantly, the manhunt is organized and coordinated not by citizens but by the FBI.

4. THE DRAGNET EFFECT

1. The 1921 Federal-Aid Highway Act allocated seventy-five million dollars per year to states for building national highways. States were required to link 7 percent of their roads with those in other states. The Bureau of Public Roads worked to designate certain roads as interstate highways and to standardize road signs (Lewis 1997, 18). Efforts at national highway building increased during the Depression as part of the Works Progress Administration effort to provide jobs (Lewis 1997). The tremendous increase in the number of paved roadways was especially helpful to criminals. While the road mileage increased 50 percent between 1904 and 1930, the number of paved roads increased 365 percent (Kaloupek 1938, 9). Paved roads allowed for swift travel, so criminals could easily cross city, county, and even state lines, rendering the decentralized system of city, town, county, and state police forces inadequate to the task of keeping up with these criminals.

2. One particular problem of rural police was the tremendous increase in area they were required to cover with minimum resources. As crime spread to rural areas

during the 1920s and 1930s, the rural sheriff was unable to provide protection for the thousands of square miles that might be in his jurisdiction due to the increasing use of the automobile: "The motor car quickly assumed a conspicuous place in the problem of crime control. It continues to figure in the records of most criminal cases. But as criminals developed a new technique through speedier flight, law enforcement agencies adapted the automobile to their needs. Horse and buggy law enforcement was replaced by police cruisers and scout cars capable of equal—or greater—speeds" (Olander 1942, 12).

3. See, for example, Cummings (1935), Geiger (1929), "Good Work with Radio Motorcycles" (1939), Harrel (1931), *The Illinois Crime Survey* (1929), Olander (1931, 1942), and Smith (1929a, 1929b, 1933, 1940).

4. The idea of using communications technology in crime fighting was not entirely new. Carolyn Marvin (1988) documented how police forces were among the earliest users of the telephone, establishing phones in station houses and call boxes in urban neighborhoods beginning in the 1870s. The idea of using wireless technology as an aid in policing dates back to the 1910 case of Harvey Crippen, who killed his wife in London. When he attempted to escape to Canada by boat, the London police telegraphed the captain of the ship he had boarded with Crippen's physical description, which led to his arrest (Marvin 1988; Ranson 1937). In the early 1900s, different people experimented with putting radio receivers and transmitters in cars (Ranson 1937). Perhaps one of the most famous cases of the early use of radio involves the 1923 kidnapping of the son of E. F. Alexanderson. Ironically, Alexanderson was the man responsible for the creation of the electric wave generator, known as the Alexanderson alternator, that allowed Reginald Fessenden to become the first radio pioneer to transmit voice rather than Morse code (Douglas 1987). When his son was kidnapped, Alexanderson immediately broadcast all the details—the descriptions of two men, how they made their getaway, and so on. One of the rare radio owners of the era heard the broadcast and matched the description to some people who had rented a cottage from him. This event drew international attention to the possibility of using radio in police work. The Michigan State Police began experimenting with wireless in 1922, but it is the city of Detroit that can claim to have had the first working two-way police radio system, which began operation in 1928 (Olander 1942).

5. Auto theft was one of the key crimes addressed by the earliest users of both police radio and teletype.

6. For popular accounts of the magic of police radio see "Catching Aliens by Radio" (1937), "Discouraging News for Criminals in Westchester County" (1930), "Electric Police Stations" (1926), "Ether Waves vs. Crime Waves" (1922), "The Invisible Man Hunter" (1929), Michigan State Police (1936), Miles (1939), "Radio—The Latest Crime Detector" (1925), "Radio Patrol Most Effective Crime Deterrent" (1935), "Radio Shoots Typed Words through Space" (1925), Teale (1936), and "Want a Policeman: From 'Short Wave' to Television" (1937). For professional accounts, see

"Abbreviation for Police Radio Messages" (1934), Casey (1938), Cutchins (1938), Dickennson (1936), "F.C.C. Allocates High Frequencies for Police Radio" (1937), Friede (1934), Geiger (1929), Glasgow (1930), Hussey (1937), Kent (1931), Manderbaugh (1937), "New Fashions Turn Up in Police Radio" (1937), Olander (1931), Peters (1930), "Police Radio Service Today" (1935), "Police Radio Meets Interference" (1935), "The Police Yearbook" (1939), "Radio Becomes a Good Right Arm" (1937), Skidmore (1936), "Small Cities Going to Radio" (1936), Watt (1936), and Wolfe (1936).

7. See, for example, Cantril and Allport (1935), Barnouw (1939), Firth and Erskine (1934), and Wylie (1939).

8. One-way radio was used by a limited number of cities in the early 1920s. Police cars were fitted with mobile *receivers* only. Unable to radio back to the station, officers were still required to find a phone box and call the station to register receipt of the transmission. The relative slim advantage afforded by the one-way radio was grossly outweighed by the cost of the receiving and dispatch units, essentially forestalling widespread use of radio until the development of mobile two-way radio.

9. This article is located in the Papers of Harold Wolfe Collection, Box 1, Folder "Newspaper Clippings."

10. The first "modern" state police force was formed in Pennsylvania in 1905. While its administration was centralized, its organization was largely decentralized, consisting of militialike units spread throughout the state, each assigned to cover a certain part of the state. While initially relying on horse and foot patrols, in addition to cars, the Pennsylvania State Police eventually moved to using only patrol cars (Kaloupek 1938; Mayo 1917; Smith 1940; Vollmer and Parker 1935). Other states did not form statewide police or highway patrol systems until the 1930s; Iowa's was formed in 1935 (Kaloupek 1938).

11. Michigan was one of the first states to try statewide radio broadcasting. Although it cost a total of $55,000, the state decided to equip each sheriff's office with a radio dispatch unit so that crime fighting could be coordinated at the state level. In 1929, after the Michigan State legislature approved funds for the construction of state police radio stations, the state police force met resistance from the Federal Radio Commission, which at that time was flooded with requests for wavelength assignments. In the ensuing battle between the State of Michigan and the FCC, Governor Fred Green informed the FCC that Michigan would run the station in any event, testifying that "if the radio commission believed it is more important that the ether be filled with jazz music and advertisements than that criminals be apprehended and punished, that is the commission's privilege. We do not think that way and we are not going to be influenced or controlled by anyone who does" (Federal Radio Commission 1931). By 1930, Station WRDS was up and running on a Federal Radio Commission–assigned frequency. This information comes from the Donald S. Leonard Papers, Box 29, Folder "Radio Committee

1932." Leonard had an active career in law enforcement in the state of Michigan, moving through the ranks from his beginnings as a trooper in the 1920s to commissioner in 1946. One of his key areas of interest was police communications systems. These records are part of the holdings regarding his involvement with the International Association of Chiefs of Police. In addition, Leonard was actively involved with the Associated Police Communications Officers.

12. The seemingly instantaneous arrival of police and detectives serves as a source of humor in the March 30, 1940, episode of *The Fred Allen* program. A regular segment of the program was the presentation of skits by the Mighty Allen Art Players (a predecessor of *Saturday Night Live*'s Not Ready for Primetime Players). When a "song plugger" is "plugged," Allen's detective character instantly arrives at the scene. When the plugger's brother asks him how he arrived so quickly, the detective himself is dumbfounded! Such humorous skits frequently spoofed cultural conventions of the day, and as Hilmes (1997) argues, this includes radio programs.

13. This notion of constancy needs some adjustment for the period in question. Twenty-four-hour broadcasting was not the norm, but few would expect this during the Depression era. The extension of time through the electric light, urban amusements, and commercial activity was a process still underway. From the perspective of today's media consumers, radio service of that period must seem limited. Depression-era listeners might indeed have experienced radio—the first medium to offer a constant flow of programming into the private sphere of the household—as "constant."

14. Nick Browne (1984), in reference to television, referred to this experience of flow as the "super-text," arguing that the overall flow of programming was more important to the experience of broadcasting than discrete segments.

15. Hay and Packer (2004) examine the development of police radio through the trope of safety.

16. A letter from the program supervisor for *Gang Busters* to the production manager of the Washington, D.C., affiliate station asks for this information:

> Can you help me out?
>
> In a GANG BUSTERS broadcast we plan to present within the next few weeks, we would like to include some statistics, and our files are either outdates on the following points, or we lack information entirely.
>
> Can you get for me from the F.B.I and other sources known only to you Washington boys:
>
> Number of uniformed police officers throughout the United States.
> Number of detectives.
> Number of FBI men.
> Number of Secret Service men.
> Number of Postal Inspectors.
> Number of Customs Service men.
> Number of State Troopers.

Number of short-wave police radio sending sets.

Number of scout and patrol cars, throughout the country.

Number of Miles of telephone wires throughout the country.

Number of Scientific Crime Detection Laboratories in the country.

A phone call seems to be the only way to get such information nowadays, and for obvious reasons they want your pedigree and everything else before giving out this information, so I figured the fastest and most efficient way was to impose on your cooperation.

If you can get this information to me as soon as possible—round figures will do—I'll appreciate it very much. ("Bruno Salek" 1943)

5. THE SHADOW OF DOUBT AND THE MENACE OF SURVEILLANCE

1. There was no guarantee about how audiences interpreted the programs and about whom they might identify with in the narrative. Some audience members might well have identified with the criminals and their plight against the seeming omnipresence of the State as embodied by the police. The dragnet effect discussed in chapter 4, which worked to construct an idea of police omnipresence as a positive development, might be interpreted by some listeners as a threat.

2. As discussed in chapter 3, *Gang Busters* did the exact opposite, representing female criminals as particularly vicious, often associating them with animals of prey, such as in "The Blonde Tigress" (1939) and "The Tiger Woman and Her Slave" (1936). Whereas the program often worked to suggest environment was the cause of male juvenile delinquency and hence, by inference, of male criminality in general, female criminals were "born bad" and did bad things from the start.

3. The newspaper clippings are located in the WOR Collection, Box 1, Folder "Livacoli Gang."

4. The newspaper clipping is located in the WOR Collection, Box 2, Folder "Arthur Boccadero."

5. Peters (1999) suggests that while commercial radio broadcasters worked hard to close the gap between the voice over the radio and the body that produced it, a creepy excess always remained. He writes, "The Shadow knew that under commercial broadcasting's carefully wrought artifice of intimate familiarity lurked the loneliness of the long gaps, the eerie calls of distant voices, and the touch of oozing ectoplasm, strange flesh from afar" (218). One way this anxiety was quelled was by invoking signs of bodily suffering. The strange thing about the Shadow, however, is that while he cannot be seen, he is still bodily present. Over the course of the program, while cloaked in invisibility, the Shadow is shot, punched, confined and left to die, and even sprayed with a skin-eating acid. The Shadow invokes the anxiety caused by a disembodied presence and, by the continued reminders of his bodily presence, quells such anxieties at the same moment.

6. Russo (2002) explores the significance of the shift in Kato's identity from Japanese to Filipino after the attack on Pearl Harbor.

7. Publicity material is located in the George Trendle Papers, Box 58, Folder 6.

8. The undated program description is located in the George Trendle Papers, Box 58, Folder 6.

CONCLUSION

1. Discussed in Ranson (1937, 1).

BIBLIOGRAPHY

The WOR Collection is housed at the Library of Congress Motion Picture, Broadcasting and Recorded Sound Division in Washington, D.C.

Recordings are listed in a separate section. New technologies have made old-time radio programming increasingly easy to access. Recordings here come from multiple sources but primarily through CDs from OTRCAT.com and the download service OTRFTP.com.

"Abbreviations for Police Radio Messages." *American City* 49 (October 1934): 13.

Adorno, Theodor. 1994. "Analytical Study of the NBC 'Music Appreciation Hour.'" *Musical Quarterly* 78, no. 2: 325–77.

Altman, Rick, ed. 1992. *Sound Theory/Sound Practice.* London: Routledge.

———. 1994. "Deep-Focus Sound: Citizen Kane and the Radio Aesthetic." *Quarterly Review of Film and Video* 15, no. 3: 1–33.

Arnheim, Rudolf. 1936. *Radio.* Trans. M. Ludwig and H. Reed. London: Faber & Faber.

Bain, R. 1939. "The Policeman on the Beat." *Scientific Monthly* 48, no. 5: 450–58.

Bakhtin, Mikhail. 1981. *The Dialogic Imagination: Four Essays.* Trans. Caryl Emerson and Michael Holquist. Austin: University of Texas Press.

Barnouw, Eric. 1939. *Handbook of Radio Writing: An Outline of Techniques and Markets in Radio Writing in the United States.* Boston: Little, Brown.

Bates, Theodore, to John Ives. 1936, May 8. WOR Collection, Box 1, Folder "Homer Van Meter."

Blumer, Herbert. 1933. *Movies and Conduct.* New York: MacMillan.

Blumer, Herbert, and Philip Hauser. 1933. *Movies, Delinquency, and Crime.* New York: MacMillan.

Bordua, David, and Albert Reiss, Jr. 1966. "Command, Control, and Charisma: Reflections on Police Bureaucracy." *American Journal of Sociology* 72, no. 1: 68–76.

Breuer, William B. 1995. *J. Edgar Hoover and His G-Men.* Westport: Praeger.

Brinkley, Alan. 1989. "The New Deal and the Idea of the State." In *The Rise and Fall of the New Deal Order, 1930–1980,* ed. Steve Fraser and Gary Gerstle, 85–121. Princeton, N.J.: Princeton University Press.

Browne, Nick. 1984. "The Political Economy of the Television (Super) Text." *Quarterly Review of Film Studies* 9, no. 3: 183–95.

Bryson, L., ed. 1936. *America's Town Meeting of the Air: How Can We Solve the Crime Problem?* New York: American Book Company.

Cantril, Hadley. 1940. *The Invasion from Mars: A Study in the Social Psychology of Panic.* Princeton, N.J.: Princeton University Press.

Cantril, Hadley, and Gordon Allport. 1935. *The Psychology of Radio.* Salem, N.H.: Ayer.

Carey, James, and J. J. Quirk. 1992. "The Mythos of the Electronic Revolution." In *Communication as Culture: Essays on Media and Society,* 113–41. London: Routledge.

Casey, D. 1938. "Jersey City's Pioneer Two Way Radio." *American City* 53 (March): 47–48.

"Catching Aliens by Radio." 1937. *Popular Mechanics* 68 (July): 50–53.

"Catching Crooks Red-Handed by Police Radio Broadcast." 1930. *Literary Digest* 101 (January 18): 45–47.

Cawelti, John G. 1976. *Adventure, Mystery, and Romance: Formula Stories as Art and Popular Culture.* Chicago: University of Chicago Press.

Charters, Werrett Wallace. 1933. *Motion Pictures and Youth: A Summary.* New York: MacMillan.

Chion, Michel. 1999. *The Voice in Cinema.* New York: Columbia University Press.

Clarens, Carlos. 1980. *Crime Movies: From Griffith to the Godfather and Beyond.* New York: Norton.

Cmiel, Kenneth. 1991. *Democratic Eloquence: The Fight over Popular Speech in Nineteenth Century America.* Berkeley: University of California Press.

Cohen, Lizbeth. 1990. *Making a New Deal: Industrial Workers in Chicago, 1919–1939.* New York: Cambridge University Press.

Conway, Helen, to Phillips H. Lord. 1936, April 30. WOR Collection, Box 1, Folder "Homer Van Meter."

Cooper, Courtney Ryley. 1935a. "Criminal America: The Mixing Bowl of Crime." *Saturday Evening Post* 207 (April 27): 5–7+.

———. 1935b. *Ten Thousand Public Enemies.* Boston: Little, Brown.

Cummings, H. 1934. "The Menace of Organized Crime." *Vital Speeches of the Day* 1 (October 8): 26.

———. 1935. "Co-ordination of Law Enforcement in the Movement against Crime." *Vital Speeches of the Day* 1 (January 28): 273–75.

Cunningham, R. F., to Phillips H. Lord. 1936, April 27. WOR Collection, Box 1, Folder "D'Autremont Brothers, Part 1."

Cutchins, J. 1938. "Modern Police Equipment." *American City* 53 (February): 47.

Denning, Michael. 1996. *The Cultural Front: The Laboring of American Culture in the Twentieth Century.* London: Verso.

———. 1998. *Mechanic Accents: Dime Novels and Working-Class Culture in America.* 2nd ed. London: Verso.

Dickennson, E. 1936. "Crime Lessons via Radio." *American City* 51 (May): 15.

"Discouraging News for Criminals in Westchester County." 1930. *American City* 42 (April): 150–51.

Doherty, Thomas. 1999. *Pre-Code Hollywood: Sex, Immorality, and Insurrection in American Cinema 1930–1934.* New York: Columbia University Press.

Douglas, Susan. 1987. *Inventing American Broadcasting, 1899–1922.* Baltimore: Johns Hopkins University Press.

———. 1999. *Listening In: Radio and the American Imagination.* New York: Times Books.

Dove, George N. 1982. *The Police Procedural.* Bowling Green, Ohio: Bowling Green University Popular Press.

Dunning, John. 1998. *On the Air: The Encyclopedia of Old-Time Radio.* Oxford: Oxford University Press.

"Electric Police Stations." 1926. *Literary Digest* 88 (January 30): 21.

Enright, Richard E. 1923. *Addresses of Police Commissioner Richard E. Enright, New York City, by Radio on Police Problems, September 5, 1923–October 30, 1923.* New York City.

Ernst, Robert. 1991. *Weakness Is a Crime: The Life of Bernarr Macfadden.* Syracuse, N.Y.: Syracuse University Press.

"Ether Waves versus Crime Waves." 1922. *Literary Digest* 75 (October 7): 25.

Fabian, Ann. 1993. "Making a Commodity of Truth: Speculations on the Career of Bernarr Macfadden." *American Literary History* 5, no. 1: 51–76.

"F.C.C. Allocates High Frequencies for Police Radio." 1938. *American City* 53 (February): 17.

Federal Radio Commission. 1931. *Report of the Federal Radio Commission.* Washington, D.C.: Federal Radio Commission.

Fink, Howard. 1981. "The Sponsor's v. the Nation's Choice: North American Radio Drama." In *Radio Drama,* ed. Peter Lewis, 185–243. London: Longman.

Firth, Ivan, and Gladys Erskine. 1934. *Gateway to Radio.* New York: MacAulay.

Fogelson, Robert. 1977. *Big-City Police.* Cambridge: Harvard University Press.

Fones-Wolf, Elizabeth, and Nathan Godfried. 2007. "Regulating Class Conflict on the Air: NBC's Relationship with Business and Organized Labor." In *NBC: America's Network,* ed. Michele Hilmes, 61–77. Berkeley: University of California Press.

Forman, Henry James. 1933. *Our Movie Made Children.* New York: MacMillan.

Foucault, Michel. 1979. *Discipline and Punish: The Birth of the Prison.* Trans. Alan Sheridan. New York: Vintage Books.

Friede, H. 1934. "Street-Signal Boxes and the Patrolman in the Age of Radio." *American City* 49 (November): 45–46.

Gang Busters. "The Akron Cop Murders" [unpublished script]. 1937. WOR Collection, Box 3.

———. "Alex Bogdanoff, Part 1" [unpublished script]. 1936. WOR Collection, Box 1.

———. "Arthur Boccardero." [unpublished script]. 1936. WOR Collection, Box 2.

———. "Blonde Tigress, Part 1" [unpublished script]. 1939. WOR Collection, Box 9.

———. "Blonde Tigress, Part 2" [unpublished script]. 1939. WOR Collection, Box 9.

———. "Bonnie and Clyde, Part 1" [unpublished script]. 1936. WOR Collection, Box 1.

———. "Bonnie and Clyde, Part 2" [unpublished script]. 1936. WOR Collection, Box 1.

———. "Busche Brothers" [unpublished script]. 1937. WOR Collection, Box 3.

———. "Bruno Salek" [unpublished script]. 1942. WOR Collection, Box 10.

———. "The Chicago Kid" [unpublished script]. 1937. WOR Collection, Box 3.

———. "Dago Paretti" [unpublished script]. 1936. WOR Collection, Box 1.

———. "D'Autremont Brothers, Part 1" [unpublished script]. 1936. WOR Collection, Box 1.

———. "D'Autremont Brothers, Part 2" [unpublished script]. 1936. WOR Collection, Box 1.

———. "Eddie Doll" [unpublished script]. 1936. WOR Collection, Box 7.

———. "Edward Metelski." [unpublished draft script]. 1936. WOR Collection, Box 2.

———. "Edward Metelski" [unpublished final script]. 1936(a). WOR Collection, Box 2.

———. "Fats McCarthy Gang" [unpublished script, final draft]. 1936. WOR Collection, Box 1.

———. "Fats McCarthy Gang" [unpublished script, first draft]. 1936. WOR Collection, Box 1.

———. "Fleagle Brothers" [unpublished script]. 1937. WOR Collection, Box 3.

———. "Gray Anthony Gang" [unpublished script]. 1936. WOR Collection, Box 1.

———. "Homer Van Meter" [unpublished script]. 1936. WOR Collection, Box 1.

———. "Jessie Wendell" [unpublished script]. 1942. WOR Collection, Box 10.

———. "Livacoli Gang, Part 1" [unpublished script]. 1936. WOR Collection, Box 2.

———. "Livacoli Gang, Part 2" [unpublished script]. 1936. WOR Collection, Box 2.

———. "Midget Fernekes, Part 2" [unpublished script]. 1936. WOR Collection, Box 1.

———. "Sacramento Post Office Robbery" [unpublished script]. 1936. WOR Collection, Box 1.

———. "Safe Crackers and Vault Makers" [unpublished script]. 1937. WOR Collection, Box 3.

———. "Scarnici Case, Part 1" [unpublished script]. 1936. WOR Collection, Box 1.

———. "Scientific Cases" [unpublished script]. 1942. WOR Collection, Box 4.

———. "Scientific Cases" [unpublished script]. 1937. WOR Collection, Box 4.

———. "Seattle Safe Crackers" [unpublished script]. 1937. WOR Collection, Box 3.

———. "Slot Machine Murders" [unpublished script]. 1939. WOR Collection, Box 7.

———. "The Tiger Woman and Her Slave, Part 1" [unpublished script]. 1936. WOR Collection, Box 2.

———. "Tony, the Stinger" [unpublished script]. 1936. WOR Collection, Box 2.

———. "Two Gun Crowley" [unpublished script]. 1936. WOR Collection, Box 1.

———. "Willie 'The Actor' Sutton, Part 1" [unpublished script]. 1936. WOR Collection, Box 1.

———. "Willie 'The Actor' Sutton, Part 2" [unpublished script]. 1936. WOR Collection, Box 1.

Geiger, C. W. 1929. "Equip Berkeley Police Cars with Radio Sets." *American City* 41 (November): 154.

Gitlin, Todd. 1983. *Inside Prime Time.* New York: Pantheon.

Glasgow, Roy. 1930. "Police Radio Tends to Discourage Crime." *American City* 43 (December): 152.

G-Men. "Bremer Kidnapping" [unpublished script]. 1935. WOR Collection, Box 58.

———. "Cannon Case" [unpublished script]. 1935. WOR Collection, Box 58.

———. "Dillinger" [unpublished script]. 1935. WOR Collection, Box 58.

———. "Eddie Doll" [unpublished script]. 1935. WOR Collection, Box 58.

———. "Fleagle Brothers" [unpublished script]. 1935. WOR Collection, Box 58.

———. "Osage Murders" [unpublished script]. 1935. WOR Collection, Box 58.

———. "Urschel Kidnapping" [unpublished script]. 1935. WOR Collection, Box 58.

"G-Men Collect Six Million Clues." 1936. *Literary Digest* (October 17): 5–6.

Goodman, David. 2007. "Programming in the Public Interest: *America's Town Meeting of the Air.*" In *NBC: America's Network,* ed. Michele Hilmes, 44–60. Berkeley: University of California Press.

"Good Work with Radio Motorcycles." 1939. *American City* 54 (January): 7.

Grams, Martin, Jr. 2004. *Gang Busters: The Crime Fighters of American Broadcasting.* Churchville, Md.: OTR Publishing.

Gunning, Tom. 1995. "Tracing the Individual Body: Photography, Detectives, and Early Cinema." In *Cinema and the Invention of Modern Life,* ed. Leo Charney and Vanessa R. Schwartz, 15–45. Berkeley: University of California Press.

Hall, Stuart, Charles Critcher, Tony Jefferson, John Clarke, and Brian Robert. 1978. *Policing the Crisis: Mugging, the State, and Law and Order.* New York: Holmes & Meier.

Harmon, Jim. 1992. *Radio Mystery and Its Appearances in Film, Television, and Other Media.* London: McFarland.

Harrel, Frank. 1931. "Teletypewriter Aids in Police Work." *American City* 44 (June): 81–84.

Hay, James, and Jeremy Packer. 2004. "Crossing the Media(n): Auto-mobility, the Transported Self and Technologies of Freedom." In *MediaSpace: Place, Scale and Culture in a Media Age,* ed. Nick Couldry, 209–32. London: Routledge.

Haycraft, Julius, to Phillips H. Lord. 1936. WOR Collection, Folder "Bonnie and Clyde, Episode 2."

Hayes, Joy. 2000a. "Did Herbert Hoover Broadcast the First Fireside Chat?: Rethinking the Origins of Roosevelt's Radio Genius." *Journal of Radio and Audio Media* 7, no. 1: 76–92.

———. 2000b. *Radio Nation: Communication, Popular Culture, and Nationalism in Mexico, 1920–1950.* Tucson: University of Arizona Press.

Hendy, David. 2008. "Radio's Cultural Turns." *Cinema Journal* 48, no. 1: 130–38.

Hilmes, Michele. 1997. *Radio Voices: American Broadcasting, 1922–1952.* Minneapolis: University of Minnesota Press.

———. 2008. "Foregrounding Sound: New (and Old) Directions in Sound Studies." *Cinema Journal* 48, no. 1: 115–17.

Hilmes, Michele, and Jason Loviglio, eds. 2002. *Radio Reader: Essays in the Cultural History of Radio.* New York: Routledge.

Hobsbawm, Eric J. 1959. *Social Bandits and Primitive Rebels: Studies in Archaic Forms of Social Movement in the 19th and 20th Centuries.* Glencoe, Ill.: Free Press.

Hoover, J. Edgar. 1935. "Modern Problems of Law Enforcement." *Vital Speeches of the Day* 1: 682–87.

———. 1936. "The Influence of Crime on the American Home." *Vital Speeches of the Day* 2 (March 11): 390–94.

Hopkins, Ernest Jerome. 1931. *Our Lawless Police: A Study of the Unlawful Enforcement of the Law.* New York: Viking Press.

Hussey, W. H. 1937. "Two Men in a Radio Car: New Police Radio Installation." *American City* 52 (August): 81.

The Illinois Crime Survey. 1929. Chicago: Illinois Association for Criminal Justice.

Interstate Commission on Crime. 1936. "Proceedings of the Second Annual Meeting of the Interstate Commission on Crime." Donald S. Leonard Papers, Box 29. Bentley Historical Library.

"The Invisible Man Hunter." 1929. *Popular Mechanics* 51 (May): 712–16.

Ives, John, to Ken Stowan. 1936, June 27. WOR Collection, Box 2, Folder "Tony, the Stinger."

Johnson, Marilynn. 2003. *Street Justice: A History of Police Violence in New York City.* Boston: Beacon Press.

Jowett, Garth, Ian Jarvie, and Kathryn Fuller. 1996. *Children and the Movies: Media Influence and the Payne Fund Controversy.* Cambridge: Cambridge University Press.

Kaloupek, Walter. 1938. *The History and Administration of the Iowa Highway Patrol.* Iowa City: University of Iowa.

Kelling, G., and M. Moore. 1996. "The Evolving Strategy of Policing." In *Classics in Policing,* ed. Steven Brandl and David Barlow, 71–95. Cincinnati: Anderson Publishing.

Kent, Roscoe. 1931. "Catching the Criminal by Police Radio." *American City* 45 (November): 106.

Lacey, Kate. 2002. "Radio in the Great Depression: Promotional Culture, Public Service, and Propaganda." In *Radio Reader: Essays in the Cultural History of Radio,* ed. Michele Hilmes and Jason Loviglio. London: Routledge.

Lastra, James. 2000. *Technologies and the American Cinema: Perception, Representation, Modernity.* New York: Columbia University Press.

Lawes, Lewis. 1938. "Crime and Community." *Vital Speeches of the Day* 4 (May 15): 477–80.

Laythe, Joseph. 2002. "'Trouble on the Outside, Trouble on the Inside': Growing Pains, Social Change, and Small Town Policing—The Eugene Police Department, 1862–1932." *Police Quarterly* 5, no. 1: 96–112.

Leonard, Donald S., Papers. Bentley Historical Library, University of Michigan, Ann Arbor.

Lewis, Tom. 1997. *Divided Highways: Building the Interstate Highways, Transforming American Life.* New York: Penguin.

Lippmann, Walter. 1922. *Public Opinion.* New York: MacMillan. Reprinted 1965 by Free Press.

Loader, Ian. 1997. "Policing and the Social: Questions of Symbolic Power." *British Journal of Sociology* 48, no. 1: 1–18.

Lord, Phillips H., to Chief of Police, Salt Lake City. 1936, January 27. WOR Collection, Box 1, Folder "Sacramento Post Office Robbery."

Lord, Phillips H., to Helen Conway. 1936. WOR Collection, Box 1, Folder "Hover Van Meter."

Lord, Phillips H., to J. Edgar Hoover. 1935, August 15. The Papers of Helen Sioussat. Library of American Broadcasting, University of Maryland, College Park, Maryland. Box 30.

Lord, Phillips H., to Lt. Ledbetter. 1936, n.d. WOR Collection, Box 1, Folder "Gray Anthony Gang."

Lord, Phillips H., to Lawrence Mould. 1936, March 20. WOR Collection, Box 1, Folder "Scarnini Case, Part 1."

Lord, Phillips H., to Jesse Sarber. 1935, July 7. WOR Collection, Box 58, Folder "Correspondence, Juveniles."

Lovell, Jarret. 2003. *Good Cop/Bad Cop: Mass Media and the Cycle of Police Reform.* New York: Criminal Justice Press.

Loviglio, Jason. 1999. "The Shadow Meets the Phantom Public." In *Fear Itself: Enemies Real and Imagined in American Culture,* ed. Nancy Lusignan Schultz, 313–30. West Lafayette, Ind.: Purdue University Press.

———. 2005. *Radio's Intimate Public: Network Broadcasting and Mass-mediated Democracy.* Minneapolis: University of Minnesota Press.

Lysing, Henry. 1938. *Men Against Crime.* New York: David Kemp & Company.

MacDonald, J. Fred. 1979, *Don't Touch That Dial! Radio Programming in American Life, 1920–1960.* Chicago: Nelson-Hall.

Manderbaugh, I. A. 1937. "Police Patrols Extinguish Crime and Fire." *American City* 52 (October): 91+.

Marchand, Roland. 1986. *Advertising the American Dream: Making Way for Modernity, 1920–1940.* Berkeley: University of California Press.

Marshall, Cecil. F. 1932. *Police Administration in Davenport.* Iowa City: State Historical Society of Iowa.

Marvin, Carolyn. 1988. *When Old Technologies Were New: Thinking About Electric Communication in the Late Nineteenth Century.* Oxford: Oxford University Press.

Matowitz, George, to J. T. Vorpe. 1936, March 9. WOR Collection, Box 1, Folder "Phantom of the Flats."

Maxwell, Grant. 1979. *The Shadow Scrapbook.* New York: Harcourt, Brace, Jovanovich.

May, Lary. 2000. *The Big Tomorrow.* Chicago: University of Chicago Press.

Mayo, Katherine. 1917. *Justice to All: The Story of the Pennsylvania State Police.* New York: G. P. Putnam's Sons.

McAnally, Isaac. 1938. *Gang Busters in Action.* Racine, Wis.: Whitman Publishing.

McCann, Sean. 2000. *Gumshoe America: Hard-Boiled Crime Fiction and the Rise and Fall of New Deal Liberalism.* Durham, N.C.: Duke University Press.

McChesney, Robert. 1990. "The Battle for the U.S. Airwaves, 1928–1935." *Journal of Communication* 40, no. 4: 29–57.

———. 1994. *Telecommunications, Mass Media, and Democracy: The Battle for Control of U.S. Broadcasting, 1928–1935.* New York: Oxford University Press.

McCracken, Allison. 1999. "'God's Gift to Us Girls': Crooning, Gender, and the Re-creation of Popular Song, 1928–1933." *American Music* 17, no. 4: 365–95.

McFadden, Margaret. June 1993. "America's Boyfriend Who Can't Get a Date: Gender, Race, and the Cultural Work of the *Jack Benny Program.*" *Journal of American History* 80, no. 1: 113–34.

———. March 2003. "'WARNING—Do Not Risk Federal Arrest by Looking Glum!': *Ballyhoo* Magazine and the Cultural Politics of Early 1930s Humor." *Journal of American Culture* 26, no. 1: 124–33.

McNeely, Mrs. A. H., to Phillips H. Lord. 1936, September 12. WOR Collection, Box 58, Folder "Machine Gun Kelly."

Menken, Harriet. 1936, February 9. "Radio Personalities." *New York American.* The Papers of Helen Sioussat. Library of American Broadcasting, University of Maryland, College Park, Maryland. Box 30, Folder 12.

Michigan State Police. 1936. *Cruising with the Michigan State Police: Reprints of a Series of 18 Radio Talks Given from Station WKAR.* East Lansing: Michigan State University.

Miles, Arnold. 1939. *How Criminals Are Caught.* New York: MacMillan.

Miller, Edward. 2002. *Emergency Broadcasting and 1930s American Radio.* Philadelphia: Temple University Press.

Mitchell, John, to Phillips H. Lord. 1936, April 23. WOR Collection, Box 1, Folder "Scarnini."

Monkkonen, Eric H. 1981. *Police in Urban America, 1860–1920.* Cambridge: Cambridge University Press.

Munby, Jonathan. 1999. *Public Enemies, Public Heroes: Screening the Gangster from "Little Caesar" to "Touch of Evil."* Chicago: University of Chicago Press.

Nachman, Gerald. 1998. *Raised on Radio.* New York: Pantheon Books.

"New Fashions Turn Up in Police Radio." 1937. *American City* 52 (August): 105.

Newman, Kathy. 2004. *Radio Active: Advertising and Consumer Culture, 1935–1947.* Berkeley: University of California Press.

Olander, Oscar. 1931. "State-Wide Broadcasting System Promotes Crime Control." *American City* 43 (February): 92–94.

———. 1942. *Michigan State Police: A Twenty-Five Year History.* Lansing: Michigan Police Journal Press.

Osgood, Dick. 1981. *Wxyie Wonderland: An Unauthorized 50 Year Diary of WXYZ Detroit.* Bowling Green, Ohio: Bowling Green University Popular Press.

Peters, John. 1999. *Speaking into the Air.* Chicago: University of Chicago Press.

Peters, Ralph. 1930. "Radio Revolutionizes Police Work." *American City* 42 (February): 151–52.

"Police Radio Facts and Result in New York Municipalities." 1937. *American City* 52 (January): 51.

"Police Radio Meets Interference." 1935. *American City* 50 (January): 13.

"Police Radio Service Today." 1935. *American City* 50 (July): 39–40.

"The Police Yearbook, 1938–39." 1939. Paper presented at the International Association of Chiefs of Police, Toronto.

Potter, Claire Bond. 1998. *War on Crime: Bandits, G-Men, and the Politics of Mass Culture.* New Brunswick, N.J.: Rutgers University Press.

Powers, Richard G. 1983. *G-Men: Hoover's FBI in American Popular Culture.* Carbondale: Southern Illinois University Press.

"Proofs That Police Radio Reduces Crime." 1935. *American City* 50 (September): 17.

Publicity Material. 1935. WOR Collection, Box 58, Library of Congress.

"Radio Becomes a Good Right Arm for Police." 1937. *American City* 52 (April): 62.

"Radio Drops Crime 20 Per Cent in Nassau County." 1936. *American City* 51 (April): 15.

"Radio Patrol Most Effective Crime Deterrent." 1935. *Literary Digest* 120 (August 3): 18.

"Radio Shoots Typed Words through Space." 1925. *Popular Mechanics* 43 (October): 599–602.

"Radio—The Latest Crime Detector." 1925. *Popular Mechanics* 43 (May): 709–11.

Ranson, Jo. 1937. *Cops on the Air: Modern Police Radio Methods of Combatting Crime.* Brooklyn: Eagle Library.

Razlogova, Elena. 2004. "The Voice of the Listener: Americans and the Radio Industry, 1920–1950." Ph.D. diss., George Mason University.

———. 2006. "True Crime Radio and Listener Disenchantment with Network Broadcasting, 1935–1946." *American Quarterly* 58, no. 1: 137–58.

Reams, Frazier, to John Ives. 1936, July 8. WOR Collection, Box 2, Folder "Livacoli Gang, Part 1."

Robson, William. 1966. "Reminiscences of William N. Robson." Interview by Eric Barnouw, transcript. Radio Pioneers Project, Oral History Research Office, Columbia University, New York City.

Roediger, David. 2005. *Working toward Whiteness: How America's Immigrants Became White.* New York: Basic Books.

Root, William. 1925. *A Series of Six Radio Talks on Criminology.* Pittsburgh, Pa.: University of Pittsburgh.

Round, Lester. 1932. *Scientific Crime Detection (Parts 1 and 2): Radio Talks over Station WEAN, the Shepard Stores, Providence, Rhode Island.* Providence: Rhode Island Public Health Commission.

Rowland, Howard. 1942. *Crime and Punishment on the Air.* Columbus: Ohio State University.

Russo, Alex. 2002. "A Dark(ened) Figure on the Airwaves: Race, Nation, and *The Green Hornet.*" In *Radio Reader: Essays in the Cultural History of Radio,* ed. Michele Hilmes and Jason Loviglio, 257–76. London: Routledge.

———. 2004. "Roots of Radio's Rebirth: Audiences, Aesthetics, Economics, and Technologies of American Broadcasting, 1926–1951." Ph.D. diss., Brown University.

Ruth, David E. 1996. *Inventing the Public Enemy: The Gangster in American Culture, 1918–1934.* Chicago: University of Chicago Press.

Scannell, Paddy. 1991. *Broadcast Talk.* London: Sage.

———. 1996. *Radio, Television and Modern Life.* Oxford: Blackwell.

Sconce, Jeffrey. 2000. *Haunted Media: Electronic Presence from Telegraphy to Television.* Durham, N.C.: Duke University Press.

Sies, Luther. 2000. *Encyclopedia of American Radio, 1920–1960.* Jefferson, N.C.: MacFarland.

Skidmore, Abram. 1936. "Portable Detective Office, Nassau County Police Department." *American City* 51 (April): 15.

Skocpol, Theda. 1992. "State Formation and Social Policy in the United States."
American Behavioral Scientist 35, nos. 4–5: 559–84.

Skocpol, Theda, and Kenneth Finegold. 1992. "State Capacity and Economic
Intervention in the Early New Deal." *Political Science Quarterly* 97, no. 2: 255–78.

Slotkin, Richard. 1992. *Gunfighter Nation: The Myth of the Frontier in Twentieth-
Century America.* New York: Atheneum.

"Small Cities Going to Radio." 1936. *American City* 51 (October): 15.

Smith, Bruce. 1929a. "Rural Police Protection." *The Illinois Crime Survey.* Chicago:
Illinois Association for Criminal Justice.

———. 1929b. "Municipal Police Administration." *Annals of the American Acad-
emy of Political and Social Science* 146 (November): 1–27.

———. 1933. *Rural Crime Control.* New York: Columbia University Institute of
Public Administration.

———. 1940. *Police Systems in the United States.* New York: Harper & Brothers.

Smith, Erin A. 2000. *Hard-Boiled: Working Class Readers and Pulp Magazines.*
Philadelphia: Temple University Press.

Soderman, Harry, and John O'Connell. 1935. *Modern Criminal Investigation.* New
York: Literary Digest Books.

Sponsor Material. 1935. WOR Collection, Box 58, Library of Congress, Washington, D.C.

Sterne, Jonathan. 2003. *The Audible Past: The Cultural Origins of Sound Reproduction.* Durham, N.C.: Duke University Press.

Stott, William. 1973. *Documentary Expression and Thirties America.* Chicago: University of Chicago Press.

Susman, Warren. 1984. *Culture as History: The Transformation of American Society
in the Twentieth Century.* New York: Pantheon Books.

Teale, Edwin. 1936. "Forging New Weapons for the War on Crime." *Popular Science Monthly* 129, no. 2: 9–11+.

Thomas, Ronald. 1999. *Detective Fiction and the Rise of Forensic Science.* Cambridge:
Cambridge University Press.

Thompson, Emily. 2002. *The Soundscape of Modernity: Architectural Acoustics and
the Culture of Listening in America, 1900–1933.* Cambridge, Mass.: MIT Press.

Trendle, George, Papers. Detroit Public Library, Detroit, Michigan.

Vollmer, August. 1929. "The Police in Chicago." *The Illinois Crime Survey.* Chicago: Illinois Association for Criminal Justice.

———. 1932. "Abstract of the 'Wickersham' Police Report." *Journal of Criminal
Law and Criminology* 22, no. 5: 716–23.

Vollmer, August, and Alfred Parker. 1935. *Crime and the State Police.* Berkeley: University of California Press.

———. 1937. *Crime, Crooks, and Cops.* New York: Funk & Wagnall.

Walker, Samuel. 1977. *A Critical History of Police Reform: The Emergence of Professionalism.* Lexington, Mass.: Lexington Books.

———. 1998. *Popular Justice: A History of American Criminal Justice.* New York: Oxford University Press.

"Want a Policeman: From Short Wave to Television." 1937. *Literary Digest* 124 (December 25): 28.

Watt, J. 1936. "Radio Produces in Oklahoma." *American City* 51 (February): 17.

Whyte, William. 1956. *The Organization Man.* New York: Doubleday.

"Wickersham Report on Police." 1931. *The American Journal of Police Science* 2, no. 4: 337–48.

Williams, Raymond. 1974. *Television: Technology and Cultural Form.* Hanover, N.H.: Wesleyan University Press.

Wilson, Christopher. 2000. *Cop Knowledge: Police Power and Cultural Narrative in Twentieth-Century America.* Chicago: University of Chicago Press.

Wolfe, Harold E., Papers. Special Collections Department. University of Iowa Libraries, Iowa City, Iowa.

Wolfe, Thomas. 1936. "Motors of the Jersey City Police." *American City* 51 (January): 63–65.

Wylie, Max. 1939. *Radio Writing.* New York: Farrar & Rinehart.

Recordings

Calling All Cars. "The Bloodstained Shoe," first broadcast 5 May 1938 on Columbia Broadcasting Systems/West Coast (CBS/West Coast).

———. "Cinder Dick," first broadcast 2 July 1937 on CBS/West Coast.

———. "Crooks Are Human," first broadcast 15 August 1934 on CBS/West Coast.

———. "The Dillinger Case," first broadcast 21 March 1934 on CBS/West Coast.

———. "The Execution of John Dillinger," broadcast 7 July 1934 on CBS/West Coast.

———. "Fingerprints Don't Lie," first broadcast 11 July 1934 on CBS/West Coast.

———. "July 4th in a Radio Car," first broadcast 4 July 1934 on CBS/West Coast.

———. "Lt. Crowley Murder," first broadcast 23 October 1934 on CBS/West Coast.

———. "Murder at Sunset," first broadcast 18 May 1939 on CBS/West Coast.

———. "The Murder Quartet," first broadcast 30 October 1934 on CBS/West Coast.

———. "The Phantom Radio," first broadcast 9 November 1937 on CBS/West Coast.

———. "The Poisoning Jezebel," first broadcast 9 December 1938 on CBS/West Coast.

———. "Power and Light Holdup," first broadcast 27 June 1934 on CBS/West Coast.

———. "Skid Row Dope Ring," first broadcast 1934 on CBS/West Coast.

———. "Stop That Car," first broadcast 26 September 1934 on CBS/West Coast.

————. "Tobaccoville Road," first broadcast 7 September 1937 on CBS/West Coast.

————. "Unwritten Law," first broadcast 9 October 1934 on CBS/West Coast.

————. "Youth Rides Tough," first broadcast 28 May 1935 on CBS/West Coast.

Eno Crime Clues. "The .32 Caliber Kiss, Part 1," first broadcast 10 November 1936 on CBS.

————. "The .32 Caliber Kiss, Part 2," first broadcast 12 November 1936 on CBS.

The Green Hornet. "Parking Lot Racket," first broadcast 31 October 1939 on Mutual Broadcasting System (MBS).

————. "The Political Racket," first broadcast 5 May 1938 on MBS.

————. "The Smuggler Signs His Name," first broadcast 25 November 1939 on Blue Network.

Mercury Theater of the Air. "War of the Worlds," first broadcast 31 October 1937 on CBS.

Police Headquarters. "Antonio Moretti." 1932 electrical transcription, syndication.

————. "Dr. Thornton's Wife Disappears." 1932 electrical transcription, syndication.

————. "$40,000 Payroll Shipment." 1932 electrical transcription, syndication.

————. "Jake Miller Knifed." 1932 electrical transcription, syndication.

————. "John Fleming Confesses." 1932 electrical transcription, syndication.

————. "Laundry Truck Kidnapping." 1932 electrical transcription, syndication.

————. "Man Stealing Food." 1932 electrical transcription, syndication.

————. "Mrs. North Robbery." 1932 electrical transcription, syndication.

————. "Silver Collection." 1932 electrical transcription, syndication.

————. "Tommygun Murders." 1932 electrical transcription, syndication.

————. "Tommy Wood Killed." 1932 electrical transcription, syndication.

————. "William Spencer Killed." 1932 electrical transcription, syndication.

The Shadow. "Aboard the Steamship Amazonia," first broadcast 17 July 1938 on MBS.

————. "The Blind Beggar Dies," first broadcast 18 April 1938 on MBS.

————. "The Cat That Killed," first broadcast 21 December 1939 on MBS.

————. "Circle of Death," first broadcast 28 November 1937 on MBS.

————. "The Death House Rescue," first broadcast 26 September 1937 on MBS.

————. "Death Speaks Twice," first broadcast 15 February 1942 on MBS.

————. "Death under the Chapel," first broadcast 28 August 1938 on MBS.

————. "Firebug," first broadcast 19 June 1938 on MBS.

————. "The Ghost Building," first broadcast 12 January 1941 on MBS.

————. "The Ghost on the Stair," first broadcast 29 December 1940 on MBS.

————. "The League of Terror," first broadcast 9 January 1938 on MBS.

————. "The Leopard Strikes," first broadcast 5 January 1941 on MBS.

————. "Murder on Approval," first broadcast 21 August 1938 on MBS.

————. "The Oracle of Death," first broadcast 20 October 1938 on MBS.

————. "The Phantom Voice," first broadcast 6 February 1938 on MBS.

————. "The Poison Death," first broadcast 30 January 1938 on MBS.

————. "The Precipice Called Death," first broadcast 21 January 1940 on MBS.

————. "The Return of Anatol Chevanic," first broadcast 1 February 1942 on MBS.

————. "Ring of Light," first broadcast 23 November 1941 on MBS.

————. "Sabotage," first broadcast 16 January 1938 on MBS.

————. "The Temple Bells of Neban," first broadcast 24 October 1937 on MBS.

————. "The Three Frightened Policemen," first broadcast 16 November 1941 on MBS.

————. "Traffic in Death," first broadcast 25 September 1938 on MBS.

True Detective Mysteries. "The Buddha Man Mystery," first broadcast 8 April 1937 on MBS.

————. "The Girl in the Iron Mask," first broadcast 15 April 1937 on MBS.

————. "Horror in a Hospital Ward," first broadcast 25 March 1937 on MBS.

————. "Secrets Never Told Before," first broadcast 1 April 1937 on MBS.

INDEX

acousmetre, 217–18. *See also* Chion,
Michael; *Shadow, The*
action heroes, 35, 47
Adorno, Theodor, 102
advertising agencies, 30, 35, 38. *See also*
Benton and Bowles
Alexanderson, E. F., 252n4
Allen's Alley, 77
Allport, Gordon. *See Psychology of
Radio*
Altman, Rick, 48, 72, 78, 96–97,
247n1, 248n12
American Civil Liberties Union, 195
American Legion, 55
America's Most Wanted, 233
America's Town Meeting of the Air,
67, 68
Amos 'n' Andy, 77, 127, 248n6
antivigilantism, 138–40; in crime
drama, 107, 136, 138–40, 144, 145.
See also police-citizen relations
apprehension model: in crime drama,
36, 39–45, 83, 149, 153–56, 157, 159,
176; in policing, 17, 24–25, 75–76,
121–22, 147–50, 176, 185–86; in vigilante drama, 186, 187–88, 206. *See
also* communication technologies;

criminals: mobility; dragnet;
dragnet effect; physical mobility;
police; police-citizen relations;
police radio; radio networks: as
metaphor
Arnheim, Rudolf, 29
audiences, 30, 48–49, 50, 55–57, 61,
110, 115, 168, 189; Depression-era, 55,
56, 101, 129, 138, 144, 168, 189, 231;
juvenile, 62, 64–65, 249n2; working
class, 26, 27, 58, 61, 121, 196–97
automobiles, 1, 17, 30, 147–49, 150–53,
157, 171, 185, 230
automobility. *See* automobile; physical
mobility

Bain, R., 36, 247n2
Bakhtin, Mikhail, 149, 154
banditry: theories of, 109–11, 145
bandits, 19, 23, 24, 26, 27, 109–20,
130–31; celebrity, 105, 115; in crime
drama, 111–20; female bandits,
134–35. *See also* Bonnie (Parker)
and Clyde (Barrow); criminals;
criminals, representations of;
Dillinger, John; populism
Barnouw, Eric, 29, 94, 156, 218, 253n7

271

KATHLEEN BATTLES is assistant professor of communication and journalism at Oakland University.